Call if Lost _____ Brian Fensstermaher 6104

Jennifeh

577

D0331182

Between Sundays

A Year of

Transforming

Devotionals

for the

Toughest

Days of

Your Week

Between

Sundays

Shawn Craig

Our purpose at Howard Publishing is to:

- *Increase faith* in the hearts of growing Christians
- *Inspire holiness* in the lives of believers
- *Instill hope* in the hearts of struggling people everywhere

Because He's coming again!

Between Sundays © 1998 by Shawn Craig
All rights reserved. Printed in the United States of America

Published by Howard Publishing Co., Inc.,
3117 North 7th Street, West Monroe, Louisiana 71291-2227

98 99 00 01 02 03 04 05 06 07   10 9 8 7 6 5 4 3 2 1

Library of Congress Cataloging-in-Publication Data

Craig, Shawn, 1959–
    Between Sundays : a year of transforming devotionals for the
toughest days of your week / Shawn Craig.
        p. cm.
    ISBN 1-878990-92-6
    BV4811.C687 1998
    242'.2—dc21   98-40524
                                                                   CIP

Edited by Sue Ann Jones
Interior design by LinDee Loveland

Turn Your Eyes Upon Jesus © 1922 Singspiration Music (Admin. by Brentwood-Benson Music Pub., Inc.).

To my
Mom and Dad,

Ted and Beverly Craig,

who, in between,
live what they profess on Sundays

❧

Contents

contents

contents

Acknowledgements

In order for this dream to become reality, there have been many wonderful people who have made invaluable contributions. My thanks go out to...

Philis and the editorial staff at Howard Publishing for their patience and hard work through this whole process,

Joy Becker for encouraging me to keep writing,

Demie Rainey for her insight and editorial pointers along the way,

Pastor Gerald and my church family for loving me and allowing me time to write and sing and be gone days at a time,

Dave, Kim, and the music team for their faithfulness and understanding,

Pamela Muse for introducing me to Howard Publishing, and

Randy Phillips and Dan Dean for helping me to remember to laugh more often.

Introduction

The wise man said, "There is nothing new under the sun" (Eccles. 1:9).

I once heard a pastor who related how excited he had been on having received what he thought was a new revelation on the subject he was preparing to preach about. But as he was reading a book in his own library, he discovered his "revelation" right there in chapter 1. Not only that, he had underlined it!

This book contains nothing new. It is the overflow of what so many have poured into me over the years through books I have read and God's wonderful people whom I have met.

This book began as a personal project as I journaled what I felt God was saying to me along my own journey of faith. But as a result of encouragement from friends, I began to put some of these thoughts into book form. It was my desire to have something I could give to younger Christians to encourage them to press on to know God more intimately and to find that Jesus is truly there between Sundays.

The reader may notice that the pronouns for God are not capitalized. This is not meant to show any disrespect to our mighty God but was a mutual decision between the editor and myself regarding a particular style of writing. It may be well noted that most editions of the King James Version as well as the New International Version do not capitalize divine pronouns.

A Moment of Reckoning

But you, lazybones, how long will you sleep? When will you
wake up?—Proverbs 6:9 NLT

I am convinced that we all receive a wake-up call at least once in our lifetimes. We don't always recognize it when it happens, but later we realize that's what it was. We are blessed if we can hear and know when God is trying to shake us loose from the shackles of slumber and delirium.

The Father of our souls is looking for long-term results, not short-term gains. We may look at our lives and say, "I'm doing fine...money in the bank, healthy family, faithful to attend church, etc." But God looks at us and is not satisfied until Christ is formed in us. God's eyes are on the inner self, not the outward man (see 1 Sam. 16:7). He knows when we're due for a wake-up call.

Peter the apostle had a wake-up call in the days following the Last Supper. In the warmth of fellowship among his ministry peers, he was quick to say, "Lord, I am ready to go with thee, both into prison, and to death" (Luke 22:33 KJV). But later, in the warmth of the fire of scrutiny, he hastily denied any knowledge of Christ. Then, when he realized what he'd done and admitted how weak he truly was, his heart was broken, and a conversion took place.

God cannot fully use those who are totally self-reliant. It is from the broken places of our lives that we minister most effectively. It is from a state of utter hopelessness that we realize how much we desperately need God. Only when we reach this point are we emboldened to do what is beyond ourselves, because only then do we realize our strength is from God and not something we can conjure up ourselves.

So when your faith is shaken, when your world is suddenly turned upside down, stop and listen. Consider what's happening. It might be God's alarm clock going off in your life. Your wake-up call. Arise and shine; resist the lure of the snooze button.

⊗∞⊗

Lord Jesus, let me recognize the crucial moments of my existence. I don't want to be spiritually asleep. I want to be attentive to your workings, to your voice and your purpose.

Stand by Me

*He lifted me out of the slimy pit, out of the mud and mire; he set my
feet on a rock and gave me a firm place to stand.*—Psalm 40:2

Moses. Mighty man. Leader. Chosen by God. Now in the presence of
God…there on the mountaintop, Moses watched as God's finger chiseled
out the holy commandments for Israel. God was so close that Moses
could feel the holy light permeating his very being.

"God, show me your glory," he said bravely.

God looked at his faithful servant and smiled. Surely there was so
much he would have liked to reveal, but he knew his servant only too
well. God spoke. "There is a place near me where you may stand on a
rock" (Exod. 33:21). "I will cause all my goodness to pass in front of you"
(Exod. 33:19).

As God's glory passed by, God covered Moses with his hand so that
Moses got only a glimpse. Still, Moses' face shone for many days to come.

Later, in the last few days of his life, Moses was once again on the
mountain. This time he had not come to view God's glory but to behold
from afar the land of promise. Moses must have felt great anguish in seeing what he could never obtain because of his disobedience. But once
again…he was not alone. He was with his friend, his God.

Do you remember your first special encounter with God? I remember
mine well. The distance from my seat to the altar seemed to be at least a
mile or more. I was privileged, however, to have my dad sitting beside me.
I asked him to take that walk with me. Facing God with my sin did not
seem as overwhelming to me as long as Dad was with me.

Whether we are basking in God's glory, facing disappointment, or
confronting the truth of our transgressions, God has provided a place
where we can stand beside him. He will be with us and help us not to be
afraid. He will cover with his hand what he knows we cannot bear. And
he will give us the courage we need to encounter what we must.

∞

Father, how I love to stand beside you, to feel the strength that you alone possess, and to know you hold my hand and give me courage enough to face your
holiness. I will not be afraid, for you will hide me in your pavilion, in the secret
of your tabernacle. You will set me on a rock, that special place beside you.

An Encounter with God

*When they saw the courage of Peter and John and realized that they
were unschooled, ordinary men, they were astonished* and they took
note that these men had been with Jesus.
—Acts 4:13 (emphasis added)

Recently I was asked which three people have had the greatest impact
on my life. At first I thought it wouldn't be difficult to answer the question. But upon further consideration, I realized it wasn't easy to come up
with an answer. I've encountered many, many helpful people along the
way, most of them for just a short while, and there have been several who
have impacted my life in varying ways, large and small. I couldn't name
just three.

If someone asked me to identify the single source of life-changing
impact in my life, however, I wouldn't even have to stop and think. The
answer is *God.*

God's impact on his children's lives goes beyond the normal "bumping into" changes brought about by earthly helpers or motivators. When
Moses met with God on Mount Sinai, the glory of God shone so radiantly
on his face that when he left God's presence he had to wear a veil to
address the Israelites. When Saul, the terrible persecutor of Christians,
encountered God on the road to Damascus, he became the mighty apostle Paul, who would write more of the New Testament than any other disciple. Consider the stories of Abraham, Peter, Mary Magdalene, and all the
others whose lives were radically changed after their date with divinity.

When we encounter God—when we allow him to touch our lives and
take up residence in our hearts—we are not just impacted; we are transformed, marked for life, changed and revolutionized. And people will
notice. Just as Jacob's mysterious limp was an outward reminder to others
of his Peniel encounter with God, and just as Moses' face glowed, when
we encounter God and allow him to change us, the transformation will
be noticeable. Others will look at us and say we've never been the same
since that moment.

∞

Lord, I pray that your transformation of my life is so evident that others will
notice so that I may point the way for them to have their own encounter with
you.

The Moment of Revelation

When he was at the table with them, he took bread, gave thanks,
broke it and began to give it to them. Then their eyes were opened and
they recognized him, and he disappeared from their sight.
—Luke 24:30–31

Revelation begins when you open the door. As long as Jesus stands outside the door beckoning with his voice, there is no revelation. Christ longs for us to open the doors of our hearts, to open our spiritual eyes, so that he can come in and reveal his heart, character, and love to us.

The disciples who met Jesus on their way to Emmaus but didn't recognize him are an example to us of what it means to be spiritually blinded. These two disciples spilled out their grief over the loss of their Master and Friend, when at that very moment the risen Lord was right there with them. It was only after they had invited him into their abode that revelation took place as he blessed and broke the bread. Suddenly they recognized him, and then he was gone.

When Jesus comes into our lives and "breaks bread" by sharing his words of spirit and life, our eyes will be opened. We will get a glimpse of our Lord and of his love for us. The blinders will fall from our eyes as the Bread of Life is blessed, broken, and given. Maybe then he will vanish from our sight, not because he plays games, but because we can only receive revelation in small doses. In essence, we can only eat so much bread at one sitting!

There must be a time of assimilation of what we have received and then a giving to others. As Jesus instructed us, "Freely ye have received, freely give" (Matt. 10:8 KJV).

As we wait and listen, we will hear his voice calling. If we will open the door, he will come in. He has said, "Whoever has my commands and obeys them, he is the one who loves me. He who loves me will be loved by my Father, and I too will love him and show myself to him" (John 14:21). If you love him, listen...

∞

Dear Lord, I want to be able to hear your voice calling at the door of my heart. Let me seize the moment of the calling. I will open the door to your revelation. My knowledge of you will grow as I partake of the Bread of Life.

A Humbling Experience

[Jesus] made himself nothing, taking the very nature of a servant,
being made in human likeness.—Philippians 2:7

What a humbling experience it must have been for God to take the form of humanity and feel all the hunger, fatigue, and other discomforts that were so different from his glorious existence in the heavenly realm. But that was only the beginning. Those difficulties couldn't compare with the humiliation he suffered on the cross, dying the most horrifying of deaths, experiencing complete and utter rejection by the very ones he had come to save.

And despite all he's already done for us, still today he continues to humble himself for us. He comes down to our level of understanding to meet us at our point of need. He humbles himself to reach us at our measure of faith.

I love how Jack Deere, a former professor at Dallas Theological Seminary, tells how God met him at his level of faith. Deere was convinced that the miraculous was a thing of the past. But God slowly tore down Deere's walls of resistance until he reversed his stance. In his book *Surprised by the Power of the Spirit,* Deere explains how God patiently revealed this on a level he could understand. Being a cerebral theologian, Jack found that God was merciful enough to meet him there.

There will always be diversity in the body of Christ. One church will respond one way while another will respond in a manner that's radically different. God is big enough and yet humble enough to understand both.

∞

Jesus, thank you for humbling yourself by taking the form of man, for experiencing the joy and the suffering of life so that you could be touched with the feeling of our weaknesses and could save us. I want to remember your humility, your willingness to be a servant, and make allowances for diversity in my spiritual family.

Weekend Reflections

God surprises us. He rarely shows up where and how we expect him to. The two disciples on the road to Emmaus were walking with the Son of God and didn't even know it! Maybe their eyes were blinded by God for a greater purpose. Or maybe their minds were so closed to the possibility of Jesus' being alive that they just couldn't recognize him when he walked right beside them. What a shock it must have been when they realized that the one they so loved had been so near to them!

Leading a Bible study recently, my friend Ken Schmitt encouraged us to spend a week looking for Jesus in those around us. I was amazed how we could see the evidence of Jesus in friends, family members, coworkers, and even strangers when our minds were tuned to the idea and we actively *looked* for him everywhere we went. Pay attention! Jesus may pay you a surprise visit today through someone who touches your life.

1. Spend the next few days looking for Jesus to surprise you. Write down how he reveals himself to you in the people around you.

   _____

   _____

   _____

2. Why do you think the two men on the road to Emmaus didn't recognize Jesus? How does this apply to your situation?

   _____

   _____

   _____

3. When do you find that you are most aware of Jesus? On Sundays? On a quiet night gazing at the stars? Why?

   _____

   _____

   _____

The Call to Remember

*Consider your own call, brothers and sisters: not many of you were
wise by human standards, not many were powerful, not many
were of noble birth.*—1 Corinthians 1:26 NRSV

I love the word *remember*. It literally means to bring the picture back
to your mind. To relive it, to see it, to do it again. When a man sets a
photograph of his wife on his desk, he wants to call her image to mind.
As he looks at her photograph, he *remembers* her.

The apostle Paul wanted the Corinthians to remember something as
a way of attaining the proper attitude of mind and spirit. In essence he
was saying, "When you are tempted to boast and become prideful, recall
your humble beginnings. Bring back to your mind the picture of who you
were before Christ found you."

In the same way, Moses reminded the children of Israel, "Remember
that you were slaves in Egypt and that the Lord your God brought you
out of there with a mighty hand and an outstretched arm" (Deut. 5:15).

Why does a superstar athlete go to the ghetto and reach out to the
poor and destitute? He wants to remember his humble beginnings. He
looks at a young boy and sees himself a few years earlier when someone
reached out to him with compassion and caused him to believe that he
could escape the tyranny of poverty.

Remembering empowers us to move forward. Woodrow Wilson said,
"A nation which does not remember what it was yesterday does not know
what it is today, nor what it is trying to do. We are trying to do a futile
thing if we do not know where we came from or what we have been
about." Remembering our calling and who we were before Christ found
us does two things: It causes us to boast in the Lord instead of in ourselves, and it gives us faith in the mighty power of God. Remembering,
we can boldly stand and say, "Christ saves! Christ delivers!" because we
are living witnesses of his grace. We remember what he has done for us.

⤬

Lord, I choose to remember. I know what I was before I found you, and I give
you thanks for what I have become. I know it is only by grace that I have been
saved and have become a son of God, a joint heir with Jesus Christ. I was
bound, but now I am free! I was lost, and now I am found. I remember.

Clouded Vision

*Your eye is the lamp of your body. When your eyes are good, your
whole body also is full of light. But when they are bad, your body also
is full of darkness.*—Luke 11:34

Psychiatrists often use certain pictures and diagrams when diagnosing
a patient. By the patient's reaction to the images, the doctors are able to
gain insight into his or her perspective. The same pictures are used time
and again, yet different images will be seen at different times or by different clients.

Like those pictures used repeatedly, the situations in our lives do not
really change all that much. We all experience similar happenings and circumstances: celebrations, accidents, illnesses, milestones, accomplishments, and trials. The events, themselves, may be similar. It's our perspectives that are always changing.

When Moses sent twelve men to spy out the Promised Land for Israel,
ten came back with a bad report. When they saw the giants who occupied
that land, they saw themselves as grasshoppers in comparison!

But two of the men, Joshua and Caleb, brought back a good report.
They said, "We should go up and take possession of the land, for we can
certainly do it…. The land…is exceedingly good" (Num. 13:30; 14:7).

What gave the two groups of men such different perspectives? The ten
terrified scouts had bad eyes—clouded vision. But Joshua and Caleb had
eyes that were good—eyes of faith. They knew the Lord had led them to
that land, had promised it to them. They said, "If the Lord is pleased with
us, he will lead us into that land, a land flowing with milk and honey, and
will give it to us" (Num. 14:8).

What's your perspective on your circumstances? Are things really as
bad as you see them, or is your vision a little cloudy? Are your eyes flawed
by the elements of unforgiveness, self-pity, fear, or pride? May God help
us to clear our vision that we may truly number our blessings and claim
his promises!

∞

Lord, I sometimes have been blinded to your faithfulness and supernatural
work in my life. Give me clear spiritual vision. May I view my difficulties with
the eyes of faith and others' faults with the eyes of grace.

No Shadows There

*These are a shadow of the things that were to come; the reality,
however, is found in Christ.*—Colossians 2:17

In the light of eternity, our present circumstances take on new emphasis—or dissolve into nothingness. When we look at things from an eternal perspective, some issues that seem trivial take on new weight, while other things that seem vitally important fade in the glow of heaven's brilliance. So many things look different in God's light.

The shadows cast by the sun as it rises on a cloudless morning are many times the length of the actual objects that stand before the sun's rays. Those shadows, stretching out from various objects, are but images of the originals. And in those early morning hours, they are distorted images—much larger than the objects they represent.

The Mosaic law with its sacrifices, feasts, and celebrations cast a long, early shadow of good things that were coming for God's children. The old law could never make us truly righteous in God's sight. It wasn't real; it was just an image, a symbol, of what was real. All the lambs offered on the altar were only symbols of the real Lamb who would die on a cross. As the apostle Paul said, such rituals of Mosaic law were "only a shadow of the good things that are coming—not the realities themselves" (Heb. 10:1). The good thing that is coming—the reality himself—is Christ.

How amazing it is to realize that, since we are spirit beings confined to earthly bodies, we cannot yet contain the full measure of God's glorious presence. The blessings we have now from knowing we are his beloved children are only shadows of the unimaginable joy we will feel when we join him in paradise. "Now we see but a poor reflection as in a mirror; then we shall see face to face. Now I know in part; then I shall know fully, even as I am fully known" (1 Cor. 13:12).

∞

Lord, keep the light of eternity shining on my life so that I may see things in the right perspective. Thank you for the glimpses of your glory and your presence. I long to know you fully, and I look forward to that day when I will see you face to face.

2/25/98

THURSDAY

There's a Chink in Every Hero's Armor

How can you say to your brother, "Let me take the speck out of your eye," when all the time there is a plank in your own eye? You hypocrite, first take the plank out of your own eye, and then you will see clearly to remove the speck from your brother's eye.—Matthew 7:4–5

New believers often get a rude awakening when they encounter Christians who fall short of their expectations. To see the failure of someone we have held up as perfect is disheartening, to be sure.

Heroes are important and good, but when we see them as infallible, we are headed for trouble. As one after another falls off the pedestal we've put them on, we may even begin to believe we are the only ones staying true to God. That is the situation the prophet Elijah found himself in as he prayed for God to take his life. He saw the wickedness of his people, Israel, and believed he was the only servant of God left. (In reality, there were seven thousand others who had not bowed to Baal!)

What should we do when the weaknesses of a dear brother or sister are exposed? First of all, we must recognize our own weaknesses and ask God to remind us of our own imperfections. Then, as we ask for grace to cover ourselves, we will be more capable of showing patience and understanding to others. Next, as Richard Foster suggests in his book *Celebration of Discipline,* we must ask God to allow us to "see them with the light of God permeating every fiber of their being." What are God's hopes and aspirations for this child of his? Lift up the person into the Father's presence, and with eyes of faith, see him or her in the light of God's love. Finally, praise God for what you see.

Not only will these steps activate God's power in your fellow Christian, but best of all, they will trigger a change in you and how you view others. You will find yourself reacting differently to those who have fallen, as you see their weaknesses—and yours—from God's perspective.

∞

Lord, I free myself from the responsibility of trying to change others. I recognize that we are all fallen in our carnal nature and it is only by your grace that we stand. Let me begin to see others the way you see them through your eyes of mercy.

10

The Illuminated Word

None of the rulers of this age understood it, for if they had, they
would not have crucified the Lord of glory.
—1 Corinthians 2:8

It is often difficult to understand how those religious leaders in Jesus' time, who had devoted their lives to studying the Scriptures, could not recognize Jesus for who he was. If anyone should have known the Messiah when they encountered him, it was those men.

Their inability to accept Jesus as the Messiah is solid proof that knowledge alone is not enough. When it comes to spiritual things, there must be an enlightenment of the heart before the Spirit of God's revelation begins to flow into it. This order of doing things is something God takes pleasure in. He loves to confound the wise and reveal the hidden mysteries to the simple (see Matt. 11:25–26).

The sinful mind cannot accept God's leading. Paul said, "It does not submit to God's law, nor can it do so" (Rom. 8:7). But oh, what a transformation takes place when the mind is renewed by the Holy Spirit and the Word of God! In contrast to the sinful mind, which rejects the laws of the Spirit, the renewed and enlightened mind embraces the thoughts and purposes of God. Then, as if a big light bulb has been switched on in the heart, the mind says, "Now I see. Now I understand."

∞

Lord, I've missed out on so many things because of my spiritual blindness. May my heart and mind be illuminated to see your truth for what it really is.

WEEK 2
SATURDAY

a new perspective

Weekend Reflections

In his book *The Seven Habits of Highly Effective People,* Stephen Covey tells about a new perspective he received on a subway one morning. His hopes for a quiet ride home were dashed when a man and a couple of energetic, noisy children boarded the subway car. The children were loud, disturbing other passengers, yet the man to whom the kids belonged did nothing. Finally at the point of exasperation, Stephen tells how he, with restraint, said to the man, "Sir, your children are disturbing a lot of people. I wonder if you couldn't control them a little more."

The man, lifting his eyes from a near daze, said, "Oh, you're right. I guess I should do something about it. We just came from the hospital where their mother died about an hour ago. I don't know what to think, and I guess they don't know how to handle it either."

Stephen immediately got a whole new perspective.

1. Part of the evidence that we are walking in the Spirit comes when we see things from God's perspective. Describe a situation that is troubling you and ask God to help you see it from his perspective.

   This whole thing with Leah.

2. Write down three things that God sees differently than you do. For example, he sees a person differently because we look on the outside while he sees the heart.

3. How would your perspective change if you looked at everything you do as though you were measuring the results one hundred years from now?

12

When the Earth Trembled

The earth shook; the heavens also dropped rain at the presence of God;
Sinai itself was moved at the presence of God, the God of Israel.
—Psalm 68:8 NKJV

I have only experienced two earthquakes that I can recall, but that was two too many! The first one occurred while I was eating in a restaurant in California. I suddenly felt my chair move, and I looked up to see the beams of the ceiling shifting back and forth as if I were inside a toy house.

I remember the fear I felt that day whenever I read Psalm 68, where David recounts the scene of God's meeting with Moses on Mount Sinai. When God's presence came upon the place, David said, the force of him was so awesome that the mountain itself quaked.

Close your eyes and picture it. Imagine you are there, watching from a distance as, in one awe-filled moment, the Lord himself descends upon the mountain in fire. Smoke billows up into the heavens, and the mountain trembles at the force of his presence. There is a long heavenly trumpet blast, and then, if you're still conscious, you hear *the voice.*

Thanks be to God, we no longer come to a quaking Mount Sinai but to Mount Zion, the church covered by the blood of Christ (see Heb. 12:18–22). Still, it is the knowledge of God's power displayed on Mount Sinai that moves us to "serve God acceptably with reverence and godly fear" (Heb. 12:28 NKJV).

God help us when we find ourselves serving him with blasé and superficial worship! May God have mercy on us when we pray to him as though we were beseeching Santa Claus or the tooth fairy! Instead, we must worship him with reverence and awe, "for our God is a consuming fire" (Heb. 12:29 NKJV).

Perhaps it is time we took a lesson from nature. If the earth knows to tremble at the presence of God, how much more should our hearts tremble when we come before him?

⚜

Oh God, my God, how awesome and mighty you are! Forgive me for the times I have approached you with dulled senses and a listless heart. I love you, and yet I tremble at the thought of One so great knowing and loving me. I praise you for your grace and unfailing love.

13

3/2/99

TUESDAY

New Isn't Necessarily Better

But we must be sure to obey the truth we have learned already.
—Philippians 3:16 NLT

The kingdom of God is like a building constructed by God stone upon stone, revelation by revelation. But with all the great teachers we have had through history down to the present day, it's easy to get caught up in the excitement of discovery. Too many people run from one new revelation to another, thinking that each new one will be our miracle cure. While we should be thankful for revelations and grateful that God is speaking a fresh word to his people, we must not come to believe that the new makes the old obsolete. If the new cannot be built upon the old, the new should be discarded—that is, if the old thing we have learned is really truth.

If you've ever had a yard sale, you've probably been surprised (as I have been) to see the stuff that people will buy. Things that you have found no use for are often treasures to other people. Here in prosperous America, we're always buying the latest gadget or tool and discarding the old ones, only to wish later that we still had that good ol' Shop Vac or camera or exercise bike. We discover too late that new isn't necessarily better.

Even when new enlightenment and knowledge thrill and inspire us, the power is still where it has always been. As God reveals himself to us and we stand amazed, the new revelation should point us, in some way, to the bedrock of our faith. The blood of the Cross, the name of Jesus, the Resurrection, his grace to us and our faith in him—these are the things that must remain central. In embracing new methods of devotion, new ideas that inspire, we must not forget the tried-and-true power of prayer and study in the Word.

Go ahead and redecorate your spiritual house with new pictures on the walls. But if you're adding a new room, be careful not to chip away at the foundation. "For no one can lay any foundation other than the one already laid, which is Jesus Christ" (1 Cor. 3:11).

∞

Father, thanks for letting me share in what you are doing on the earth. I know that the power to accomplish the work you have set before me is in you. What I accomplish, I do by your strength. Jesus, you are the cornerstone and the foundation of all that lasts.

Small Beginnings Plus God Equal Great Things

Who despises the day of small things? Men will rejoice when they see the plumb line in the hand of Zerubbabel.—Zechariah 4:10

As soon as you decide you are going to obey God, don't be surprised if your faith is immediately challenged. And don't be upset if you find yourself looking foolish in the eyes of others at some point. Even some of your so-called friends may say, "Why are you doing *that?* Be reasonable! Don't you have any common sense?"

Sometimes reason and common sense can be our worst enemies, because common sense always tells us to take the way of reason while God tells us to take the way of faith. If God calls us to obey, we *must* obey, looking to him to do the impossible.

When Zerubbabel set out to build the temple, there were some who actively tried to discourage him and the other builders. They even "hired counselors to work against them" (Ezra 4:5)! Apparently, they were mocking them during the construction, saying things like "What are you doing *that* for?" But God spoke through Zechariah and said, "Who [with reason] despises the day of small things?" (Zech. 4:10 AMPLIFIED).

Reason says, "That is such an insignificant thing to do." God says, "Watch what I will do with your small things."

Never underestimate what God will do when you obey. Yes, what you're doing may look small, but God will take your five loaves of bread and feed five thousand! Lead one soul to Christ, and God may take that one and touch the world. Don't look with disgust and shame on the day of small beginnings. If God is telling you to do it, rejoice, because God will complete it, and he will be glorified.

∞

Lord, forgive me for the times when I have laughed at the small things, for the times when I have despised the small beginnings, for grumbling and complaining about the seemingly insignificant. I boldly confess today that it is in these small things that you are glorified when the great results finally come.

15

THURSDAY

Are You Sure You Want Jesus to Come?

And these are but the outer fringe of his works; how faint the whisper
we hear of him! Who then can understand the thunder
of his power?—Job 26:14

Often in church we find ourselves praying something like "Lord Jesus, come and dwell among us. Come in your power and grace and touch your people." But sometimes I wonder…Do we understand what we are asking for? What if he really answers that prayer? Would we really be glad he came?

Wherever Jesus went, there was both celebration and upheaval. Those who were delivered and healed rejoiced while others were annoyed. Some listeners hung on his every word while others hoped he would entrap himself. Cheers mixed with murmuring, and shouts of joy were accompanied by whispers of doubt. He never pleased everyone in the crowd. Isaiah prophesied concerning this, saying he would be a sanctuary for some but for others he would be a rock that would cause men to fall (see Isa. 8:14).

I'm convinced that many of us really don't want Jesus to show up in our churches. We want a god created in our image, a god like we want him to be. A safe god. Someone who will only do things when we want him to and who will stay in his place the rest of the time.

You see, when we invite the Almighty God among us, he brings his own agenda. Will he reveal himself to people with their own plans? It's like inviting Billy Graham to speak at your conference but asking him not to make any reference to Jesus Christ. Good luck!

It could be dangerous to invite Jesus to your church. He may cause a disturbance. But one thing is for sure: If he comes, your church will never be the same again.

∞

Lord, you are the Almighty God. Show me where I have forged a god in my own image. I resign myself to your agenda and your plan. Send your glory and power and give me the grace to receive.

The Power of the Submitted Life

Submit yourselves therefore to God.
—James 4:7 KJV

What do you think of when you hear the word *submit*? Some would say it means giving up your rights to an authority figure. To others, it is moving to a lesser, perhaps degrading, role.

When I think of submitting, I think of a trip I took with my family as a teenager. I had just received my driver's permit and insisted on driving every time an opportunity arose. We had rented a small motor home, and my parents had agreed to let me drive some of the time. When we were making our way through Utah, they permitted me not only to drive but to read the map and choose the best route. I selected what appeared to be a shortcut. What I did not perceive from the map was that the "shortcut" was through a mountain pass. Suddenly, I found myself driving the motor home over a small mountain road with dangerous turns. Eventually, I had to stop and turn around because the road ahead had been closed due to snow. By the time I reached the bottom of the mountain, my hands were shaking on the steering wheel, and I submitted to my parents' expertise as drivers and navigators. What a relief it was to scoot out of the driver's seat and let my dad be in charge again!

When we submit ourselves to God, we are saying, in effect, "Lord, you know the road ahead. You lead, and I'll follow." It is an act of trust, a relinquishing of control. I gladly turn the wheel of life over to his Lordship, because there are mysteries of life I will never comprehend.

What a relief it is to submit this way! What peace we have as we slide over and let God steer our lives! Our lives are not our own. They are his; he lives in us. He knows the dangerous turns that lie ahead, and we need his expertise and direction.

Herein lies the power of submission: "It is no longer I who live, but Christ lives in me" (Gal. 2:20 NKJV).

❧

Father, I gladly turn the wheel of my life over to you. I submit to your Lordship, your wisdom, and your plan. What power I realize as I do this! You raise me up, and I glorify you.

3/6/99

Weekend Reflections

In *Teaching a Stone to Talk,* Annie Dillard says, "Churches are children playing on the floor with their chemistry sets, mixing up a batch of TNT to kill a Sunday morning. It is madness to wear ladies' straw hats and velvet hats to church; we should all be wearing crash helmets. Ushers should issue life preservers and signal flares; they should lash us to our pews. For the sleeping God may wake some day and take offense, or the waking God may draw us out to where we can never return."

Faith is more than believing in God for answered prayers. It is knowing God and understanding how great and awesome his mighty power is. If we perceive God to be little more than our grandfather in heaven who fulfills our every desire, how can we trust him with our lives, much less the universe?

1. Why is an idol or graven image so detestable to God in relation to who he is?

   _____

   _____

2. The Bible tells us that the earth trembles at the power of God (Ps. 68:8). How does this relate to our understanding that we are loved and accepted by God because of the blood of Christ?

   _____

   _____

   _____

3. When is the last time you stood amazed at the power of God? What were the circumstances?

   _____

   _____

4. How can we truly love God and yet fear him? (Acts 9:31; Prov. 9:10.)

   _____

   _____

   _____

Watch, Wait, and Listen!

*In the morning You hear my voice, O Lord; in the morning I prepare
[a prayer, a sacrifice] for You and watch and wait [for You to
speak to my heart].*—Psalm 5:3 AMPLIFIED

One of the most difficult things for us to do as Christians is to wait
and listen quietly for God to speak to our hearts. So often it's easier for us
to *do* and *talk.*

I once heard someone describe a hard-working Christian woman who
found it difficult to *wait* on the Lord until someone told her that "to
wait" actually meant "to serve." Now, she could do *that.*

Like that woman, many of us are looking for a different way of waiting than, well, just *waiting.* We are afflicted with the "Martha attitude"
instead of choosing the "one thing [that] is needed," the one thing Mary
did as she sat at Jesus' feet and intently listened (Luke 10:42).

Too often we spend our time with the Lord—our prayer time—
thinking more about what we are praying for instead of thinking about
who we are praying to. Like Mary, we must learn to focus instead on the
"one thing [that] is needed," meditating on God's character, his grace, his
beauty, seeking to know him as so much more than a source of blessing
and provision.

Waiting means quietly listening. Learning to recognize his voice as it
speaks to our hearts. Fixing our eyes on him. Turning our thoughts from
the things that need to be done to the One who fills the true need of our
hearts.

❧

Oh God, quiet my heart so that I can wait in your presence, learning your
voice until my heart leaps at the sound of it...until my greatest quest as a
Christian is to sit at your feet.

WEEK 4

TUESDAY

Speak, Lord!

One thing I ask of the Lord, this is what I seek: that I may dwell in the house of the Lord all the days of my life, to gaze upon the beauty of the Lord and to seek him in his temple.—Psalm 27:4

We all communicate on different levels. Some of us tolerate silence only in very small doses; we feel uncomfortable unless we are swimming in a sea of verbiage. Still others of us are happy to sit, listening to the quiet. And God relates to us all.

I once asked a relative what true love meant to him. He said it's when two people can't stand being apart—not necessarily that they have to be always side by side but at least in the same room, he explained. I think he's right. Since he shared that idea, I have often noticed how couples in love enjoy just being together, not always talking but just being near each other. Sometimes a husband and wife will settle into easy chairs and read separate books or magazines "together." Some lovers take long walks and hardly talk at all. Other couples, especially the younger ones, stay on the phone for hours, not really saying anything, just knowing that a certain someone is on the other end of the line.

We feel the same need for nearness when we're deeply in love with the Lord. We don't always have to be praying to him to show our love for him. And he doesn't have to always be speaking to our hearts to show us he's there. Once, after lifting up quite a long list of needs to the Lord in prayer, I paused for a moment and said quietly, "Speak, Lord," as I had so often done before. No sooner had I said this than I sensed the heart of my Father saying, without my actually hearing the words, *Must I always speak when you ask?*

That's when it occurred to me that perhaps God sometimes wants us to simply be there with him with no grocery list of requests, no agenda, no secret intentions. It's enough, I realized, just to be together with the Father and know that he and I are there in the same place. He wants not just our fellowship but a relationship...not just communication but communion.

∽

Lord, teach me not to be impatient when I don't hear your voice. Let me be happy just to sense your presence and know that we are together.

20

What Are You Listening For?

Since ancient times no one has heard, no ear has perceived, no eye has seen any God besides you, who acts on behalf of those who wait for him.—Isaiah 64:4

Do you ever feel like saying, "Just do something, God! I know you're up there. Say something!"? Surely that's how Isaiah felt as he cried out, "Oh, that you would rend the heavens" (Isa. 64:1). In other words, "I know you're up there, God! Just *do* something!"

I am convinced that God shows himself more than we realize. I believe he speaks to us, but our hearts are not always tuned to the necessary wavelength.

I am reminded of the story of the country dweller who went to visit his friend in New York City. As they walked down one of the busy streets, there, amid all the busyness, the visitor remarked that he heard a cricket chirping. His city friend looked at him in disbelief and said it would be impossible to hear a cricket above all the noise of the city. Walking over to a planter, the visitor reached down and pulled out the cricket. "Man hears what he listens for," he said.

God does not scream to make himself heard above the noise in today's busy lifestyles. Instead, he is there for those who turn off their natural ears and listen with their hearts for his still, small voice.

He spoke through Isaiah, saying, "When I called, no one answered, when I spoke, no one listened" (Isa. 66:4). God "shows Himself active on behalf of him who [earnestly] waits for Him" (64:4 AMPLIFIED). God is ready to reveal himself and to speak to those who will earnestly wait and listen.

Who are you waiting for? What are you listening for?

⮾

Lord, teach my heart to hear your voice, to recognize it among the many voices I hear each day. As I learn to earnestly wait, I will rejoice in your work on my behalf.

21

WEEK 4

THURSDAY

He Who Hath Ears to Hear, Let Him Hear

The sheep listen to his voice. He calls his own sheep by name and leads them out.... His sheep follow him because they know his voice.—John 10:3–4

I am frustrated from time to time when an old friend calls and puts me through the agony of guessing who he or she is. If the caller is someone I haven't talked with in a long time, I may not be able to link the voice with a face. On the other hand, I quickly recognize the voices of those people I speak with regularly. Usually, all they have to say is hello, and in that instant I know who's calling.

The same is true when God speaks to us. If we're in touch with him frequently, if we often sense him speaking to our hearts, we know instantly that it is God's voice we hear. But if we don't listen for it, if it's been a long time since we were quiet enough to hear him speaking to us, we may not recognize what's happening.

The only way we can quickly recognize God's voice is to hear it often. In frequent times of communion with him, we learn the sound of his voice, the warmth of his love, the encouragement of his grace.

Then we wait, as Mary waited at the tomb. And when, in that quietness, he calls our names, we will instantly respond, "Rabboni!" We recognize him as he calls to us because we have sat at his feet and heard his voice time and time again.

Lord, teach me to recognize your voice quickly. Whether I am alone or in crowds of people, I want to hear and identify your voice. Be my shepherd, Lord, and I will be one of your sheep who knows and responds to what you say.

A Sure Word

*The boy Samuel ministered before the Lord under Eli. In those days
the word of the Lord was rare; there were not many visions. Now
Samuel did not yet know the Lord: The word of the Lord had
not yet been revealed to him.*— 1 Samuel 3:1, 7

Oh, to hear a sure word from the Lord! How often we find ourselves
in situations where we so desire to know God's word for that moment.
We long to be like the prophet Samuel, a man who spoke the Word of
the Lord with surety and boldness. The Bible says, "The Lord was with
Samuel as he grew up, and he let none of his words fall to the ground"
(1 Sam. 3:19). Everything Samuel declared came to pass. Now, that is
quite a testament!

But Samuel's gift of prophecy could not come until he learned to
know God's voice. Since his earliest years, Samuel had ministered before
the Lord. When God first spoke to him, Samuel did not recognize the
voice of God, but as he learned to listen and obey, he came to know and
speak the sure word of the Lord.

Do you recognize God's speaking in your heart? If not, keep studying
his Word and praying for his presence in your life. There will come a time
when you know the sound of his voice. Then, as you minister to others,
you will be the voice of God in their lives. You will say something and
find later that your words were exactly what God was saying.

Listen for God's voice and be quick to obey in matters that at the time
seem insignificant. Then God will entrust you with matters of greater
importance. Over time, because of the character God has built in you,
you will find joy in all of his words, and you will rejoice in the power of
those words to bring life.

∞

Lord, I desire to know your voice, to speak as an oracle of God, to bring a
sure word at the right time so that others will be called to hear and obey your
voice as well. I surrender my desire to speak great things before I learn to
speak as a child. Thank you for being patient with me as I learn when to listen
and when to speak.

Weekend Reflections

"Then a voice came from heaven, 'I have glorified it, and will glorify it again.' The crowd that was there and heard it said it had thundered; others said an angel had spoken to him" (John 12:28–29).

What does God's voice sound like? When the Father spoke from heaven when Jesus was baptized, apparently not everyone heard the same thing. Some said it thundered; some heard an angel. Jesus heard His Father.

The fact remains: Not everyone is listening when God speaks, and not everyone understands. Only those who know God will truly hear what God has to say. Seven times in Revelation, within the space of two chapters, the Scriptures declare, "He who has an ear, let him hear what the Spirit says to the churches."

1. Have you ever heard God's voice? What did it sound like?

   _____

   _____

   _____

2. Examine several references in Scripture where God spoke. What description is used? (for example, 1 Kings 19:12—a whisper)

   _____

   _____

   _____

3. In your time alone with God, set aside a larger portion of time to be still and listen. Write down what you believe God says to you.

   _____

   _____

   _____

   _____

4. How can we judge whether or not we are hearing the voice of God?

   _____

   _____

   _____

Stumbling Over the Stumbling Stone

They stumbled over the "stumbling stone." As it is written: "See, I lay in Zion a stone that causes men to stumble and a rock that makes them fall, and the one who trusts in him will never be put to shame."—Romans 9:32–33

You probably have seen those pictures that seem like one thing to some people and something else to others. One person looks at such a picture and sees an old lady while another sees a beautiful young miss. What seems so obvious to one viewer is not so apparent to someone else. That's the way it was for the religious people of Jesus' day. They were anxiously awaiting the Messiah's appearing. But when he came, they didn't know him. They looked right at God and saw something else. Jesus said distress would befall them "because [they] did not recognize the time of [their] visitation from God" (Luke 19:44 NRSV). They were looking for God...and stumbled right over him.

Today, we are capable of making the same mistake. In our quest for knowledge, discipline, and goodness, we can miss the whole point—fellowship with the One who makes us good. We search for him and think we have found him, only to later discover we have embraced counterfeit Christianity. The enemy of our souls wants us to believe that the form is real. He wants us to get so caught up in running the race that we fail to walk with Jesus.

Maybe you're searching for Jesus and looking too hard. He's a lot closer than you think. The apostle Paul said, "Men would seek him and perhaps reach out for him and find him, though he is not far from each one of us" (Acts 17:27).

❦

Oh God, don't let me be one of those who misses the point. I want to see. I want to know the time of my visitation.

Hide and Seek

*You will seek me and find me when you seek me with all
your heart.*—Jeremiah 29:13

We humans often enjoy seeking after something as much as we enjoy possessing it. Perhaps it's because God knows us so well, knows our love of seeking after things, that he seems to delight in sometimes being elusive. As believers, we know he is there, but we don't always sense his presence. When we seek him, he sometimes reveals himself to us one glory at a time. He lets us catch a glimpse of him here…then there. And slowly in our quest to know him, his character unfolds before us—and within us—like a stunning masterpiece that appears one brushstroke at a time.

Think of Elijah, who spent forty days and nights on Mount Horeb. Elijah probably looked for God in the wind that suddenly swirled around him and then in the earthquake that shook the mighty mountain and in the fire that blazed down upon him. But God, perhaps delighting in being elusive, was not in any of the obvious places. Instead, Elijah finally found the Almighty God of the universe where he might have least expected him: in a still, small voice.

It would be so much easier today if we could find God in the obvious places: the booming thunder or the roaring surf or some other kind of natural phenomenon. But usually that is not where he chooses to be found. Instead, he seems to show up in the most unexpected ways…as a babe in a manger…or as a stranger on the road to Emmaus. So often, like Jacob considering the ladder that rose to heaven, we only recognize after the fact that God was there.

God knows us and understands us. He knows we cherish a prize more dearly if we've expended some effort in finding it. And he loves to be found.

∞

Lord, I pray that when I cannot readily sense your presence, my faith will motivate me to diligently seek you in every part of my life. Help me to realize that you are always near. Open my eyes, sharpen my senses so that I can see you in the everyday and in the unexpected.

Mountain Experiences

After leaving them, he went up on a mountainside to pray.
—Mark 6:46

The first time I stepped up to the edge of the Grand Canyon, the view literally took my breath away. The overwhelming beauty and grandeur of this natural wonder transfixed me. People I could see hiking near the bottom looked like ants. Miles and miles of the untamed Colorado River snaked through the canyon, a small company of rough-and-ready rafters having the ride of their lives. In that moment I could sense nature gloriously bellowing out its song of praise to its Creator. It was an experience unlike anything I'd ever known.

I like to think that perhaps it was a magnificent experience like the one I enjoyed at the Grand Canyon that explains, at least in part, why Jesus often went to the mountain. Maybe on the mountain he was able to clear his mind of the mundane and fix his eyes again on the eternal purpose at hand. The homes and villages that spread below him across the valley were amazing evidence of man's workmanship, but the mountain... ah...the mountain was familiar. This was his creation. His word had formed every peak and given life to every plant and creature that clung to the rocky soil. He went to the mountain to pray. Perhaps he prayed about another mountain—a hill, actually—that he would climb before too much longer.

It was on that smaller mount that the Father would demonstrate his love for us again, fixing a point between heaven and earth where God could meet mankind without judgment. For there, justice was served and mercy kissed that mount with each drop of blood.

Today, like Jesus, we go to the mountain. We go to enjoy the view—and to feel close to God. If we cannot literally go, we can always close our eyes and trek up Mount Calvary...and there remember and experience a love beyond anything we've ever known.

∞

Shepherd of my soul, I will follow as you lead me up the mountain. There, let me see things from your perspective and pray as you teach me to pray.

3/25/99

To See Jesus

They came to Philip, who was from Bethsaida in Galilee, with a
request. "Sir," they said, "We would like to see Jesus."
—John 12:21

From the Scriptures we can rightfully conclude that there are several realms beyond what we can see with our natural eyes. (The apostle Paul speaks of at least three. See 2 Cor. 12:1–2.) We should be more than just a little interested about such things, about viewing the supernatural. More than just a natural curiosity about the unknown, we should feel a hunger to see Jesus.

We will see him only as our natural passions fade. Our spiritual senses become focused only when the carnal is laid aside. So do not expect visions of glory to spring up in the middle of your physical surroundings. We must first "cast down" the temporal images before we can see the spiritual (see 2 Cor. 10:5 KJV). As one fades from view, the other just naturally comes into focus.

As Helen Lemmel wrote so effectively, "Turn your eyes upon Jesus. Look full in his wonderful face. And the things of the earth will grow strangely dim in the light of his glory and grace."

If we wish to see Jesus, we must deliberately and decisively turn away from idols, from selfish desires and ambition, from lazy and slothful devotion. As we turn away from these things of the world and turn instead toward our Lord and what is Holy, we will begin to understand and know what was there all along but could not be discerned. The more we exercise our spiritual senses and put to death the carnal, the more enlightenment will be poured out on us.

❧

Lord, what things have consumed my vision? May the real desire of my heart be to see your world, to turn my eyes to heavenly things, and to fix you as the goal of my affections.

Who Is Seeking Whom?

*But if from there you seek the Lord your God, you will find him if you
look for him with all your heart and with all your soul.*
—Deuteronomy 4:29

"I don't know. There is just no passion in my faith anymore. I mean,
I go to church on a regular basis, but it's like God has forgotten that I
exist. I don't sense him like I used to. He seems so far away."

We have all heard such laments—or maybe thought them ourselves
on occasion. But God does not violate his principles, and he has said,
"Never will I leave you" (Heb. 13:5). So what is happening when we feel
this way? Could it be that we have ceased to seek him? Could it be that
we're pursuing happiness or a successful career more intently than we're
seeking God?

The fact is we must deliberately decide every day to seek the Lord.
It's a decision we make for ourselves regardless of our circumstances. As
Joshua said, "Choose for yourselves this day whom you will serve" (Josh.
24:15). Serving God must be a lifestyle, not just an emotional, one-time
decision. Service demands "all your heart and all your soul" (Josh. 22:5).
We're to seek him earnestly and call out to him, not with a halfhearted
whimper, but with a plea for divine fellowship that arises from our innermost beings.

When I read the psalms of David, I become envious of such a friendship with God. But David did not find this close relationship through a
religious once-a-week encounter. He daily encountered God. His desire
was a constant thirst. We hear this heart-cry when he says, "As the deer
pants for streams of water, so my soul pants for you, O God" (Ps. 42:1).

If you would know God's presence and sense his heart, cultivate your
desire. Set out on your own search for God. Seek him, and you will find
him just as they did, not far away but very close indeed.

⊗⊗

Oh Lord, cause my desire to grow. Replace this wandering heart of mine with
a seeking heart, a heart that longs to know you, to hear your voice, to see
your face. Enlighten my path with the lamp of your Word. There are many
paths that seem to lead to you. Let me choose the right one, the one that
leads to your presence.

3/27/99

Weekend Reflections

God says, "You will seek me and find me when you seek me with all your heart" (Jer. 29:13).

An intimate relationship doesn't just happen. A great friendship is forged by communication, fellowship, and the fire of tough times. So it is with God. If we would really know him intimately, we must pursue knowing him. We must spend time with him—talking, listening, inviting him to walk with us through life's pleasure and pain.

1. The psalmist wrote, "As the deer pants for streams of water, so my soul pants for you, O God" (Ps. 42:1). What similarities can be drawn between the thirsty deer and man or woman who is in pursuit of God?

   _____

   _____

   _____

   _____

2. What three steps can you take now that will encourage you to pursue after God?

   _____

   _____

   _____

3. Communication, fellowship, and walking together through tough times strengthen a relationship. Are any of these missing from your friendship with God? Are you weak in any of these areas? Which ones?

   _____

   _____

   _____

A Slave by Choice

I put this in human terms because you are weak in your natural selves.
Just as you used to offer the parts of your body in slavery to impurity
and to ever-increasing wickedness, so now offer them in slavery to
righteousness leading to holiness. —Romans 6:19

How much energy did you expend offering yourself to sin before you became a new creature?

Often, when we look back, it seems to have taken us no effort at all to serve sin. But in reality we may have done many things to nurture that lifestyle. After all, it takes money, time, and other personal sacrifices to measure up to the world's standards and keep up with the pace of the party crowd. The more we expend ourselves on earthly pleasures, the more those pleasures demand of us...until they enslave us. Things that once brought pleasure soon become insatiable desires that gnaw away at us and are never fulfilled.

The key to living a victorious Christian life that resists this kind of bondage is to offer ourselves as servants of God. As we yield to God's righteousness and purity with the same energy and effort we once expended on fulfilling our selfish desires, we can become slaves to righteousness instead of slaves to wickedness. Instead of a desire for something impure, the desire for God's presence can grow within us, becoming a thirst that is quenched only when we are in fellowship with him. This is the "slavery to righteousness leading to holiness."

Are we offering ourselves to God so that Christ is formed in us? Or are we expending our energy to resist God's work in us and enslaving ourselves instead to "impurity and to ever-increasing wickedness"?

∞

Today, Lord, I yield myself to the working of your Spirit. I willingly offer myself to you as an instrument of righteousness so that Christ may be formed and revealed in me.

surrender

WEEK 6
TUESDAY

The Living Way

Having therefore, brethren, boldness to enter into the holiest by the
blood of Jesus, by a new and living way, which he hath consecrated
for us, through the veil, that is to say, his flesh.
—Hebrews 10:19–20 KJV

When we stand at the foot of the Cross, we may feel like the children of Israel must have felt as they stood before the curtain in the temple that separated them from the Holy Place. On the other side of that veil was the awesomeness of God, which stood in stark contrast to their own human frailty. And on the other side of the Cross of Christ is life with Christ, which is a far cry from the "dead life" we live without Christ. But in order to share that glorious new life with the Father, we must follow the Son through the veil of death.

When we are faced with the holiness of his glory, we see ourselves in a new light and recognize that part of us must die. So we go the way that millions have gone before, the way of the Cross, to nail that part of us that is not like him to the tree.

Dying to self may seem a lonely process, but we do not make this passage alone. There is One who meets us at death's door. As David said, "Though [we] walk through the valley of the shadow of death," we do not fear, for he is with us. Even his rod and staff are comforting because they let us know that he is near (Ps. 23). And on the other side of the valley is true life in Christ. From darkness to light…from death to life.

So we do not dread the way of death after all, because he is there. He takes our hands and guides us safely to the other side of the Cross into sweet communion with the Father.

∞

Lord, thank you for walking the way of suffering before me. You know the loneliness of the narrow way. You took the sting of death onto yourself so that I can now have comfort in knowing you love me even in those difficult moments when I struggle to put to death another part of myself. Let me see death to my old self as a joyful time when our relationship is restored to the fullest.

Concern or Pride?

*My heart is not proud, O Lord, my eyes are not haughty; I do not con-
cern myself with great matters or things too wonderful for me. But I
have stilled and quieted my soul; like a weaned child with its mother,
like a weaned child is my soul within me.*—Psalm 131:1–2

Oh, the many masks of pride! In this passage, the psalmist astutely
links pride with worry, a pairing that came as a surprise to me the first
time I read these verses. But how true it is: pride does, indeed, lie beneath
the guise of needless concern. Most worry is rooted in selfishness, self-
centeredness, and pride. In contrast, people who are giving and unselfish
tend not to concern themselves with things they cannot change. They
don't spend much time worrying about themselves or what *might* happen
in the future.

When Jesus commissioned the apostle Peter, "Feed my sheep," he also
indicated what would happen at the end of Peter's life, even telling him
the kind of death he would have. Certainly, this was not an easy thing for
Peter to swallow. He immediately pointed to John and asked, "Lord, what
about him?" (see John 21:17–19).

Jesus' answer echoes down the ages to our ears today: "What is that
to you? You must follow me" (John 21:22). Our responsibility is to follow him, letting God deal with others as he sees fit, leaving up to him
those "great matters or things too wonderful."

To follow Jesus is to lay down our selfishness and pride and, in so
doing, to relinquish our needless concerns and worries about things
beyond our control. We're simply to deny ourselves—even denying ourselves self-indulgences such as worry—and take up the cross and follow
him (see Matt. 16:24). To follow him is to trust that he will lead us down
the best road for us, that he will care for us and be faithful to us. As the
psalmist did, we choose to still and quiet our souls in his presence—abdi-
cating the responsibilities of those "great matters" or "things too wonderful" and believing God is big enough to handle them without our help.

❧

Lord, you are so great and awesome. You handle great matters with ease and
wisdom. Help me to give up my pointless anxiety and concern, laying all my
cares on you, knowing how much you care for me.

surrender

Where Are You?

*And they heard the sound of the Lord God walking in the garden in
the cool of the day, and Adam and his wife hid themselves from the
presence of the Lord God among the trees of the garden. Then the Lord
God called to Adam and said to him, "Where are you?"*
—Genesis 3:8–9 NKJV

When God asks a question, it isn't to gather facts. He already knows
all the answers! God asks questions for our sake, not for his. It is the
course God often chooses to bring us to a confession of truth. When God
asks a question, it's time to "fess up!"

Where are you right now? Are you trying to hide from God, rejecting
his love because you have too much pride to repent and admit your sin-
fulness? As Adam learned, when we run from the truth, we only deceive
ourselves. There is no place to hide from God. And consider this:
Although God knew Adam and Eve were guilty, it was not in judgment
that he pursued them. The first issue was love, *then* judgment. His first
question of them was not, "What have you done?" but, "Adam, where are
you?"

Adam ran. Love pursued.

Today God asks us the same question. Where are you? Are you trying
to hide from his presence? What deed has brought you such shame that
you would turn away from his love? Confess—and run to him.

∞

Lord, I hear you walking in my life sometimes, and I run away. But you already
know my deeds, my heart. I will turn to you, Father. Where else can I go? "You
alone have the words that give eternal life" (John 6:68 NLT). I will rejoice at the
sound of your voice.

Reserved

If you listen carefully to what he says and do all that I say, I will be an enemy to your enemies and will oppose those who oppose you....Then he took the Book of the Covenant and read it to the people. They responded, "We will do everything the Lord has said; we will obey."
—Exodus 23:22; 24:7

What would happen if, in our churches on Sunday morning, everyone stood up and said wholeheartedly, "We will do everything the Lord has said; we will obey"? What power and glory could you know if you would declare the same? The truth is this is exactly what God expects. He resists the proud but gives grace to the humble. And what greater humility is there than saying, "We will do everything you say, Lord"?

There are many who are ready to receive Jesus as their Savior. There are few who are willing to receive him as their Savior *and Lord*. But he will not be Savior unless he is also Lord. Often the people who are not living an abundant, overcoming life are the same ones who gasp, "Surely God does not want me to give up *this!*" Or they ask, "Must I really be baptized?" Having this attitude is like hanging a sign on part of their heart that says "Reserved for Myself." As long as we are not fully obeying, we will not be fully blessed. As long as the church is halfhearted in its service and devotion, it will not experience the power the church of Acts had.

On the other hand, when we hear his voice and obey everything he says, God will not only be on our side, he will fight for us. As he told the Israelites, "I will be an enemy to your enemies and will oppose those who oppose you."

∞

Jesus, I declare you are not only my Savior but also my Lord. Is there any place I have reserved in my heart for myself? What have you asked me to do that I have failed to obey? Show me the truth, Lord. I will do everything you say.

35

4/3/99

surrender

Weekend Reflections

Someone once asked William Booth, founder of the Salvation Army, about the secret of his success. After several moments of quiet reflection, he said, "There have been men with greater brains or opportunities than I, but I made up my mind that God would have all of William Booth there was."

God is not looking for half-surrendered soldiers. He asks for full surrender.

1 Is there something you know God is asking you to do that you have been resisting? What has been your excuse?

_____

_____

_____

_____

2. Do you fear a full surrender to God? Why?

_____

_____

_____

_____

3. The psalmist said, "I do not concern myself with great matters or things too wonderful for me" (Ps. 131:1). *Surrender* includes the relinquishing of "needless concerns and worries of things beyond our control." What "great matters" do you need to surrender to God?

_____

_____

_____

_____

love

Why Did God Make Man and Woman So Different?

*"For this reason a man will leave his father and mother and be united
to his wife, and the two will become one flesh." This is a profound
mystery—but I am talking about Christ and the church.*
—Ephesians 5:31–32

Think of it: What if men and women were just alike? Marriages would be smoother, there would be fewer problems in the workplace, and the world in general would be a happier place. Or would it?

God has compared marriage to his relationship with his church. Thus we can learn a lot about God as we look at the institution of marriage and the relationship that goes along with it. For example, God created the woman in such a way that for her to be intimate there must be relationship. If she could be intimate without relationship, there would be no need to pursue the "getting to know each other" process. The relationship must not be looked at as the means to an end, such as sexual intimacy, but should be appreciated itself, for what it is. We should actually come to enjoy the road there and not just the getting there.

Through all this we see the heart of God, how he desires a relationship with us and not merely the "I'll really love you, God, if you'll just answer my prayer" kind of association. In time, we actually begin to enjoy the "getting to know you" journey. It becomes the heart of our passion, our real goal, more than just a means to receiving what God will do for us as a result.

In marriage we see a symbol of God's undying commitment to us. God is in this for the long haul. He isn't interested in just short-term results. We are in covenant together. We commit to loving him, and he commits to loving us even while we are changing and growing.

This is the kind of love that must be in a marriage and in our relationship with God. Not "I'll love you when," but "I love you still."

∞

Lord, I know you as my Savior and Lord. But I also want to know you as Father and Friend. I am grateful for your commitment to love me through the process of becoming. In return, I pray that I would have a strong resolve to find a deeper place of intimacy with you.

love

TUESDAY

Mine, Yours, and His

_If you cling to your life, you will lose it; but if you give it up for me,
you will find it._—Matthew 10:39 NLT

It's one of the first words we learn to say. Babies quickly learn the power of this forceful utterance. When another little unsuspecting tyke comes too close to a cherished possession, watch the baby clutch whatever he or she is afraid of losing, furrow that little brow, and shout, "Mine!"

We learn this word early, and we struggle throughout our lives to give it up. Even though we learn to share our possessions, other things are not so easy to turn loose of. Consider the following:

- Our children interrupt our favorite TV shows, wanting to play with us.
- Our sleep is interrupted by a call from the Holy Spirit to intercede for someone we barely know.
- Our spouses get sick on our day off work.

Though we may not say the word out loud, our actions may shout _Mine!_ in situations such as these. The word itself does not have to be spoken for others to know how we feel. Here are some other ways we may be subtly exhibiting our selfishness:

- Remind everyone of what belongs to us.
- Put what makes us happy above what makes others happy.
- Fill our conversation with the pronouns _I, me,_ and _my._
- Complain when our loved ones spend too much time with others.
- Frequently remind others of the gifts we have given.

Instead of getting the desired results of friendship, love, and acceptance, by such antics we actually drive our loved ones away. When our eyes are fixed so rigidly on our own needs, we fail to see the needs of others.

Cling, clutch, grip, and grab—and life will slide right through your fingers. But Jesus offers us the real recipe for abundant life: When we open our hands and our hearts and let go of those things we once clung to so selfishly, abundant life will come pouring in.

∽

Father, every good thing I have is from you. I am so grateful! However, there are some things I have clung to, thinking that I own them. I lay them before you and consecrate them now.

True Love Is Vulnerable

Do your best to come to me quickly, for Demas, because he loved this world, has deserted me and has gone to Thessalonica. Crescens has gone to Galatia, and Titus to Dalmatia. Only Luke is with me.
—2 Timothy 4:9–11

True love requires us to be vulnerable, honest, and frank. It always includes risk and uncertainty, because, unfortunately, not everyone we love will love us back and not everyone who loves us will do so forever.

Paul wrestled with disappointment and loneliness when his other associates abandoned him and he was left with only Luke. But he also reaped a rich harvest from the seeds of love he had sown throughout the region.

Though everyone you love will not love you back, your love will not be wasted. Only the Lord of the harvest knows when and where you will reap from the seeds of love you have sown. But rest assured: There will be a harvest, and if you have sown your love generously, you will also reap generously (see 2 Cor. 9:6). Sow anger, reap anger. Sow selfishness, reap isolation. Sow friendship, reap friends. No one ever said it better than C. S. Lewis in his book *The Four Loves:*

> To love at all is to be vulnerable. Love anything, and your heart will certainly be wrung and possibly be broken. If you want to make sure of keeping it intact, you must give your heart to no one, not even to an animal. Wrap it carefully round with hobbies and little luxuries; avoid all entanglements; lock it up safe in the casket or coffin of your selfishness. But in that casket—safe, dark, motionless, airless—it will change. It will not be broken; it will become unbreakable, impenetrable, irredeemable.... The only place outside Heaven where you can be perfectly safe from all the dangers of love...is Hell.

God, you are the ultimate example of what true love should be. You loved, and yet the world did not love you back. Lord, I choose to love others because you have loved me. You give me the power to love because I am loved by you.

4-8-99

love
THURSDAY

Passion Makes a Difference

Yet I am not ashamed, because I know whom I have believed.
—2 Timothy 1:12

It is an accepted fact that only 30 percent of what we communicate is verbal. The rest of the message we're sending is carried by such unspoken things as our tone of voice and our body language. Our passion for what we are sharing comes out more obviously in *how* we say it rather than in *what* we say. As Emerson said, "What you *are* speaks so loudly I cannot hear what you say."

If we are going to be effective witnesses of the power of Jesus Christ, we must share the good news passionately. Others must not only hear the truth we're sharing but, by seeing the passion with which we carry the message, also understand how urgent this message is. They need to feel the affection we have for the gospel and sense the love we have for the Savior. But unless we are totally convinced, ourselves, that what we are saying is true, there will be no passion in the way we express it to others.

This passion arises from confidence. As the apostle Paul stated, "I am not ashamed because I *know whom* I have believed" (emphasis added). It's not just that we know the facts. We know *him*. And that gives us the assurance to believe what he has said and done. The relationship factor is the key to passion.

We can know all the right things to say—have a great formula of sound theology—but if there is no passion, no confidence, or conviction in our colloquy, we may have "lookers" but no "takers."

∞

Lord, renew the passion of my heart. Let the fervency of my relationship with you shine through the words I say so that others may believe you are alive in me. May the fire of the Holy Spirit burn out my complacency, pride, and insecurity and in its place kindle a new boldness and confidence.

Learning to Be Gentle

But we were gentle among you, like a mother caring for her little children.—1 Thessalonians 2:7

Gentleness may be the most often forgotten attribute of Christ. No one was more focused and determined to complete his mission than Christ himself, yet he knew how to be gentle when it was fitting. He was a "gentleman."

Gentleness is not always a convenient response, especially for some of us men. Often it seems so much easier to us to simply barge in, take control, demand attention, and complete whatever action is needed. Occasionally, that kind of response is appropriate. But often, an attitude of gentleness is much more beneficial and nurturing to all concerned.

Gentleness can be a natural response because it is a fruit of the Spirit. As we allow the Spirit to work within us, it will bear fruit, and gentleness will flow from us just as naturally as joy. I like to say that gentleness brings a certain "fragrance" to other fruits of the Spirit such as joy and faith. Consider how much easier it is to hear truth wrapped in the fragrance of gentleness rather than having it blasted at us in a harsh and arrogant way. Love, too, goes a lot further when it's steeped in gentleness rather than soaked with demands.

To become more Christlike, we must become more like the One who said, "Take my yoke upon you and learn from me, for I am gentle and humble in heart, and you will find rest for your souls" (Matt. 11:29).

Lord, I confess that I am not always gentle when I need to be. You are the perfect combination of gentleness and strength, and in you I find the power to be gentle.

41

Weekend Reflections

Love should not be something we keep but something that is given. As Jesus said to Peter, "Do you love me?... Feed my sheep" (John 21:17). In a similar way, Mother Teresa said it like this, "Love, to be real, must cost. It must hurt. It must empty us of self" (*USA Today*, November 17, 1986).

1. What are the top three things about your spouse that you're most thankful for.

   _____

   _____

   _____

   _____

   _____

2. Love includes risk and vulnerability. When was the last time you were really transparent with someone?

   _____

   _____

   _____

   _____

3. Selfishness kills love. What three unselfish things will you do this week for someone you love?

   _____

   _____

   _____

   _____

   _____

Was He an Angel?

*Then they also will answer Him, saying, "Lord, when did we see You
hungry or thirsty or a stranger or naked or sick or in prison, and did
not minister to You?"*—Matthew 25:44 NKJV

It was a Tuesday evening about nine o'clock. I had just finished
rehearsal with the worship team and rhythm section. I was exhausted,
hungry, and ready to go home. I was ready to turn out the lights when a
man who looked to be in his early forties stepped through the door. He
walked to the front of the meeting room, saw the piano, and asked if he
could play.

The man was untidy, to say the least. He was wearing several layers of
clothes, and they were all rumpled and soiled. His blond hair was cut
neatly, but it looked as if it hadn't been shampooed in days.

I reluctantly told him he could play, so he sat down at the piano and
began to play songs I didn't recognize. After several minutes, I told him I
needed to lock up and go home. He said, "Sure," and quit playing. We
chatted for a couple of minutes, and I asked him his name.

"Oh, you don't need to know my name," he said. "I'm nobody."

I tried to reason with him, telling him he *was* somebody. He continued to kindly but firmly say, "Look, I know what you're trying to do.
Don't bother." We walked out, and I locked the door and said good-bye.

Later it occurred to me, *What if he was an angel?*

Suddenly, I was overwhelmed with the joy of even thinking about
such an encounter. I wanted to go back and find him, hoping we could
talk some more. Then I felt such shame over my selfishness. I was ready
to serve him if he was an angel. But when I had thought he was just
another vagrant looking for a handout, I was too tired.

Jesus said, "I tell you the truth, whatever you did not do for one of the
least of these, you did not do for me" (Matt. 25:45). In some amazing way,
I am actually ministering to Jesus when I minister to the least of his.

❦

Father, forgive me for the times I have turned away from reasonable service.
Help me to see the genuine opportunities where I can serve you. Let me love
others with your compassion and bless them in the same way you have
blessed me.

service

Good Impressions

We were not looking for praise from men, not from you or anyone else.
—1 Thessalonians 2:6

The goal of ministry service must be to point others to Jesus, not to ourselves. Our aim is not to impress them with our abilities, to have them think, *My, isn't he eloquent!* The sign of effective ministry is when others exclaim, "My, isn't Jesus wonderful!"

This means that as we minister we lay down our desire for affirmation, our need for praise and applause. We will be effective ministers when people walk away feeling impressed with Jesus more than with our own gifts and abilities.

Jesus told us, "Anyone who does not take his cross and follow me is not worthy of me. Whoever finds his life will lose it, and whoever loses his life for my sake will find it" (Matt. 10:38–39). The cross is the symbol of death, but here it is not *his* death that is symbolized but ours: death to selfishness and pride. In our total commitment to him, we show our willingness to lose our life for his sake. And we choose not to glory in our sacrifice but in his.

Lest we should think God unkind, we must remember that it is the losing of our lives that brings real life. This is the point when we really begin living. As one dear sister of the faith said, "You think you're livin' now? Honey, you ain't lived 'til you been livin' for Jesus!"

We preach the gospel of Christ, not *our* gospel. We lift up his Cross, his life, his greatness, and lay down our own. And in doing so, we find new and abundant life.

∞

Father, I pray that through me your light will shine. By what I do, may others be impressed with you more than with me. May they see your life in me as I lose myself in you.

What's in It for Me?

A new command I give you: Love one another. As I have loved you, so you must love one another.—John 13:34

When folks are "too nice," we often suspect that they have ulterior motives. It seems rare to find people who bestow kindness when they have nothing to gain.

Truly unselfish love can only come from God. This is the kind of love described in those familiar verses in the Gospel of John: "For God so loved the world, that he gave his only begotten Son" (3:16 KJV) and "Greater love hath no man than this, that a man lay down his life for his friends" (15:13 KJV).

God had nothing to gain by loving the world except fellowship with his creation. That is all he asks of us: to love him and to be loved by him. Yet he came down to earth and suffered the cruelest of human fates so that he could be with us forever.

Sometimes the way we take advantage of his love seems blatantly shameful. Too often when we come before God's presence, our first tendency is to pull out our wish list: "God, since I know I have your attention…" Instead of asking only for selfish benefits, we need to ask God to give us hearts that have a passion for communion with him. We need to thank him for the unequaled love he shows us—and ask him to help us show that same love to others.

May God grant us the grace to seek him for the sake of selfless, unpretentious love. There is no other way we can do it, for he is the only source of such unselfish love.

∞

Father, there is no fountain of life besides you. When I love, let it be with the love of Christ. When I hate, let it be only what you hate.

service

Loving Jesus

Again Jesus said, "Simon son of John, do you truly love me?" He
answered, "Yes, Lord, you know that I love you." Jesus said,
"Take care of my sheep."—John 21:16

Jesus' instructions to us to serve one another do not go over too well in a society that lives by the rule "Look out for number one." But those who know God also know that the one who is serving is the one who truly receives. We learn this lesson by following his example. We also learn it because sometimes he places us in positions where we have no other options!

We show our love for Christ by serving others, and our attitudes as we serve them show how genuine our love for him really is. If our attitude is *What a chore!* we are showing that our love for Christ may not be as deep as we would like it to be.

One of the greatest ways to find joy in service is to picture ourselves serving Christ. For example, instead of seeing ourselves helping a whining child or comforting a helpless invalid, we see ourselves serving Christ. This is where true freedom to serve becomes possible. We do it as though we are "working for the Lord, not for men" (Col. 3:23).

"Take care of my sheep," Jesus tells us.

"Lord, you know that I love you," we reply.

"Take care of my sheep," he echoes.

And then he guides us toward the pasture...

∞

Lord, if I would love you today, I know that I must love my brothers and sisters. Give me the eyes to see those around me in the light of your love. Instead of seeing their faces, may I see yours.

The Motivational Factor

*And though I bestow all my goods to feed the poor, and though I give
my body to be burned, but have not love, it profits me nothing.*
—1 Corinthians 13:3 NKJV

What motivates you in the work you do for Christ? Why do you do what you do? Is it out of a sense of obligation? Do you believe it is required of you because you are a child of God? Or is it from your drive to succeed, to be somebody?

The apostle Paul said that even if we give everything we have to the poor and even if we give our bodies "to be burned," it profits nothing if we don't have love.

"Nothing?" we ask. "You mean all those times I gave to the local mission and worked in the nursery at church amount to nothing just because I don't have love?"

That's right. Nothing. Absolutely nothing.

In Jesus' life and words we see the only real reason for service: "I am come that they might have life," he said (John 10:10 KJV). His whole mission was accomplished because God so loved us.

True love gives. The only work, the only sacrifice acceptable to God is the one given out of love. Any other is tainted with the smell of self-service, and love, the Bible teaches us, "is not self-seeking" (1 Cor. 13:5).

∞

Father, you are the source of the love I share with others. I look to you to fill me with your pure love so that I may love what you love.

service

Weekend Reflections

The true foundation for serving others is seeing the face of Christ in those we serve, no longer seeing them as ordinary people but as eternal spirits who will spend forever somewhere. It was C. S. Lewis who said in *The Weight of Glory*, "You have never talked to a mere mortal...but it is immortals that we joke with, work with, marry, snub and exploit—immortal horrors or everlasting [splendours]."

1. Jesus revealed service as the path to greatness. Write down some examples of great people who practiced this kind of greatness.

   _____

   _____

   _____

   _____

   _____

2. What are you doing to serve Christ by serving others?

   _____

   _____

   _____

   _____

3. Have you served "angels unawares" (Heb. 13:2 KJV)? When? How does it compare with ministering to "the least" (Matt. 25:40)?

   _____

   _____

   _____

   _____

   _____

All of Me

*O Lord, you have searched me and you know me. You know when I
sit and when I rise; you perceive my thoughts from afar. You discern
my going out and my lying down; you are familiar with
all my ways.*—Psalm 139:1–3

An old adage defines a friend as "one who knows all about you—and
likes you anyway." Few of us are secure enough to let our real selves show
except to those friends and relatives who are closest to us. We become
actors, learning at an early age to portray a different, more polished role
in public—in conversation, in play, and in work.

We may become so accustomed to this acting that we don't even realize we're doing it. Yet God knows. He knows every part of us, every secret
role we play, every hidden thing we do. He's perfectly familiar with that
part of us we consider too playful and immature or too brassy and dramatic. The part that, when it shows, causes us to shudder and hope no
one notices. But God sees. And he loves us anyway.

What freedom we find when we realize we can stand before our Creator without dread, knowing he sees every intimate part of us and yet does
not despise those traits that we consider less than desirable. God knows
all our ways because he wove together all our parts (see Ps. 139:13).

David completely understood that God made him, knew him, and
loved him. For only by knowing this could the king allow himself to
dance "with all his might" before the procession that brought the ark back
to town. When someone criticized the young ruler for his rather undig-
nified behavior, David answered simply, "It was before the Lord, who
chose me....I will celebrate before the Lord" (see 2 Sam. 6:14–21).

God saw it all…every part of David's character: the courage and the
childlike joy, the honor and the humility. And he knew it would take all
of those ingredients for David to become the great king God wanted him
to be. In the same way, God has given us diverse traits and characteristics
so that we can be the people he wants us to be.

⌘

Lord, I acknowledge that you created me, and I thank you for all that I am,
even for the parts of me that sometimes seem so undesirable. Thank you for
loving all of who I am.

49

The Way to Defeat a Bully

Then you will know the truth, and the truth will set you free.
—John 8:32

Most of us probably have had to deal with a bully or two sometime in our lives, especially during our youth. For me, the incident I most vividly recall happened in third grade. I was in a new school in a new city and had not yet made many new friends. The bully's name was Eddie, and he was a pest in every sense of the word.

He was always punching me—never really hurting me, but hitting just hard enough to annoy me. I remember trying to avoid him, but it seemed he always knew where to find me. I can't remember the day the conflict finally ended, but eventually we came to respect each other.

The enemy of our souls is much like Eddie. He always knows where we are, and his most common weapons are annoying nuisances more than anything else. He uses deception, condemnation, boasting, and other practices that usually don't really hurt us immediately as much as they knock us around and seek to wear us down.

If you keep running into condemnation in your life, you can know assuredly that it is either from Satan or from your own soul. The Bible tells us so: "For God did not send His Son into the world to condemn the world, but that the world through Him might be saved" (John 3:17 NKJV). God's weapons—such things as truth and love—are not like Satan's at all. God uses truth to dispel self-doubt, and we must do the same. It is the most effective way to defeat our enemy.

What did Jesus do when he met an adversary? He spoke the truth. Whether it was being tempted in the wilderness or facing the hostile Pharisees, he continued to speak the truth. Truth is freedom. Even though it may hurt in the beginning, truth is the way to freedom.

Do you want to defeat the bully of your soul? "Stand firm then, with the belt of truth buckled around your waist, with the breastplate of righteousness in place" (Eph. 6:14).

∞

Lord, your truth sets me free. I lift the shield of faith and take the sword of the Spirit and firmly resist the enemy. I'm so glad you don't use condemnation to change me. Instead, you speak the truth in love and make me free.

Words of Life

Reckless words pierce like a sword, but the tongue of the wise brings healing.... Pleasant words are a honeycomb, sweet to the soul and healing to the bones.—Proverbs 12:18; 16:24

Stop for a moment and consider words—long ones, short ones. Individually, most are harmless enough. But the right combination of words can evoke strong feelings of affection, compassion, hatred, or disgust.

While the right words can bring healing, words said with little or no thought can pierce like a sword right through to the heart. When we are the target of such words, we have a choice about how to respond: We can receive them as lies, or we can hold to what God has already declared.

The biblical account of Gideon has him "threshing wheat in a winepress to keep it from the Midianites" (Judg. 6:11). Then an angel of the Lord came and sat down under a nearby oak tree. He said, "The Lord is with you, mighty warrior" (v.12). Though Gideon felt like a cowering and defeated man, God spoke words of life to him, and Gideon chose to believe what God said in spite of his feelings and the evil report of the day.

Friend, we must choose to believe what God says rather than believing the harsh words others may level against us. The apostle Paul wrote, "Let God be true, and every man a liar" (Rom. 3:4). God cannot lie. What he says is true. Read some of what God says about you:

> Are not two sparrows sold for a penny? Yet not one of them will fall to the ground apart from the will of your Father.... So don't be afraid; you are worth more than many sparrows. (Matt. 10:29, 31)

> But you are a chosen people, a royal priesthood, a holy nation, a people belonging to God, that you may declare the praises of him who called you out of darkness into his wonderful light. (1 Pet. 2:9)

> How great is the love the Father has lavished on us, that we should be called children of God! And that is what we are! (1 John 3:1)

Do not let others' critical remarks cause you to forget your heritage. You are a child of God—created, chosen, and cherished.

✺

Lord, I turn to you. You alone have "the words of eternal life" (John 6:68).

Have You Heard What God Says about You?

But now, this is what the Lord says—he who created you, O Jacob, he who formed you, O Israel: "Fear not, for I have redeemed you; I have summoned you by name; you are mine."—Isaiah 43:1

I sat and listened as a young man told me of his failures. "All my life they predicted I would never amount to anything," he said. "I finally believed them."

Our world is full of people who are held captive by the lies of others. Perhaps as a child they often heard, "You are worthless. Can't you do anything right?" Or later on they may have been told, "You shouldn't try to do that. Face the facts. You don't have what it takes."

Some strong-hearted people are able to throw off this kind of negative feedback, but in others the wounds are buried so deep that the person may not even recall them at a conscious level. But the message isn't forgotten.

As we open our hearts to the Father's tender mercy, his healing love does radical things to us. It closes the wounds cut by those harsh words so long ago, and we find our true reason for existence, our purpose for living. Best of all, we begin to experience real joy within.

But sometimes those accusing voices of the past still call out to us. When they do, we must listen for God's words of truth and life and immediately prepare our minds for battle, choosing to believe the words of the Lord over the words of the accuser. We must reject the old lies by lifting them up and exposing them to the light of God. This is what I believe the apostle Paul meant when he said to "take captive every thought to make it obedient to Christ" (2 Cor. 10:5).

Regardless of how many lies we have listened to and believed, we need to know what God has to say about us: that we are treasures in his eyes and that we cannot even count the times he thinks of us! We must choose now to believe what God says about us rather than to believe other people's lies—and even our own.

⊗

Jesus, at times I have wondered what the truth is. But you said that you are the truth. I will come to you and listen for the truth, and I renounce and reject the false.

Something Out of Nothing

*God deliberately chose things the world considers foolish in order to
shame those who think they are wise. And he chose those who are
powerless to shame those who are powerful.*
—1 Corinthians 1:27 NLT

Have you ever found yourself saying, "But God, I don't have the ability to do this! Surely, there is someone who could do it better!" If you have, you are a perfect candidate for the job!

God seems to delight in calling people who think they are not qualified. When God called Moses to be Israel's deliverer, Moses' reply was, "O Lord, please send someone else to do it" (Exod. 4:13).

The reason God calls those who feel inadequate is clear: *He does not want us depending on our own resources but on his.* When Gideon and his army were preparing to face the Midianites, God told him to send most of the men home so that Israel would not boast that their own strength had saved them (see Judg. 7:2). The three hundred men who remained were a greater force with God on their side than the original army of thirty-two thousand without God.

God definitely can use our abilities, but he receives the greatest glory from men and women who may not possess a wealth of talent but are available and compliant in their spirits. The greatest leaders have been and always will be those who stay in touch with their own frailty. They know their weaknesses and depend on God to make up the difference.

God knows we aren't perfect. He is very much aware that we are human and will make mistakes. Still, he chooses us and declares us righteous. He takes the mediocre and makes them fantastic! He uses the meek and gives them the inheritance. He uses the simple things to confound the wise. That's our God!

∞

God, have you commissioned me to do something I have neglected? Is there an area of my life where I have not trusted you and leaned upon your strength? Show me those things, Lord. I will depend on your heavenly, supernatural resources to empower me to do what I cannot do aside from you.

self-acceptance

Weekend Reflections

Self-acceptance begins with knowing we are loved by God. If God accepts us, we can accept ourselves. This self that we accept, of course, is the self we find in Christ. As C. S. Lewis said, "The very first step is to try to forget about the self altogether. Your real, new self...will not come as you are looking for it. It will come when you are looking for him" (*Mere Christianity*).

1. How can your unique qualities serve the body of Christ?

   _____

   _____

   _____

   _____

   _____

2. What are some visible changes you see in your new self that are totally different from your old self?

   _____

   _____

   _____

   _____

   _____

3. What do you dislike about yourself? Lay it out before God. What does he have to say about your opinion?

   _____

   _____

   _____

   _____

   _____

The Blesser or the Blessed?

It is more blessed to give than to receive.
—Acts 20:35

For many of us, humility may be the most elusive of Christ's attributes. Once we think we are safely on the road toward the goal, seemingly out of nowhere the ugly head of pride pops up, and we realize once again just how far away from humility we really are.

When I was greeting churchgoers after services one Sunday, a particularly large, unkempt, older lady asked if she could have a hug. I obliged, and she happily wrapped her dimpled arms around me and squeezed. I also received a wet kiss on the cheek. Afterward, I was feeling sort of lofty about my willingness to be a blessing to this overly sweet, rather childish misfit when a quiet voice within me said, *Who was blessed, you or her?*

In my heart I knew the truth.

The example Jesus set for us on earth was as a humble servant, not as a pompous dignitary. He taught us to serve, not to judge. He urged us to love one another selflessly regardless of wealth, status, or outward appearances. He told his disciples that when they helped the hungry, the poor, the imprisoned—"the least of these"—they were helping him (see Matt. 25:35–40). And he said, "Whoever welcomes this little child in my name welcomes me; and whoever welcomes me welcomes the one who sent me. For he who is least among you all—he is the greatest" (Luke 9:48).

That's what I sensed him reminding me that day after church: *When you accept a heartfelt hug and a kiss of enthusiastic greeting from an overweight, disheveled champion of the faith, you're receiving it from me.*

Yes, I was the one who was blessed that day. As I received the woman's kindness, I was accepting the love of Christ. As she planted her wet lips against my cheek, it was Christ's kiss I received. She was the blesser, and I was the blessed.

❧

Lord, how many times have I turned away from others and, in doing so, turned away from you? I choose to serve. Forgive me for the times you have blessed me through others and I haven't noticed.

Pride Unmasked

A man's pride brings him low, but a man of lowly spirit
gains honor.—Proverbs 29:23

Have you ever seen pride hidden under the guise of self-sacrifice?

This is the heart that says, "Nobody else seems to see the needs I do. I'm the only one who cares enough to do anything." We are easily deceived by such an attitude because, frankly, self-sacrifice is not one of the places we would expect to find pride. After all, isn't denying the self the best way to crucify pride?

Certainly, we're taught the godliness of self-sacrifice. But some of us have a tendency to glory in that sacrifice, to call attention to our noble deeds. Our challenge, then, is to serve humbly and quietly, to find joy in the service itself, and to work in areas that do not directly improve our image or our reputation.

We must always be mindful of our need to serve God in all we do. And we must understand that it is God who prompts us to serve in the first place and who gives us hearts that can love unselfishly. By serving others we carry the love of God to others—the love we have first experienced ourselves. Mother Teresa did not serve those needy ones for her own well-being but as a natural overflow of the love she had experienced. If our love is to be like God's love, it cannot be "self-seeking" (1 Cor. 13:4–5).

Self-sacrificing service with no thought of receiving something in return puts God's love into action. It is birthed from divine compassion and comes straight from the heart of Christ, the One who looked on the multitudes with compassion and saw them as helpless "sheep without a shepherd" (Matt. 9:36). To save them—and us—he became the Good Shepherd, laying down his life for his hurting little lambs. That compassion, completely lacking pride, is our example.

∞

Lord, there is no sacrifice I can make that compares to yours. I will resist the temptation to glory in service and instead choose to serve for your glory.

Do This, and the Devil Will Run!

God opposes the proud, but gives grace to the humble.
—James 4:6

Many of us have quoted this verse to those struggling with temptation: "Resist the devil and he will flee from you" (James 4:7 KJV). But we often forget the first part of the verse: "Therefore submit to God."

Simply resisting the enemy is not enough to make him flee. If you want to put a demon on the run, submit to God and resist the temptation of pride and haughtiness. The enemy cannot stay in the presence of one who is truly submitted to the Father.

Do you want the grace (favor) of God to be upon you? Submission is the key. Pride says, "I can do this." Submission says, "I can do all things *through Christ*" (Phil. 4:13 NKJV).

James also wrote, "Humble yourselves in the sight of the Lord, and he shall lift you up" (4:10 KJV). We have a choice to make. God can allow us to fall flat on our faces so that we become humble and submitted, or we can humble ourselves. I don't know about you, but I choose the latter.

And notice that James said we're to humble ourselves "in the sight of the Lord." If we publicly humble ourselves, we may feel tempted to glory in it—to feel proud of our humility, thinking, *Look at me. I'm sacrificing for the Lord.* But when we humble ourselves in places nobody sees, there is less temptation for pride. This is the kind of humility that God honors and rewards. Public humility may bring the praise of men, but private humility will bring the public grace and favor of God.

❧

Holy Lord, awesome in power and might, I submit to you—to your authority, to your lordship, to your power. There is no God besides you. I choose humility. Forgive me for pride and arrogance.

THURSDAY

humility

The Key Ingredient of Greatness

Wherefore let him that thinketh he standeth take heed lest he fall.
—1 Corinthians 10:12 KJV

The truly great are not impressed with themselves. They don't sit around thinking about their "standing." They are in touch with their humanity and aware of how temporary life really is.

When I think of greatness, one man who always comes to mind is Billy Graham. I once saw an interview where he was posed the question, "When you get to heaven, is there any major question you would like to ask God?"

He quickly replied, "Yes. I want to ask the Lord why he chose me."

Those who are great usually don't realize how great they really are. It is not a matter of insecurity or a lack of confidence. The truly great are very confident, but their attitude is not so much *self*-confidence as it is *God*-confidence. It is the expectancy and hope that springs from knowing *whose* we are is more important than *who* we are.

The apostle Paul addressed a quarrel that occurred at Corinth among those who were boasting about whose ministry they were saved under. Some bragged, "I was baptized by Apollos," while others replied, "Well, I was baptized by Cephas" (see 1 Cor. 1:11–15).

Paul appealed to them, "Neither he who plants nor he who waters is anything, but only God, who makes things grow" (1 Cor. 3:7).

You and I get the pleasure of participating in God's garden. Some of us are tilling the soil, some are planting the seed, and some are watering. But it is God who makes things grow.

What is the key ingredient to greatness? What do great men and women strive for? They don't work for greatness. No, they humble themselves in obedience—and in doing so, find greatness. Their example is the greatest man who ever lived, One who did not aim for prestige but "made himself nothing" (Phil. 2:7). Then the God who makes things grow exalted him to the peak of greatness.

∞

Lord Jesus, I acknowledge your greatness. Help me to walk circumspectly, aware of the trap of pride and the deceitfulness of self-promotion. Without you I can do nothing, but with you I can do all things.

Who Me, God?

*My message and my preaching were not with wise and persuasive
words...so that your faith might not rest on men's wisdom,
but on God's power.*—1 Corinthians 2:5

Do you feel inadequate? Congratulations! You've met the first require-
ment for becoming an instrument of God!

God rarely chooses the most competent persons to do his work.
Frankly, his choices seem more likely to be based on availability than ability. Consider the perceived inadequacies of these Bible heroes: Abraham
thought he was too old, Moses thought he couldn't speak well enough,
Saul was from the wrong family, Gideon was too weak, and David was too
young. In each case God capitalized on their insufficiency and did what
appeared to be impossible. Abraham fathered a child. Moses led a nation,
Saul became king, Gideon became a war hero, and David brought down
the town bully!

I love that about God, don't you? So often he passes right by the
champion standing in the spotlight and chooses instead the One Most
Unlikely to Succeed as his chosen representative. He seems to enjoy calling the terrified wallflower who stutters, "S-s-surely you don't mean me,
God! Why, look at my brother Aaron. He is much more qualified than I."

God says, "No. I chose *you.*"

What's your excuse? Maybe it's "But I've never done that before!" or
or "I didn't go to college."

Isn't it funny how we sometimes argue with God, thinking we're
telling him something he doesn't know? Believe me, he is well aware of
our every deficiency. Still he chooses us and says, "My grace is sufficient
for you, for my power is made perfect in weakness" (2 Cor. 12:9).

∞

Lord, what have you called me to do that I have excused myself from doing?
Not by might nor by power, but in the strength of your Spirit, I will move out
to accomplish what you've set before me (see Zech. 4:6).

Weekend Reflections

God says the way to greatness is service. The road to the top requires us to humble ourselves "before the Lord" (James 4:10). C. S. Lewis spoke of this humility when he said, "The Eternal Being, who knows everything and who created the whole universe, became not only a man but (before that) a baby, and before that a fetus inside a woman's body. If you want to get the hang of it, think how you would like to become a slug or a crab" (C. S. Lewis, quoted in *Jesus Christ: The God-Man* by Bruce Demarest).

1. Many successful businesses have discovered the principle that service leads to greatness. Write down some observations about why it has brought about their success.

   _____

   _____

   _____

   _____

   _____

2. Identify some famous figures who began to "believe their own press" and soon met with destruction (see Prov. 16:18).

   _____

   _____

   _____

   _____

   _____

3. Why does humility come before honor (see Prov. 18:12)? Identify some examples of this truth.

   _____

   _____

   _____

   _____

   _____

The Mysterious Ways of the Lord

He took the blind man by the hand and led him outside the village.
When he had spit on the man's eyes and put his hands on him, Jesus
asked, "Do you see anything?"—Mark 8:23

There are many accounts of Jesus healing the sick. In most instances he simply touched them and they were healed. In his compassion he reached out to the masses, touching the untouchable, loving the unlovely.

But in the case of the blind man at Bethsaida, Jesus spat on the man's eyes. He spat on the man! Why would he choose to heal someone in such an unusual, even shocking, way? Perhaps it's because God refuses to be boxed in by our boundaries. Just when we think we have everything all figured out, he changes the methodology, and we're left to guess at his reasoning. Such puzzles are part of the mysterious Divine that caused David to cry out, "Show me your ways, O Lord, teach me your paths" (Ps. 25:4).

I believe these glimpses into the divine ways of God are invitations. They appeal to us to study and meditate on the amazing and inspiring life of Christ and to enter the higher realms of relationship with him where we may discover his purposes and plans for our own lives. Yes, and even gain greater understanding. Not every *why* and *how* will be answered, but the more we know him, the more we trust him. The more we walk with him, the more we rely on him. The greater our confidence in his awesome ability and mysterious design, the more our souls are at rest.

Lord, teach me your ways. Lift me up to that higher plane so that I can hear your voice and get a glimpse of the heavenly design. I know you see the big picture while my view is limited.

mysteries

The Thoughts of the Lord

*As the heavens are higher than the earth, so are my ways higher than
your ways and my thoughts than your thoughts.—Isaiah 55:9*

Have you ever looked at the heavens and wondered, *God, what are
you doing?* It boggles the human mind to contemplate the workings of
Holy God. In fact, there are not many things of the spiritual realm that
make much sense to the natural mind. This is why we must set our minds
above carnal, human reasoning. As Paul wrote, "Those who live according to the sinful nature have their minds set on what that nature desires;
but those who live in accordance with the Spirit have their minds set on
what the Spirit desires" (Rom. 8:5).

To set our minds on spiritual things, we must abandon our old
thought systems, because the old ways of thinking do not work in a spiritual kingdom. We're instructed, "Let the wicked forsake his way and the
evil man his thoughts" (Isa. 55:7).

There will always be those who feel compelled to reason everything
out as if there must be a logical explanation. But some things simply cannot be sorted out with natural reasoning. Although our thoughts can be
lifted into another, heavenly realm, we still will not understand all of
God's workings. What we *can* know is that God *is* working in our lives.
We can believe that.

∞

Almighty God, my mind races with confusion. There is so much I don't understand. But I lift my mind to you now, to keep it firmly rooted in you. As I do,
your thoughts begin to consume my thoughts, and I find peace.

To Be Continued

*To them God has chosen to make known among the Gentiles the
glorious riches of this mystery, which is Christ in you, the
hope of glory.*—Colossians 1:27

Everyone loves a good mystery. There's just something about having only a part of the answer that rattles our curiosity and makes us anxious to know the rest of the story. Perhaps there's a bit of the detective in all of us that wants to see if our suspicions are accurate.

Before Jesus ascended to the Father, his disciples tried to solve the mystery he had introduced them to. "Is now the time that you will restore the kingdom to Israel?" they asked.

"It is not for you to know what only my Father knows," Jesus replied (see Acts 1:6–7, my paraphrase).

Today we, too, ask questions that God will not answer yet. Jesus meant what he said; some things are not for us to know. Instead of trying to discern what God has said is indiscernible, we should focus on the mystery of knowing Jesus Christ more intimately.

There is so much about him to explore, yet we can only know part of the story until we join him in heaven. As Paul wrote, "Now we see but a poor reflection as in a mirror; then we shall see face to face. Now I know in part; then I shall know fully" (1 Cor. 13:12). The story is ever unfolding...to be continued.

When does the exploring end? As missionary Isobel Kuhn wrote in her book *By Searching* (Moody Press, 1959), "In one sense, it is finished when our hand, stretched out to God,...feels the answering grasp and knows that He is there. But in another sense the searching never ends, for the first discovery is quickly followed by another, and that by another."

ॐ

Oh the mystery of your grace, my Lord. You always keep me coming back for more of you. Little by little, I am discovering the riches of my inheritance in you. Stir up in me the hunger to know you more. Breathe on the sparks of my heart so that they will blaze with a passion to see your glory.

The Wonder of It All

Once more I will astound these people with wonder upon wonder; the wisdom of the wise will perish, the intelligence of the intelligent will vanish.—Isaiah 29:14

In an acronym for *worship*, I think the *w* should stand for *wonder*, for how can we truly worship God without a sense of wonder? He is so much greater than our knowledge of him, and that greatness causes us to wonder about the part we do not know. Wonder also explains why worship cannot be confined to quiet moments in cathedrals. Worship happens when we stand beneath a clear Montana sky and wonder at the artistry that created such a backdrop. It happens when we pause to listen to the surf crashing against a California coast or hear the trills of a canary or gaze at the tiny fingers of a newborn baby. Pondering such things should move us toward worship.

Some have called Christmas the season of wonder because it's a time when we wonder how God became a baby crying in a stable, how heaven orchestrated an angelic concert for a handful of shepherds, and how a place such as little Bethlehem was chosen for Jesus to make his entrance. Considering this, it should not surprise us that the prophet Isaiah said, "His name shall be called Wonderful" (Isa. 9:6 KJV), meaning literally "full of wonder."

Our God is full of wonder, and saying we do not understand everything about him may be one of the smartest things we can ever say!

∞

Great Creator of all things, your name is Wonderful. I am full of wonder when I consider who you are, and I stand amazed at your majesty. I worship you, for you are greater than all. The heavens cannot contain you; foolish is the man who thinks he can comprehend who you are.

A Kingdom of Fools

*But God hath chosen the foolish things of the world to confound the
wise; and God hath chosen the weak things of the world to confound
the things which are mighty.*—1 Corinthians 1:27 KJV

No wonder nonbelievers think we are fools—we who were common,
destined to lives without notoriety, now claiming to be loved by a king
who declared us so valuable that he offered his life in exchange for our
freedom. This king promised that if we would believe in him, he would
receive us into a kingdom not of this world—a kingdom where the simple
reign as princes and priests alongside him, where unimaginable wealth is
so commonplace that the streets are paved with gold and the rarest of jew-
els are so plentiful that they're used as construction material.

No wonder they think us fools when we say we are already sitting
with our king in the heavenly places. When we brag that he loves us so
much that he has written our names in the palm of his hand. Imagine
what they think when we say this all-powerful king, who from his holy
imagination spoke the worlds into existence, still spends countless
moments thinking of us.

No wonder they think us fools when we claim that not only does he
know our names but he hears our silent prayers as well and knows when
we rise and when we sleep. No wonder they scoff when we say he let the
convicted go free by paying the ransom of the guilty, the shamed, and
debase. No wonder they laugh when we say he has been seen washing the
feet of ordinary peasants, much as a servant would.

Who would believe such a fairy tale? Who would call such a king a
king at all?

"Where could such a kingdom be?" they say.

"Ah," we answer, "it's a lot closer than you think. In fact, 'the kingdom of heaven is at hand'" (Matt. 3:2 KJV).

∞

Almighty God, what a wonder you are! You have dumbfounded the sages and
philosophers with the simple things and have taken the weak and made them
strong. If I am a fool, let it be for the sake of your kingdom.

mysteries

Weekend Reflections

Some things are not meant for us to know. The wonder of such "unknowables" reminds us why he is the Almighty God and we are the created ones. In A.D. 399, Saint Augustine said, "People travel to wonder at the height of mountains, at the huge waves of the sea, at the long courses of the rivers, at the vast compass of the ocean, at the circular motion of the stars—and they pass by themselves without wondering" (quoted by Dr. Paul Brand and Philip Yancey in *Fearfully and Wonderfully Made*). There is always a reason for wonder.

1. What questions are you wrestling with in your heart right now?

_____

_____

_____

_____

2. What are some possible reasons that you perceive no immediate answers?

_____

_____

_____

3. Set aside a time of "wonder" in your worship time. What are some amazing aspects of God that you can wonder about?

_____

_____

_____

_____

_____

_____

Golden Bowls

The four living creatures and the twenty-four elders fell down before the Lamb. Each one had a harp and they were holding golden bowls full of incense, which are the prayers of the saints.—Revelation 5:8

If you have been a believer for any amount of time, you no doubt have experienced those occasions when your prayers seem about as powerful as a defective bottle rocket. They seem to rise up about ten feet and fizzle. Surely we've all had those times when we pray but feel unable to sense God's presence. When these experiences happen repeatedly, we begin to think, *I might as well not pray today; my prayers seem so empty.*

Have you ever talked to someone who didn't seem to be listening? Sometimes, however, it's not that they're not listening, it's just that they are not giving us the response we want.

In the same way, when God does not respond to our prayers immediately or in the way we would prefer, it doesn't mean he isn't listening to us or that he isn't aware of our situation.

God sees our tears. His ears are attentive to our cries, as David said (see Ps. 34:15). He sees our faithful obedience, even when the anointing is not there and the heavens seem plated with brass. Consider the biblical character Cornelius, a "God-fearing" centurion but a man who had not experienced faith in Jesus Christ and knew nothing of the power of the Holy Spirit. Yet one day an angel of God appeared to him and declared, "Your prayers and gifts to the poor have come up as a memorial offering before God" (Acts 10:4).

Our prayers are precious to God. He sees all that we do and hears every word we speak to others and to him. Take courage and remain faithful. Your prayers are lifted up to him in "golden bowls."

∞

Lord, thank you for always hearing my prayers, even when I wonder if you are listening. Help me to remember your promises and remain faithful and obedient in those moments of doubt and uncertainty.

Honest to God

The Lord is near to all who call upon Him, to all who call
upon Him sincerely and in truth.
—Psalm 145:18 AMPLIFIED

When we pray, there is one thing God is certainly looking for: honesty. Are we praying the truth? Are the words we speak sincere, arising from an earnest heart?

Jesus rebuked the Pharisees for hypocrisy in their prayers, and today he commands us, "Do not keep on babbling like pagans, for they think they will be heard because of their many words" (Matt. 6:7). Our Lord is not concerned with whether we are packing every moment of our prayer time with constant speaking. Rather, he is looking for an honest heart that will pour out before him its innermost thoughts and desires as if to say, "Lord, I lay all this before you. Now, you sort it out."

C. S. Lewis said in *Letters to Malcolm,* "The prayer preceding all prayers [should be:] May it be the real I that speaks." The real person is the only one God wishes to listen to, to commune with. He wants to hear from us, not some religious character we have created because of our fear to be honest with God and let him see who we really are.

So when we pray, we open ourselves and pour out our hearts to the Father genuinely and totally. In doing so, we obey Jesus' words, "When you pray, do not be like the hypocrites" (Matt. 6:5). We joyfully come to him in honesty.

∞

Lord, I lay aside the temptation to cover my transgressions and flaws. I want to be honest with you. Holy Spirit, walk with me through the corridors of my heart and examine it with me.

Say It with Your Mouth, Not Just Your Heart

I tell you the truth, if anyone says to this mountain, "Go, throw your-self into the sea," and does not doubt in his heart but believes that what he says will happen, it will be done for him.—Mark 11:23

Many people, especially men, have a hard time expressing their feel-ings. Perhaps it's because they don't want others to know what they're feel-ing and thinking. But in many cases these people don't express their hearts because they think it should be obvious to others what they think and feel. (And God forbid they should waste time expressing the obvious!) How many times have *you* made the mistake of not speaking up because you wrongly assumed your friends or family members already knew how you felt?

Just as we should express our feelings, we should also speak out about what we believe. It isn't enough to believe silently in our hearts and never express what we know to be the truth. God expects it of us! Consider the confessions of those who were strong in faith. Before Abraham saw the animal to be substituted for his son, he proclaimed, "God will provide himself a lamb" (Gen. 22:8 KJV). Joshua and Caleb believed in their hearts that they could defeat the giants in the Promised Land, confidently pre-dicting, "We are well able to overcome it" (Num. 13:30 KJV). And the little boy David believed so completely in his God that before he threw the first stone, he said, "This day the Lord will hand you over to me, and I'll strike you down and cut off your head" (1 Sam. 17:46).

Yes, God knows what we believe in our hearts, but he wants us to say it as well as believe it. The Bible teaches us, "The tongue has the power of life and death" (Prov. 18:21). By speaking of things we can't see with our natural eyes, we activate our faith and plug into God's power. Jesus himself said, "If anyone *says* to this mountain…"

Say what you believe, and believe what you say. That is the kingdom principle.

∞

Lord, I believe in my heart, and I say it with my mouth: "You are Lord of all." Nothing is too difficult for you. Open my eyes to see the power in what I say and to think before I speak.

He Spent the Night in Prayer

*Now it came to pass in those days that He went out to the mountain
to pray, and continued all night in prayer to God.*
—Luke 6:12 NKJV

Sometimes people who must make pivotal decisions with long-range implications spend days asking what their friends think or consulting with the "experts" or seeking advice from self-help gurus—and less than five minutes seeking God's will about the issue at hand.

But before Jesus chose his twelve apostles, he spent the night in conversation with his Father. Even though he was the Son of God, he did not feel it a waste to spend the whole night in prayer. By his example he taught us that major decisions require major prayer and that one of the best ways to use our time is in communion with God.

The first verse of the first psalm tells us, "Blessed is the man who walks not in the counsel of the ungodly" (NKJV). We cannot have peace or wisdom regarding our circumstances when we spend our time seeking the advice of "the ungodly." And who are the ungodly? Those whose minds are not in the process of being transformed (see Rom.12:2).

Jesus did not seek wisdom from the ungodly. Instead, he sought the wisdom of the Father. He spent the night in prayer when he chose his board of directors. What about you? Do you pray when you hire or fire someone? When you change jobs, careers, or locations, do you seek your Father's counsel? Do you have other important decisions that would benefit from godly wisdom? (Are there any other kinds of decisions?) Are you willing to spend the night in prayer? Will you converse with your heavenly Father about these things, or do you choose what seems to be an easier way—discussing these issues with those who offer only ungodly wisdom?

∞

Jesus, I want to walk as one of your blessed children—not in the counsel of the ungodly but in the light of your wisdom. "Order my steps in thy word" (Ps. 119:133 KJV). What is your word concerning my life and the decisions I must make? Give me a greater hunger to spend time with you, to hear your word of life, your wisdom, and your counsel.

Sweating It Out

And being in agony, He prayed more earnestly. And His sweat became
like great drops of blood falling down to the ground.
—Luke 22:44 NKJV

Sometimes we just have to sweat. It's usually not an enjoyable experience, but we all do it. And if you have lived in the humid climate of the southern United States, you may have done more sweating than you would have dreamed possible! Our bodies are complex things. God created them so that when we get too hot, we perspire, and the moisture on our skin exposed to the surrounding air begins to cool us down. As I said, it's not always fun, but it's certainly necessary.

Jesus sweated as he prayed in Gethsemane. Foreseeing the horror he was about to face, he dropped to his knees and wrestled with the knowledge of what lay ahead. In agony he prayed, "Father, if it is Your will, remove this cup from Me" (Luke 22:42 NKJV).

When we fall on our knees in agony before the Lord, laying out our questions and frustrations before him, he may not give us the answers we want. We would most likely prefer a set of numbered responses carefully replying to all our questions, but walking and talking with God rarely bring that kind of resolution. More often than not, we come away from our prayer time with more questions than answers, questions that are meant to woo us back to God. And so back we come again to enter his presence and wrestle with our agony until we sweat. Until we finally can say, "Not my will, but yours be done."

It's like the first time you asked your parents, "What should I do?" and they looked back at you and said, "What do *you* think you should do?" And with that, the sweating began.

❦

Lord Jesus, there are so many questions I can't answer by myself. I pray that you will continue to reveal the answers to me. But if you don't, I pray that I will have the ability to trust you even then, knowing your spirit will lead and guide me into all truth, and to wrestle in prayer until I know what you want me to do.

prayer

Weekend Reflections

God has made provision for the salvation and deliverance of every man, woman, and child, but it is only granted to those who receive it. His heart breaks for every hurting child of the world, but he waits for one of us to minister love in his name. He longs to "heal our land," but he waits for the people called by his name to humble themselves and pray. He yearns to linger and talk with you if you would but seek to know him.

Your unbelief will interrupt potential blessings of God. Will you choose to believe today in the power of prayer?

1. When you wait and listen in prayer, what thoughts do you wrestle with? What does this reveal about your heart? (See Matt. 6:7)

   _____

   _____

   _____

   _____

2. James 5:17 tells us that Elijah "prayed earnestly." When was the last time you prayed earnestly? What were you praying about?

   _____

   _____

   _____

   _____

3. God has chosen the prayer of faith to release his power. What might happen if you don't pray?

   _____

   _____

   _____

   _____

   _____

The Sin of Idolatry

You shall not make for yourself an idol in the form of anything in
heaven above or on the earth beneath or in the waters below.
—Exodus 20:4

The word *idolatry* makes most of us think of ancient people in far-off lands bowing down to stone images. Or we picture the children of Israel paying homage to the golden calf. While these scenes definitely qualify as idolatry, we're wrong if we think this practice ended in ancient times or that it doesn't exist in today's "civilized" society.

In its simplest form, idolatry is appealing to something or someone else besides God. It says, "You can do for me what I cannot do for myself." Many people today idolize wealth or prestige or status symbols. They let these things take precedence over everything else in their lives.

Another common form of idolatry today is people idolatry, and its adherents may not even realize they're caught up in its practice. They idolize another person, believing the lie that they cannot live without his or her love and approval. They may see their relationship as simply love or admiration or simple affection. But if their lives completely revolve around the other person, if they consider themselves as valuable only because they "belong" to that person, then they've slipped from love or friendship into idolatry. As Dr. Neil Warren wrote a few years ago in a journal article, "If you attribute to anything the power to determine your worth as a person, you have made a god out of that."

God did not declare idolatry a sin just so he could hand down another restriction. He gave us this commandment because he knows the end of such a path. He knows there is no one and no thing in the universe that can fill the neediness of our souls except him.

⊗

Lord, walk through my heart and expose any idols by the brilliance of your Holy Spirit. I choose you, and I will have no other gods before you. You are my shepherd; I shall not want.

Finding Your Way Back

*Repent therefore and be converted, that your sins may be blotted out,
so that times of refreshing may come from the presence of the Lord.*
—Acts 3:19 NKJV

Ever get lost at the state fair or in a big amusement park, maybe about the age of nine or ten? No doubt you were standing there, looking at the new roller coaster for just a second with Mom or Dad close by. Then, the next thing you knew neither parent was anywhere to be found. Your heart probably stopped, but more than likely you didn't want anyone to know how scared you were. So you took off walking. Still no Dad. You walk another direction. No Mom. At that point panic may have set in and you doubtlessly wanted to yell, "Dad? Mom?" But you didn't want to embarrass yourself, so you quietly darted here and there, lungs heaving, eyes brimming with tears.

Then, among all the noises of the midway, came that familiar voice. "Johnny! Suzy! Over here!" Relief flooded over you, and for an instant you probably wanted to dash to your parents and cling to them forever!

The children of God lose their way just as earthly children get lost from their parents. It's usually difficult to say exactly when or how it happens. They are standing next to God, and then something else catches their attention. And when they look around again, they find themselves in an unfamiliar place of unbelief.

People usually don't lose their way because of some great challenge to their faith. More often it is a gradual dulling of the spiritual senses, a distraction here, a little step in the wrong direction. Then one day real tragedy occurs, real difficulty sets in, and they realize they are lost. They start looking around, wondering where God is.

If this happens to you, don't be too proud to swallow your pride and call out to him. Don't think you are too mature to admit you were wrong. Just cry out, "Father?" Then wait quietly. Soon, in the peace of his presence, you will hear him say, "My son. My daughter. Over here."

⚭

Lord, sometimes out of selfish ambition I have let my eyes be turned from you. Just like Peter, I find myself sinking into the stormy waters. Then I cry out to you, and you save me. Soon I'm walking on the water again.

More Than Emotion

*Anyone who does not take his cross and follow me is not worthy
of me.*—Matthew 10:38

Given the right set of circumstances, a person will commit to almost anything. A man or woman may say "I love you" because of the fire of the moment in a night filled with passion. But if he or she can still say those words—and mean them—while standing alone in the harsh light of morning, then the words are more than a feeling; they signify devotion. In the intimacy of the Last Supper, the disciple named Peter vowed that he was so devoted to our Lord that he stood ready to die for him. But around the harsh fire of scrutiny, he had a different emotional response.

Sometimes our emotions may fool us into thinking we've committed ourselves wholly to God. We may show such sorrow for the sins we committed that we're convinced no one could ever doubt our sincerity. But manufactured remorse does not conform us into the image of Jesus. Emotional responses to sin are only the reactions of the human psyche. True conversion—genuine repentance, abject humility, and total commitment—comes only through Holy Spirit conviction along with an assent of the will.

This is not to say that emotional responses are wrong or improper. But we must be aware that we can have an emotional response without true repentance as well as true repentance without an intense emotional response. We need godly sorrow for our sin, not a purely physical response. Just as tears alone don't necessarily indicate apology, the fact that we feel remorse or sorrow does not necessarily bring about change. Only when Jesus lives in us—only when we are totally, irrevocably devoted to him—do we move from emotional immaturity to spiritual completeness. Repentance is more than being sorrowful—it is choosing God's way above our own. It is laying down our lives in exchange for his. It is relinquishing the worldly scepter to lay hold of the Cross.

❧

Jesus, I want to feel your response to my sin. When I grieve for my failure, let it be with your heart. Show me the cross I must carry and give me a willing heart to bear it. I now set my mind to do your will, to choose your way, and to allow your life to live through me. Holy Spirit, come!

repentance

Crossing Over

*I tell you the truth, whoever hears my word and believes him who sent
me has eternal life and will not be condemned; he has crossed over
from death to life.—John 5:24*

Crossing over from death to life requires us to face up to death itself,
to step up to the grave and stare boldly into its depths. When Jesus visi-
ted a graveyard near the small town of Bethany, he did just that. He
walked up to the tomb of his friend Lazarus and stared death in the face.
What a lesson he taught that day when he told the mourners, "Take away
the stone!" (John 11:39).

Now, if Jesus had the power to raise Lazarus from the dead, he certainly had the power to roll away the stone that covered the tomb. But it
was important that the mourners open the grave themselves. Mary, the sister of Lazarus, explained their hesitation. "But, Lord," she said, "he has
been there four days!" (v. 39). Jesus knew exactly what was in that tomb.

Inside of us there may be a tomb like Lazarus's—a place where we
have buried sin. Now death has taken its toll, and what is there is not a
pretty sight. Jesus wants to call us out of that tomb, raise us up from that
grave, but he will not remove the stone for us. Only we can do that.

And sometimes, even when we want so desperately the new life he
offers us, we hesitate beside the stone. "But God, there are things in there
that have been there a long time. It's bad in there, Lord! By now it really
stinks!" He knows.

"Come now, let us reason together," he said. "Though your sins are
like scarlet, they shall be as white as snow" (Isa. 1:18).

When the world began, the Everlasting Word spoke, and light
invaded the darkness. Today the Incarnate Word, Jesus, waits to invade
the dark graves of our hearts. The same One who said, "Lazarus, come
out!" (John 11:43) is calling to us now. Don't hesitate! Be courageous!
Roll the stone away, and let the Living Word shine into the darkness. Let
him call you into real life in him.

∞

Come, Living Word. I roll away the stone that has covered my own personal
graveyard. Speak your life into my heart; send your holy light to invade the
darkness of my life. The old me has died, and now I will arise to walk with you.

Who Turned the Light On?

Many of the Samaritans from that town believed in him because of
the woman's testimony, "He told me everything I ever did."
—John 4:39

Darkness envelops you like a thick, black veil. You can't see a glimmer of light anywhere. Shapes and forms seem to appear as your ears tune in to the slightest sound with acute, pinpoint accuracy. Your heart pounds, and you long for light from anywhere. Then a familiar voice interrupts the silence. A shaft of light pierces the darkness. And in an instant your heart is quiet, your fear is gone…for now you are not alone.

Light shines the brightest for those who have experienced the blackest midnight.

The Samaritan woman at the well was shocked when Jesus, a Jew, asked her for a drink of water. But that shock was nothing compared to the rest of the conversation. In a few moments Jesus told her, "You are right when you say you have no husband. The fact is, you have had five husbands, and the man you now have is not your husband" (John 4:17–18).

You might expect the woman to fire back a defensive answer lathered with shame or anger. Instead, when Jesus revealed her sordid past, this Samaritan woman responded with gratitude. She ran to her friends saying, "Come see this man!" (see v. 29). Her actions illustrated the psalmist's words, "The entrance of thy words giveth light" (119:130 KJV). Jesus' words shone into the darkness of her life and exposed her sinful deeds.

Now, if you have ever been in the dark—I mean *real* darkness—you know that when someone finally turns on the light, you're grateful, even if that light exposes things you aren't too happy to see! In the same way, when Jesus speaks to our darkness, even though his light exposes what we thought was hidden in our closets, our response, like the Samaritan woman's, should be one of gratitude, for now we can see the path to freedom

Don't stay there, cowering in the dark. Open the door of your heart and let God's light-giving, night-shattering words in.

∞

Lord Jesus, I willingly open the door of my heart to the light of your life-giving Word. I am not afraid of what you will see. I refuse to allow darkness to live in me. I want to live in the light.

repentance

Weekend Reflections

When we turn our faces to God for answers regarding a dilemma we're facing, or when we seek his counsel for a decision, he first demands that we destroy every idol. He can't do this work for us. If we have forged them, we must destroy them. This is the essence of repentance.

Idols have no power in themselves. But each thing we idolize is a foothold of Satan—proof that we already have been deceived by him and that he has already set up camp in our hearts.

1. Describe an area of your heart you don't want God to see—an area you don't talk with him about.

   _____

   _____

   _____

   _____

2. Neil Warren wrote, "If you attribute to anything the power to determine your worth as a person, you have made a god out of that." Who determines your worth?

   _____

   _____

   _____

   _____

3. Repentance includes surrender. What idol or sin in your heart is God waiting for you to destroy?

   _____

   _____

   _____

   _____

Alone in Death, Together in Life

*I tell you the truth, unless a kernel of wheat falls to the ground and
dies, it remains only a single seed. But if it dies, it produces many
seeds. The man who loves his life will lose it, while the man who hates
his life in this world will keep it for eternal life.*—John 12:24

Do you remember your very first day of school? Remember how your
little heart thumped in your chest when you climbed on that big yellow
bus all by yourself? Each step seemed like a mountain, and it felt as if the
whole world were rating your courage.

You probably wanted Mom or Dad to go with you on that bus, but
it wasn't possible. That was one trip you had to take alone. Your parents
could encourage you, but they couldn't do it for you. They couldn't take
a seat beside you and hold your hand. Eventually, you had to make the
choice to grow up and face the challenge alone.

Somehow you made it through that first day. When school was out,
you jumped off the bus and found those loving arms waiting for you.
Looking back from that vantage point of safety and security, it actually
felt pretty good to know you had conquered that first-day mountain,
didn't it?

Our trip to Calvary is a lot like that first bus ride to school. When it
comes to dying to self, no one else can do it for us. God will encourage
us, but he will not do for us what we alone can do. Only we can crucify
the flesh.

Is there a sin that easily besets you? Do you cry for God to kill the sin
in you? It's up to you to lay it aside. Christ has already done all he can do.
He laid down his own life as an example for you. Though many stood and
watched him struggle down the Via Dolorosa, he still faced Golgotha
alone. No one else could go to the cross in his place.

So we climb on the bus, struggle to climb those steps, and follow him
in his death. Then, when we arrive at the end of our own Via Dolorosa,
we find him waiting for us with open arms.

∞

Father, you have paved only one road to life, and it leads through the cross. I
choose death to my old life so that by faith I can obtain real life. Show me if
there are things in my life that I need to die to. I want to live!

resurrection

The Word of Life

That which was from the beginning, which we have heard, which we have seen with our eyes, which we have looked at and our hands have touched—this we proclaim concerning the Word of life.—1 John 1:1

How often we may wish we could see and touch Jesus, as John did, to literally walk and talk with Jesus, to sit at his feet and listen. We cannot do that in this life, but he has left us something of himself: his Word. The Gospel of John begins with these familiar words: "In the beginning was the Word, and the Word was with God, and the Word *was God*" (John 1:1, emphasis added).

Today we can't touch the physical Jesus, but we can literally touch something that is a part of God, his written Word. We can hold in our hands something that is more God than it is paper and ink. There, upon each page, his character is delicately revealed. Phrase after phrase reveals who he is. Verse after verse declares his love for mankind. Again and again we read how he longs to fellowship with his creation, with his children—with us. The more we study, the more he discloses himself to us. And because of what Christ has done, there is no veil between our hearts and his glory. We freely look into the Most Holy and gaze upon his beauty and goodness.

As we speak his Word aloud, we breathe the very life of God into the room—against darkness, against despair, against sickness. It all must bow its knee to the reality of the power of the Holy Word.

As we study and set God's Word in our hearts, he fills our beings with himself, from glory to glory. As we come to know his Word, we come to know him. And as we know him, we know our reason for being. As we know our reason for being, we know life. *Real life.*

How do I know? The Bible tells me so: "The words I have spoken to you are spirit and they are life" (John 6:63).

◆◇◆

Oh, wonderful Word of Life, thank you for revealing yourself to us. Thank you for leaving us something we can see and hold and embrace in our hearts. You have magnified your Word even above your name. I glory in its power and the true beauty that gives me real life.

Living Energy

To this end I labor, struggling with all his energy, which so powerfully works in me.—Colossians 1:29

Spiritual growth is a struggle as we continually face the old Adam in one way or another. But this is one struggle we should consider as a friend, a sign that we are "growing up in Jesus" (see Eph. 4:15 KJV), growing into his likeness. If there is no struggle, we may very well be coddling the old nature.

The courage to persevere in this struggle, thankfully, does not come from sheer will power alone. Although will power helps us get up and begin, it is God's resurrection energy that gives us the strength and the courage to endure. And there is no limit to the work it can do in our lives. As Paul said, it "so powerfully works" in us. After all, it is energy powerful enough to roll the stone away from a tomb and raise Christ's lifeless form from the grave! Friend, you talk about powerful energy, this is it!

This same power energizes our spirit beings to life as we "count ourselves dead" (see Rom. 6:11). The apostle Paul explained it this way in his letter to the Romans: "But if Christ is in you, your body is dead because of sin, yet your spirit is alive because of righteousness. And if the Spirit of him who raised Jesus from the dead is living in you, he who raised Christ from the dead will also give life to your mortal bodies through his Spirit, who lives in you" (8:10–11).

The giving of life that Paul described is not the resurrection of the dead that is yet to come but life *now* in the Spirit.

What struggle are you facing today? Has God set a mountain before you? Has he revealed something new that causes you to fear or be anxious? Don't be afraid. Don't shrink from the challenge. Tap into the resurrection energy of Jesus Christ that "so powerfully works" in you.

∞

Thank you, Jesus, for giving me that same power that raised you from the dead. I now consider myself dead to sin yet powerfully alive by your Spirit living in me.

81

resurrection

Jesus...Our Hope

But now is Christ risen from the dead, and become the firstfruits of them that slept.—1 Corinthians 15:20 KJV

When Jesus arose from the grave, so did hope for every man. On the cross, Jesus bore not only our sin but he carried our sorrow, every feeling of despair and every grief we might ever experience. He took all that pain into himself, and he triumphed over it. He descended to the lowest place and ascended to the highest that we might overcome through him.

In this life we will have trouble and sorrow, but Jesus said, "Be of good cheer; I have overcome the world" (John 16:33 KJV). He arose, and he stands on top of every mountain of despair that seems insurmountable to you.

And that, my friend, is hope.

You see, for Christians, hope is not in the facts but in the truth...in Jesus. Our hope rests in who we know, not in what our senses tell us. We may feel hopeless, but that feeling doesn't change the truth that Jesus lives. When we wake up to that fact, we realize that God's truth triumphs over everything else.

Are you overwhelmed with loss, with anguish, or with disappointment? Proclaim the truth that rises above the bare facts of your present circumstances—Jesus lives! See yourself with the disciples after the crucifixion, devastated and forlorn. Then run together with them from the empty tomb, carrying the news: He is risen!

Hope returns, joy springs up in you once again as you realize that death could not defeat him, nor could the weight of all the world's sorrow and grief—*your sorrow and grief*—destroy him. Jesus lives! He who has overcome the world lives in you.

∞

Lord, thank you for the hope that awakens in our hearts as we remember what you have overcome. You arose from the dead, revealing to us that we, too, can overcome anything that lies ahead. Knowing this, we face the future with confidence and assurance.

The Foolishness of the Cross

resurrection

This so-called "foolish" plan of God is far wiser than the wisest plan of the wisest man, and God in his weakness—Christ dying on the cross—is far stronger than any man.—1 Corinthians 1:25 LB

Everybody loves a winner. If our team wins and the star quarterback has a great game, we somehow feel a part of that victory. But let that same team lose a couple of games, and it's no longer "ours." Why? Because in defeat the team is perceived as weak, and no one wants to claim ownership of a failure.

This attitude was probably prevalent in biblical times just as it is today. It might even partly explain why the disciples deserted Jesus at the cross. Yes, they feared risking their own necks by publicly identifying with him after his arrest; that was one part of it. But another part was that it was humiliating for them to have their champion, their leader, the one they had protected from the adoring crowds, hanging naked on a cross.

In the eyes of the world, Jesus' crucifixion was a symbol of weakness. A cross was a place for fools. The people knew the scripture that said, "He that is hanged is accursed of God" (Deut. 21:23 KJV), and in their minds Jesus had become accursed. He was the laughingstock of the Jews. To be identified with him was to be identified with a silly man. A fool.

That terrible ridicule is one of the most amazing things about the cross. God took something that was declared foolish and made it the most powerful event in the history of the world. The One who was cursed and spat upon as he died became stronger than any man, stronger even than death!

There are still some who roll their eyes when they see a cross. If we are not careful, we, too, can push the Cross aside for something the intelligentsia deems more sophisticated, more palatable. We may even subtly embrace the message that mankind is good and doesn't need the Cross.

But the truth is, without the Cross mankind is doomed. We will overcome, not by our greatness, but by the word of our testimony and our steadfast dependence on the blood of a humble Lamb.

∞

Lord, forgive me for ever stepping over the Cross to cling to some shell of true reality. I declare my whole dependence on the power of the Cross and your resurrection. May the Cross always be my glory and strength.

resurrection

Weekend Reflections

God turned what seemed to be a humiliating ending into the greatest comeback the world has ever known. He can turn around your hopeless ending too. Don't be so sure your situation will end in defeat if God is involved in it! The truth is, only when we are at the end of ourselves are we positioned so that Christ can be glorified in us.

1. In what areas of your life has God resurrected life out of death?

_____

_____

_____

_____

_____

2. How can you best celebrate the resurrection today?

_____

_____

_____

_____

3. Consider the energy it took to raise Christ's body from the dead. As you pray, visualize this resurrection energy at work. Describe what you see being done.

_____

_____

_____

_____

_____

_____

Grace to Stand In

Wherefore let him that thinketh he standeth take heed lest he fall.
—1 Corinthians 10:12 KJV

*Amazing grace, how sweet the sound that saved a wretch like me…*One of the *most* amazing things about God's grace is that we usually need it most when we think we don't need it at all.

It's easy to cling to God's gift of loving forgiveness when we feel like wretched failures, realizing how helpless we are without his sustaining power, how hopeless our future is without his love. In our misery, we recognize his strength and our weakness. When we're on our knees, humbly begging for forgiveness, we know we need God's gift of grace. But the truth is that we need his grace all the time. And we may need it most when we're standing proudly, heads high, feeling smug about what we've done. When we're standing at the finish line, claiming our accomplishments as our own work instead of God's working through us, it's *then* that we truly need his forgiveness and his love.

Standing there in the spotlight of honor, we may not be aware of our need for grace, but God knows better. He knows we can shine in glory only because of his providence; he knows we're able to stand only because of his grace. And we know it, too…when the spotlight dims and the accolades turn to criticism and we finally come to our senses. Then we fall to our knees—fall into those patient, everlasting arms—and once again remember the source of our strength.

There, on our knees, realizing our need for his grace and completely dependent upon it, we are weak, but he is strong. And in his grace, he will lift us up to stand again.

✺

Heavenly Father, thank you for your mercy that is everlasting. Let me always be aware of your grace, not only when it is obvious to me that I need it but also in those times of success when you allow me to shine. Even in my overconfidence, help me to remember your faithfulness.

6-1-99

grace

TUESDAY

Do I Have to Stand Up?

By [Christ] also we have access by faith into this grace wherein we stand, and rejoice in hope of the glory of God.—Romans 5:2 KJV

When we're feeling inadequate and unworthy, it may feel more appropriate to *kneel* in God's grace than to stand with our heads upright. There may even be times, after we've stumbled off his path, that we wish we could show our contrition by crawling to him and lying on our faces for a predetermined number of days until we earn his favor once again. Yes, sometimes that would be easier than going to the cross, beholding the suffering Christ, and standing there expectantly...accepting the flow of his forgiveness and grace.

But standing is the stance he has chosen for us. To come to him any other way says that his grace is not enough. Therefore, when we are buffeted and weary from fighting the world's temptations, when we feel like failures, we do not resort to collapsing on our faces in self-pity. Instead, we "put on the full armor of God, so that...[we] may be able to stand [our] ground, and after [we] have done everything, to stand." (Eph. 6:13).

That is it. We just keep on standing. In his grace and in his armor, we stand, and his grace holds us up until our courage returns, and once again, we not only can stand but we can fight in God's power and might "when the evil day comes."

∞

Father, thank you for lifting me up so that I stand before you despite my failures. Let me glory in the power of your Cross and in the grace in which I stand.

Empty-Handed

*In him and through faith in him we may approach God with freedom
and confidence.*—Ephesians 3:12

How do you see yourself as you approach God? Are you cowering, trembling in fear of what he might say? Or are you hopeful that because of your works of righteousness, this time God will be proud of you? When you approach God in either of these ways, you stand on the foundation of your own abilities—your weaknesses or your strengths.

Even as firm believers in grace, too often we still find ourselves trusting in the merit of our own achievement. Perhaps we mistakenly think that our faithful devotion will give us quicker access into his presence when, in truth, the only thing that makes us worthy to stand before him is the blood of Christ. Without it, we would have to look upon his glory from afar. While our spiritual exercises put us in the place where the Holy Spirit can move and work in us more freely, they're not the thing that gives us the right to stand confidently before him.

God yearns for us to come to him. But we must come empty-handed, boasting of nothing but the grace of our Lord, resisting the temptation to gather up our golden achievements and run to him thinking, *Now he will accept me.* We please the Lord by our obedience and faithfulness, but his acceptance of us is based on nothing less than the holy blood of Jesus.

So, friend, lay them down...all your trophies and accomplishments. Praise God for what he has empowered you to do. Thank him for the transformation that is taking place through his Word and by the power of his Spirit but lay it down before you enter his courts. Go in with empty hands and an open heart and say, "Here I am, Lord." Then stand there in the robe of righteousness that Christ has given you and watch as he fills your empty hands and your open heart with the immeasurable riches of his glory.

⁂

Father, I come, resisting the temptation to list the reasons why you should accept me. I choose to trust in you alone, to believe that your grace is sufficient for me, just as I am.

grace

Unlimited Patience

But for that very reason I was shown mercy so that in me, the worst of sinners, Christ Jesus might display his unlimited patience as an example for those who would believe on him and receive eternal life.
—1 Timothy 1:16

It is difficult for us to fathom the grace and long-suffering of our Lord. We find ourselves equating God's patience with our own, which is limited and partial. But it is the unlimited patience of the Lord that gives us hope—hope that while we are changing and growing he will continue to love and befriend us.

I once met a young man who told me, "I just can't live the Christian life. I don't have what it takes to be that good."

I assured him he was exactly right! Not one of us has, in ourselves, what it takes to "live the life"; that is why we need a savior. Face it. If we could do it by ourselves, there would be no need for Jesus. But we can't. That's why he came to earth—to empower us to do what we could not do on our own. Christ's resurrection power raises us up from spiritual death to freedom so that we can declare with Paul, "If God is for us, who can be against us?" (Rom. 8:31).

Even when we continue to wrestle with old habits, bad attitudes, and jaded hearts, God's love for us never wavers. Our weakness makes God's unlimited patience all the more evident. The apostle Paul, including himself among those who tried God's patience, said he was shown mercy as "an example for those who would believe on him and receive eternal life." That idea was reinforced by Peter, another believer who had stumbled. He wrote, "Bear in mind that our Lord's patience means salvation, just as our dear brother Paul also wrote you with the wisdom that God gave him" (2 Pet. 3:15).

⊗

Oh God, I am thankful for your unlimited patience; you never give up on us but have high hopes and plans for our success. You see us as victors and overcomers in this life, and we are...by your Spirit that is at work in us even now, causing us to talk, walk, and act like you, our Father.

Finding Grace

Let us then approach the throne of grace with confidence, so that we may receive mercy and find grace to help us in our time of need.
—Hebrews 4:16

Grace is an attribute of God's character, a part of who he is. He does not create grace when we need it; instead, it is constantly available in him. Grace is something we simply find as we approach his presence. Mercy, on the other hand, is something we can ask for.

As children, we learn how to obtain mercy by various ways, even by deception, so that we can sometimes bypass the discipline that is rightfully ours. A good parent may grant mercy when necessary, but his or her love and grace will remain constant, even in light of a child's disobedience.

Similarly, we do not ask God to love us; he just does. There is no need to ask for grace; it's just there. The only condition is that we approach God's throne and find it. And we also find another gift there: righteousness. It is this righteousness that gives us the ability to stand before the throne with confidence, boldly confident that God knows us and loves us.

Father, I'm ever grateful for your abundant gift of grace that awaits me at your throne. In all my seeking, let me long for what you long to give me.

grace

Weekend Reflections

Grace is a daily need. It's not something we use only at the point of the new birth experience. And it's so much more than words from a religious creed. It is part of a theology that Oswald Chambers described as "immensely practical." Yes, it is by grace we have been saved, but it is also in grace that we stand (see Rom. 5:2), and it is grace that helps us in our needy times (see Heb. 4:16).

1. Dietrich Bonhoeffer said grace is free, but it is not cheap. Knowing the price that has been paid, how should we walk, then, in God's grace?

   _____

   _____

   _____

   _____

   _____

2. Grace is a gift, not a prize. Describe the difference.

   _____

   _____

   _____

   _____

   _____

3. How do you display the grace of God?

   _____

   _____

   _____

   _____

   _____

Are You Successful?

Be strong and very courageous. Be careful to obey all the law my servant Moses gave you; do not turn from it to the right or to the left, that you may be successful wherever you go.—Joshua 1:7

Many people feel absolutely driven to succeed. Some high achievers seem willing to sacrifice almost anything for the sake of their endeavors. They think they will be successful if they acquire great wealth and have friends who pat them on the back and say, "Man, you've got it made!" Others think they'll be a success only when they've climbed to the top of the corporate ladder and acquired a more impressive title.

Such goals are nonsense, according to Solomon, one of the wisest men who ever lived. He described these worldly endeavors and achievements as nothing but "vanity" (Eccles. 2:11 KJV), "meaningless, a chasing after the wind" (NIV). Instead, he advised us to pursue a nobler goal: to "fear God and keep his commandments" (Eccles. 12:13). *Obedience,* he said, is the only way to measure true success. We are successful when we are obedient to what God has called us to do.

God has given each of us a mission of responsibility, and our work, our responsibility, may be very different from someone else's. Jesus was successful because he was obedient to his assignment, the work the Father sent him to do. "My food," said Jesus, "is to do the will of him who sent me and to finish his work" (John 4:34). Jesus' work was his "food"—in other words, his sustenance. He lived to do the Father's will, not his own.

We should not look upon obedience with dread and apprehension. For most of us, obeying God's mission for our lives does not mean a lonely life devoid of material prosperity. Success cannot be measured by sacrifice any more than it can be measured by abundance. The Bible tells us that "to obey is better than sacrifice" (1 Sam. 15:22). Obedience doesn't necessarily mean sacrifice; it *does* mean being faithful to what he has called us to do. Whose success are *you* striving for?

∞

Lord, please make clear to me the mission you have called me to. Teach me to gauge my success by my faithfulness to doing your work, not comparing it to what others may or may not do. Let me find joy in obedience, living the fullest when I am faithful to my calling and my purpose.

obedience

Do It Now!

So, as the Holy Spirit says: "Today, if you hear his voice..."
—Hebrews 3:7

Are you responsive to God's voice in your heart? "Today, if you hear his voice," how quickly will you act upon what he says?

Many of us may not act quickly to do what God says because we find it difficult to clearly recognize his voice. We spend more time trying to decide whether it really is God who's speaking to us than we do in acting upon what he is saying!

I recall pastor Rick Shelton describing how a fellow Christian would often ask him something like, "Were you in a spiritual battle yesterday at 2:00 P.M.? I felt like something was wrong." The pastor's response was, "When that 'feeling' comes to you, don't wonder what the problem is, just do what God says to do!"

God does not give us knowledge about a situation just for our information but so that we can act on it by praying, giving, blessing, or whatever means we have. Just think of the battles that could be won, the disasters that could be prevented, the tragedies that could be avoided if only Christians would be quick to act upon the word from the Holy One!

Is God calling you to pray for someone, to intercede on a friend's behalf? Do it now! Has he revealed to you a friend's urgent need? Do you hear a heart crying out to know the Savior? Act now! We need to be so responsive to his voice that when he says go, we go, and we keep going until he says stop.

∞

Lord, help me see the time I waste and the needs I fail to fulfill because of my hesitation to do your will. Encourage me to act quickly, realizing the gravity of the things you reveal to me, and give me the strength to do all that you would have me do.

The Best Way

*The devil led him up to a high place and showed him in an instant
all the kingdoms of the world. And he said to him, "I will give you all
their authority and splendor, for it has been given to me, and I can
give it to anyone I want to. So if you worship me,
it will all be yours."—Luke 4:5–7*

In times of frustration, when Jesus calls us to his Cross and works to develop his attributes within us, we find ourselves crying out, "Surely, Lord, there is a different way!"

Sometimes his way is not the road we would readily choose for ourselves, but we follow where he leads us because we know that to become as gold we must go through the fire.

Jesus knows what it's like to strive toward the goal by following a harsh path that's not of our choosing. He came to earth to redeem the world, but the way to that goal was the way of the Cross. It wasn't the way he might have chosen for himself. In Gethsemane, he even asked the Father if there was some other way.

Actually, there *was* another way. Satan offered Jesus the kingdoms of the world without the agony of Golgotha. The goal was right, but Satan's way was wrong. Jesus knew that the only right way was the Via Dolorosa, the road to the cross.

God's purpose for your life is specific, and the way he has outlined is the perfect route for reaching this goal. There may be other ways, but there is only one perfect will of God.

Jesus humbled himself and was obedient unto death. He kept the Father's intent clearly in front of him, and he walked the path that was perfectly designed from the foundation of the world. Are you willing to be obedient, to follow the Shepherd of your soul, without looking for a different way?

If we are to walk with him, we must choose his way...the best way.

∞

Lord, the obedience you ask for may seem hard in the beginning, but I know it's the only way to my destiny. The truth is that "the way of the unfaithful is hard" (see Prov. 13:15). Your paths lead to righteousness, peace, and joy.

THURSDAY

Fill Me Up, Lord

He put a new song in my mouth, a hymn of praise to our God. Many will see and fear and put their trust in the Lord.—Psalm 40:3

I have counseled many Christians who have become disheartened because of their own weaknesses. Many of them have been born again, and they become disillusioned the first time they fall. Then they are further disillusioned when they continue to struggle to be faithful in the disciplines of the Christian life—repeatedly seeming to fall short. Of course, the accuser of the brethren, the enemy, is hastily there to make sure they feel plenty of guilt and condemnation!

In this state of self-condemnation and helplessness, what a joy it is for them to discover that it is God himself who causes us to be faithful. The apostle Paul said he is the One who gives us this desire: "For it is God Who is all the while effectually at work in you [energizing and creating in you the power and desire], both to will and to work for His good pleasure and satisfaction and delight" (Phil. 2:13 AMPLIFIED). And who is eligible for these workings of the Spirit? Those who are empty of their own will—those who give up the worries and failures and inadequacies that seem to overpower them and fill themselves instead with the grace and goodness and power of God.

You see, it is only when we have emptied ourselves of everything else that we can be filled with God. Christ was the perfect example of this emptying and refilling. Paul wrote that he "emptied Himself, taking the form of a bond-servant, and being made in the likeness of men. And being found in appearance as a man, He humbled Himself by becoming obedient to the point of death, even death on a cross" (Phil. 2:7–8 NASB). God does his best work within us when we allow our will to be crucified on Christ's cross and pray, "Thy kingdom come. Thy will be done" (Matt. 6:10 KJV).

The more you yield to this emptying and filling, the quicker the Spirit can work in you. In the position of surrender, of emptiness, and of helplessness, God readily fills with strength those who ask for it.

∞

Father, fill me up with your power to work for your pleasure. I lay down my will and fill myself with your will, your kingdom, right here and now.

There's No Use to Hide

So they inquired further of the Lord, "Has the man come here yet?"
And the Lord said, "Yes, he has hidden himself among
the baggage."—1 Samuel 10:22

When a young man named Saul was chosen by God to be Israel's first king, he became a changed man by the anointing of the Holy Spirit. What high expectations everyone had for their first king!

But when Samuel called a town meeting to present the new king to his people, nobody could find him. God had called Saul and the Holy Spirit had changed him, but when it came time for him to step into the leadership role God had prepared him for, Saul ran and hid in the luggage!

It's hard not to laugh at Saul's behavior, because most of us have felt like hiding sometimes when we think too much is expected of us. Saul's story teaches us that just because we're terrified of doing what God has told us to do doesn't mean we're not qualified as an anointed child of God to do it! Our Father is persistent when it comes to those he chooses. If he says we're capable of the task, then he will give us the abilities to do it.

Consider others who thought that by running they would be disqualified from doing the job God had set before them. How about Jonah, hiding on a ship? Elijah running from Jezebel and hiding in a cave? The disciples hiding after Jesus was crucified? All of these men were called and equipped for the mission, but they lacked the courage to move forward. Instead, they retreated into hiding.

As humans, we would probably be inclined to give up on someone who reacted so fearfully. But God, in his long-suffering love, persistently pursues us. Just about the time we think we're safely out of his reach, God announces to the world, "He has hidden himself among the baggage."

There's no use to hide, my friend. He sees the path you've chosen. He knows your hiding place. If he has called you, he has confidence in you. So come out of that cave, get off that ship, climb out from behind the baggage, and run to his side. There is nothing to fear.

∞

Lord, nothing is hidden from you. Forgive me for running away from the work you set before me. I will never find another home like your presence. I choose to abide there and to work there. Where else can I go?

obedience

Weekend Reflections

There is no such thing as partial obedience where God is concerned. It's all or nothing. Partial obedience is rebellion (see 1 Sam. 15). When Saul withheld some of the spoils of war, even though he did it in the name of God, the prophet said, "To obey is better than sacrifice" (v. 22).

1. Dietrich Bonhoeffer said, "Only those who obey can believe, and only those who believe can obey." How is your faith in Christ the foundation of your obedience?

   _____

   _____

   _____

   _____

2. Consider examples of so-called "partial obedience" and their grim results (Saul's actions in 1 Sam. 15 and the actions of Ananias and Sapphira in Acts 5). How do these accounts affect your attitude toward faith and obedience?

   _____

   _____

   _____

   _____

3. Have you ever obeyed at the risk of having people think you're a radical? What happened as a result of your "radical" obedience?

   _____

   _____

   _____

   _____

   _____

The Kingdom Belongs to a Child

*And he said: "I tell you the truth, unless you change and become like
little children, you will never enter the kingdom
of heaven."*—Matthew 18:3

The kingdom of God cannot be earned. It is inherited. Only those willing to walk as God's children will find themselves as his inheritors.

This was impressed upon me one day before a church service. I was preparing for ministry while joyful and upbeat preservice music played in the sanctuary. A young man with Down syndrome had already entered the sanctuary and was waiting for service to begin. Suddenly, without warning, he took off across the front of the sanctuary, leaping and dancing. In his simple way, oblivious to anyone else, he unabashedly expressed his joy.

Watching the happy gyrations of that young man, I was reminded of the power and grace that belong to those who come into God's presence as children. Oh, that we could come before him with the same kind of freedom and simple faith! No work, no sweat, no struggle. Just an open heart of faith that looks up to the Father with full expectancy and total dependence on him.

As long as we walk into his presence with arrogance, leaning on spiritual maturity and pretending we have our lives all together, God's kingdom remains out of reach to us. It is reserved for those of us who come into his courts looking up into his greatness and remembering our smallness. To us he extends his hand, touches us with his royal scepter, and says, "Ah, my child. The kingdom belongs to you."

∞

Father, I want to participate in your kingdom. I want to know what it is to grow up as your child, taking delight in discovering your kingdom purposes. What have I missed because of pride and arrogance? Please, Lord, take me there again.

Childish or Childlike?

*Then there arose a reasoning among them, which of them should be
greatest. And Jesus, perceiving the thought of their heart, took a child,
and set him by him.—Luke 9:46–47 KJV*

Mankind's innate need to feel important doesn't have to become sin.
We all want to know that we have significance, that our existence matters.
But when that need becomes a childish quest to be exalted for the sake of
power and self-centeredness, we'd better brace ourselves. Here comes the
fall!

If I had been Jesus in this scene described in Luke 9, I would have
been most irritated. One would have hoped that after all the teaching and
training these men had received from the Master teacher, they would be
getting the picture. But the same dispute would soon raise its head
again—at the Last Supper, of all places! In the middle of the conversation
in which Jesus shared with them how one of them would betray him, they
argued again about which of them was the greatest (see Luke 22:22–24)!

But Jesus did not overreact in either setting. He didn't throw up his
hands and exclaim, "Don't you guys get it?" He did not rebuke his disciples for their desire to be great; instead he revealed to them the way to
greatness: "Whoever welcomes this little child in my name welcomes me;
and whoever welcomes me welcomes the one who sent me. For he who is
least among you all—he is the greatest" (Luke 9:48).

There is a subtle difference in the two words *childish* and *childlike.*
But there is a world of difference—a *heavenly* world of difference—in the
two words' meanings. To be self-centered is to be childish. To be Christ-
centered we must become childlike. Small. Needy. The least of all. "Of
such," said Jesus, "is the kingdom of heaven" (Matt. 19:14 KJV).

∞

Lord Jesus, thank you for the example you left us. You came, not to be
served, but to serve. And in doing so you showed us the way to greatness.
Expose the childishness in me so that I can grow out of it and become a child
in your kingdom.

Don't Mock the Seed

He told them another parable: "The kingdom of heaven is like a mustard seed, which a man took and planted in his field. Though it is the smallest of all your seeds, yet when it grows, it is the largest of garden plants and becomes a tree, so that the birds of the air come and perch in its branches."—Matthew 13:31–32

Bethlehem…Nazareth…small-town life. A manger…a stable…a small group of shepherds—not the typical fanfare for the birth of a king. Jerusalem…Israel—a small world. A staff of twelve including a few seafarers…a tax collector…a thief—hardly a typical way to build a kingdom.

Yet this was the beginning of a revival that would turn the world upside down. A kingdom that would never end.

We didn't grow mustard when I was a kid, but we did grow corn. It was amazing to me then—and still is—how that small kernel can be planted and grow into a huge stalk six to eight feet high with several ears of corn, each with hundreds of kernels. Jesus said this is the way his kingdom works. From a tiny seed to eternal glory.

Don't judge whether the kingdom of God is among you just by the numbers. Numbers alone do not verify God's presence. Out of the smallest church may come one soul who will preach to thousands. Don't fall for the lie that God cannot work through small towns or businesses. From one worker in an unknown company may come a new technology that will change the world.

Don't mock the tiny seed. You don't know what's inside. From the smallest word of encouragement, the simplest explanation of the gospel, God may grow a tree of life that will provide food for the anguished soul and shade for the famished heart. He's done it before. Nearly two thousand years ago he planted a small tree on a hill called Golgotha. And millions are still running there to find healing and life.

❦

Lord, what are the small seeds around me that you are growing? What spiritual work have I been blinded to?

Bearing One Fruit

The fruit of the Spirit is love, joy, peace, patience,
kindness, goodness, faithfulness.
—Galatians 5:22

There are various kinds of fruit of the Spirit, yet they are all balanced parts of the same whole. For example, joy without love would be incomplete. Joy standing alone comes across as brassy and even pretentious. But joy with love is pleasant and uplifting to those it touches.

Or consider faithfulness without peace. Faithfulness would be fatiguing if it stood detached. But faithfulness with peace is nourishing, comforting. We faithfully endure through various temptations while remaining at peace about the outcome, joyfully envisioning our reward to come. As James said, "My brethren, count it all joy when ye fall into divers temptations" (James 1:2 KJV).

This kind of fruit will instinctively come as our roots sink deeper into the Savior. The better we get to know him, the more refreshing this fruit becomes. Unprepared and unrehearsed, it springs from us because it comes from the One whose life flows from God through us to his children. We don't have to strain or work or coerce it from us. After all, it is not something we create in ourselves. This fruit is *his* love, *his* joy, *his* peace, patience, kindness, goodness, and faithfulness, branching out of us to shade others with the richness of his kingdom. We become living expressions of the Lord Jesus on the earth, demonstrating the power of the Holy Spirit, bearing fruit to his glory. If we are abiding in him, growing in him, we cannot be fruitless.

∞

Jesus, teach me to abide in you so that I will bear much fruit to your glory. Help me to grow deeper into you so that I can be a living, thriving expression of your everlasting life in a lifeless world.

Forcefully Advancing

From the days of John the Baptist until now, the kingdom of heaven has been forcefully advancing, and forceful men lay hold of it.—Matthew 11:12

When we declare Jesus as our Savior, we must also declare him as Lord. The Bible tells us, "God has made this Jesus, whom you crucified, both Lord and Christ" (Acts 2:36). For him to be Lord as well as Savior means that we submit our wills to Christ, our Lord, while handing over our sins to Christ, our Savior, to be cleansed by the power of his blood.

Now, having a submitted will does not mean we take an apathetic, passionless approach to the kingdom, feebly mumbling, "Well, whatever God wants to do…" If we do nothing but sit and wait for the future to arrive, it will—but we won't like it!

The kingdom of God is not a happenstance sort of thing. It is a living and thriving force, moving forward to the heartbeat of God as mighty men and women get on board and advance with it. If we are to be a part of it, we must tune in to the heart of God and *move* as the Spirit leads and guides us.

Our destiny will not just happen to us all at once. It unfolds as we continually yield our wills to the Holy Spirit in the here and now, today and every day, allowing God to prepare us for what is coming, while achieving today what must be achieved.

Jesus' destiny was the throne, but before he sat on the throne, he yielded to God's will. "He humbled himself and became obedient to death—even death on a cross!" (Phil. 2:8). Every day of his life on earth, Jesus was advancing the kingdom—moving toward his destiny—as he healed the sick, loved the unlovely, and delivered his words of life. He didn't sit and wait; he aggressively followed God's will.

In the same way, we must firmly hold on to his forcefully advancing kingdom—and advance with it.

❧

Lord, I want to be a part of your forcefully advancing kingdom. I declare my will to be under your Lordship. I am tuning in to your Spirit, and I will obey. I now lay hold of that kingdom that is constantly moving at your will.

Weekend Reflections

A strange kingdom, this kingdom of God. It can't be seen with physical eyes because it's not of this world; it lives in the heart of man (see Luke 17:21; John 18:36). Even stranger, the only way one can enter this kingdom is to become like a child. It doesn't matter how many earthly crowns you accumulate. They're worthless in this kingdom—even detrimental. Oh, and get this: The king died to pay for his bride, but now he lives again. And the promised bride...well, she's a church of millions.

This kingdom of heaven is thriving today, growing all around the world. Its armies are conquering not by swords and spears but by the spoken word and the blood of the Lamb. You and I can choose to be a part of it, or we can sit idly by and watch it move on without us.

1. Since Jesus has said we must become as children to enter this kingdom, what implications does this have for you? What childlike traits do you need to aspire to?

_____

_____

_____

2. Jesus said, "The kingdom of heaven has been forcefully advancing, and forceful men lay hold of it" (Matt. 11:12). How are you laying hold of God's kingdom?

_____

_____

_____

3. What are some differences between the kingdom of God and the kingdoms of this world? For example, God's kingdom is founded on love while many earthly kingdoms are built on intimidation, fear, wealth, etc.

_____

_____

_____

_____

the kingdom of God

My Desire, His Purpose

May he give you the desire of your heart and make all your plans succeed.—Psalm 20:4

When I was traveling recently, the plane had just pushed away from the gate and was heading toward the runway when we heard an urgent banging and knocking noise below us. It was soon learned that a member of the ground crew had inadvertently been locked inside the cargo section. When he realized the cargo doors had closed and the plane was leaving, sheer panic must have struck his heart!

Many of us may think of God's will the same way that crewman thought of the airplane that day. We may believe God is always wanting to take us where we do not want to go. Some of us are sure that if we prayed, "God, I will go anywhere you want me to go," we would soon find ourselves on the next plane to Zambia or Outer Mongolia.

Is God's will for us always going to be what we least desire? Such an idea makes no sense. After all, if there is no joy in going where he sends us and doing what he asks of us, will we be as successful as he desires us to be? Even when we can't help but dread what lies ahead, we must remember that he is working in us, conforming us "to will and to act according to his good purpose" (Phil. 2:13). He will not lead us into something we have not been prepared for.

If we are doing God's will, our work may not always be glorious, but we will feel a deep satisfaction that assures us we are doing the right thing. So go ahead. Pray to do the Father's will. There is nothing to fear. His plans for you are "plans to prosper you and not to harm you, plans to give you hope and a future'" (Jer. 29:11).

∞

Lord, I am willing to walk according to your purpose for my life. I know I will find there both joy and peace as I recognize that you hold my best interests—and my future—in your hands.

Beyond the Open Door

Behold, I have set before thee an open door, and no man can shut it.—Revelation 3:8 KJV

The life of the believer has been compared to climbing a mountain, walking a road, sailing the ocean. The apostle Paul compared it to fighting the good fight. Always, the central element in such comparisons is *movement* or *becoming* as God works in us to "do of his good pleasure" (Phil. 2:13 KJV), bringing us from glory to glory.

This moving forward isn't always comfortable for us. After all, it is the familiar things that bring us security. We often oppose change because it pushes us into the unknown and requires us to evaluate and adjust to new situations. Moving into new circumstances requires us to judge what is familiar to us and discern whether the change will be a positive one. Without question, the major hindrance to forward progress is letting go of the familiar to reach for the unfamiliar.

Throughout his letter to the Galatians, the apostle Paul rebuked them for reaching back to the old law. To them it was easier to live in the past, clinging to the familiar traditions, than it was to move forward, living by faith. It was easier just to do things the way they had always been done, but Christ had brought them a new way, a better way. The new covenant required them to lay down their spiritual trophies, cast off their binding rituals, and rely wholly upon the grace of God.

What change is God trying to work in you? What revelation are you resisting because of your death grip on the old and familiar? God has set before you an open door, a fresh anointing, a new realm you have never experienced. But to enter that new world you must abandon the past and trust him to lead you safely into a greater power than you have ever known before. Paul accepted that invitation. He wrote, "This one thing I do, forgetting those things which are behind, and reaching forth unto those things which are before, I press toward the mark for the prize of the high calling of God in Christ Jesus" (Phil. 3:13–14 KJV).

∞

Lord, show me what I have been unwilling to relinquish. I want to forsake all and follow you wherever you may lead. I know your way is the best way and that true happiness lies in completely surrendering to your leading.

Making the Right Moves

Let your eyes look straight ahead, fix your gaze directly before you.
Make level paths for your feet and take only ways that are firm.
—Proverbs 4:25–26

What if we could be assured that every time we made a decision it would be the right one? It's a nice thought, isn't it? But it's not real life. The truth is, we have to make tough decisions that sometimes have long-reaching ramifications.

Some people may not understand our judgments; some may even be hurt by what we decide. But every choice we make should somehow assist us in pressing forward toward the goal, toward Jesus Christ. We must ask ourselves, "Will this choice in any way impede or delay my becoming like him? Does this decision fit into that big picture? Does it move me forward or encourage me to remain in my comfort zone?"

In the book of Proverbs, Solomon shared numerous mottoes and gleanings of wisdom that can assist us in making a good decision. When Solomon advised us to "fix your gaze directly before you" (Prov. 4:25), he was telling us not to concentrate too much on yesterday or even on what has happened today. Instead, we must look forward and upward. As he says in another proverb, "The path of life leads upward for the wise to keep him from going down to the grave" (Prov. 15:24). Our decisions should keep us moving forward in life, says Solomon, because when we stop moving forward, we begin to die. The way of abundant life is the onward, upward way, the way of growing, of becoming.

Choose this moment to be a God-pleaser and not a man-pleaser, to do, above all else, what God tells you to do. When you're faced with tough decisions, listen to his voice and his Spirit, and make those tough choices with confidence, looking with great anticipation to the future God desires you to fulfill.

∞

Lord, I choose the way of life. I will not be motivated by the fear of family, friends, or the world but by the voice of your Spirit. I thank you for yesterday and for today, but I look forward to what lies ahead, knowing that as I commit my plans to you, you will guide me to take the best path.

The Joy of Relinquishment

Consider what God has done: Who can straighten what he has made crooked?—Ecclesiastes 7:13

How long has it been since you honestly sought to know the ways of God? Most of us have to admit that too much of our prayer time is spent listing our desires and advising God on how he should do things. The prayers that are blessed are the ones that seek the heart of God, that lift our minds into another realm and earnestly seek the will of God "on earth as it is in heaven" (Matt. 6:10). With such prayers we literally bring the heavenly down to the earthly.

Don't beg God to do things your way, and don't try to straighten what God has made crooked. When you do, you set yourself against God. The Living Bible translates Ecclesiastes 7:13 as, "See the way God does things and fall into line. Don't fight the facts of nature." The Saul who became the apostle Paul learned what it was like to fight the facts God handed him. Knocked down on the road to Damascus, he heard Jesus say, "Saul, Saul, why persecutest thou me? it is hard for thee to kick against the pricks" (Acts 26:14 KJV).

Many times we feel the same thorny pricks that Saul felt but fail to recognize them. It was the wise man Solomon who said, "The way of the sluggard is blocked with thorns, but the path of the upright is a highway" (Prov. 15:19).

Have you felt a few thorns lately? It could be that you are walking down your own path instead of God's. Maybe you're trying to make a straight highway out of a narrow road that God has wound for you through some rugged mountains. Make the adjustments necessary to bring yourself back to God's course, not the other way around. Relinquish control and fall in line behind Jesus, observing his ways, watching and imitating his every move.

∞

Lord, I will not fight against you. I empty myself of my own will to embrace your will, oh God.

It's Not Natural

Through these he has given us his very great and precious promises, so that through them you may participate in the divine nature and escape the corruption in the world caused by evil desires.—2 Peter 1:4

Raised in a devout Christian home, I learned the "dos and don'ts" early in life. My schoolmates knew I didn't participate in certain things, but sometimes they would ask me, "Why not?"

As a youngster, the only thing I knew to say was, "It's against my religion."

As I grew up, I learned more about the "why not." I learned there was scriptural evidence for what I was taught so that when I was asked why, I pointed to a scripture that said, "Thou shalt not...." Yet in a greater sense, that still didn't answer the question. *Okay, so the Bible says, "Thou shalt not." But why does it say it?* I wondered.

As a child, I couldn't understand. But now, from my present perspective in life, I see a greater truth revealed: *I don't do certain things because they are not part of the nature of Yahweh, and I am one of his children.* For example, he says, "Thou shalt not lie" (see Exod. 20:16 KJV), because it is impossible for *him* to lie. It is by not lying, by being trustworthy and keeping my word, that I come to understand a cornerstone of God's character: truth.

God says, "Thou shalt not commit adultery" (v. 14 KJV), because it is against the very nature of God to break a covenant like marriage. Through the marriage covenant, we get a glimpse of the covenant-keeping faithfulness of our holy God. He is committed to us for the long haul.

As sons and daughters of God, we can partake of his divine nature. Paul said our new nature is not compelled to sin but led to holiness: "You, however, are controlled not by the sinful nature but by the Spirit, if the Spirit of God lives in you" (Rom. 8:9).

Why are some things immoral? Why are we commanded not to do certain things? Because they aren't in God's nature.

So if you're asked "Why not?" just say, "It's not my nature."

❦

Oh my Father, I worship you, for you are faithful. I am grateful that you do not lie, steal, or break covenants. Please, Lord, let your divine nature work in me, empowering me to be an ambassador of your heavenly kingdom.

Weekend Reflections

In discovering God's will, we must first lay aside our own will. George Muller wrote, "I seek at the beginning to get my heart into such a state that it has no will of its own in regard to a given matter. Ninety percent of the trouble with people is just here. Ninety percent of the difficulties are overcome when our hearts are ready to do the Lord's will, whatever it may be. When one is truly in this state, it is usually but a little way to the knowledge of what His will is" (*Bible Illustrator,* Parsons Technology Inc.).

1. By the example of Saul's encounter with God on the road to Damascus, we can see that not all opposition is from Satan. What opposition in your life may be a message from God?

   _____

   _____

   _____

   _____

2. If we would find God's will in major decisions, we must seek to obey his will in the little things. Name some little things you have been neglecting to do?

   _____

   _____

   _____

   _____

3. If you are facing a major decision, ask yourself, "Will saying yes impede or accelerate my progress in becoming like Christ?" Describe the decision you are facing and the consequences of asking this question.

   _____

   _____

   _____

   _____

Where Time Stands Still

Come with me by yourselves to a quiet place and get some rest.
—Mark 6:31

Rest. Just saying the word can sometimes bring tranquility. Often we don't realize we need rest until our eyelids get heavy and our bodies grow so weary that it becomes obvious to others that we have pushed ourselves beyond the limits of our endurance. In the same sense, we do not always realize our need for spiritual rest until we are at the proverbial end of the rope, hanging on to a few loose threads. Finally, we cry out to the Lord for rescue.

God wants us to find rest *before* we get to that place of futility—before we get to the end of the rope. He wants us to find rest for our souls in *him*. As we fall into his presence, our emotions and intellect cease their laborious struggles, and *time stands still*. He who stands on the sea of eternity gathers us up in his arms and holds us safely above the relentless pace of life's battles.

As David said, "Find rest, O my soul, in God alone" (Ps. 62:5). True spiritual rest can be found no other place.

∞

Lord, teach me to find rest in you before I even think I need it, to respond as you say, "Come with me," to rejoice in the serenity I find in the shelter of your arms, where time stands still.

spiritual rest

Falsely Accused

Cast all your anxiety on him because he cares for you.
—1 Peter 5:7

Have you ever been falsely accused by those you love? If so, you know that nothing hurts more than having loved ones believe vicious lies about you. How wonderful it is when the record is set straight and the truth comes forward.

Many people in our world believe lies about God, their Creator who loves them. They portray God as uncompassionate, uncaring, and nearing the end of his patience. Where did these ideas come from? Certainly not from God! No, it is the enemy who paints a picture of our Lord with a long, accusing finger, saying things like, "When are you going to get your act together? How many times must I forgive you?"

We must set the record straight for God. The Word clearly tells us that we have only one accuser, and it is not our Lord. Our Lord is full of compassion. He urgently calls us to him, saying, "Come unto me, all ye that labour and are heavy laden, and I will give you rest" (Matt. 11:28 KJV).

It is the accuser who says, "God doesn't care about your little worries. He has much greater things to be concerned with."

Lies. That's all such comments are. Those of us who know the truth must set the message straight, "proclaim it clearly" (Col. 4:4), as the apostle Paul did. Our Lord is loving, compassionate, and merciful. He "stoops down to look on the heavens and the earth. He raises the poor from the dust and lifts the needy from the ash heap…. He settles the barren woman in her home as a happy mother of children" (Ps. 113:6–7, 9). Though we are sinners, he bestows on us "unlimited patience as an example for those who would believe on him and receive eternal life" (1 Tim. 1:16).

∞

Father, I am casting my anxiety on you now. As I name the things I have worried about, I am giving them to you, thanking you that you care about me so much. I renounce the lies I have listened to and even believed concerning who you are and how you see me.

All Is at Rest

You will keep in perfect peace him whose mind is steadfast, because he trusts in you. Trust in the Lord forever, for the Lord, the Lord, is the Rock eternal.—Isaiah 26:3–4

Because time often seems to press in on us from all sides and our work is never done, we may believe that God must be in a similar predicament. With such an attitude, our prayers can sound like this: "Lord, have you heard the world news lately? You need to hurry and do something!" We look at the church and see its weaknesses, its seeming frailty, and we want God to fix it—and fix it fast.

But God is not up in heaven fretting, dashing about trying to see that his will is performed on earth. He is completely at rest, perfectly confident in knowing his plans will come to pass.

We get a clear picture of how God feels about our anxiety in the account of Jesus and the disciples out on the Sea of Galilee. While the disciples were frantically bailing water in the middle of a blustery storm, Jesus slept in the back of the boat. He knew what was going on, but he was not the least bit worried or alarmed.

Once God's word goes forth, it is settled. It is impossible for it not to be fulfilled. Of his word going out, God said, "It will not return to me empty, but will accomplish what I desire and achieve the purpose for which I sent it" (Isa. 55:11).

Our God is the essence of tranquility. He never gets tired or weary. When you are worried and fretting over something, picture God in heaven, calm and assured, in absolute control of his plan for you.

∞

God, you are in control. There is not a moment that you are stressed out and full of anxiety. I worship you, Jesus, because in you "all things hold together" (Col. 1:17).

spiritual rest

A Short Trip Home

The one thing I ask of the Lord—the thing I seek most—is to live in the house of the Lord all the days of my life, delighting in the Lord's perfections and meditating in his Temple.—Psalm 27:4 NLT

We can't wait to go on vacation—and we can't wait to get back home. Have you noticed that? We spend days, sometimes weeks, preparing, packing, and planning for that long-awaited trip to some new, intriguing destination only to look forward with greater anticipation a little later to getting back home to our own bed, refrigerator, and recliner.

Home is a place where we're at ease. There is no need for facades there. It's where we are most comfortable being ourselves. While our earthly dwelling is only a temporary address, our true home is in the presence of God. And getting there is as simple as a prayer empowered by faith.

Consider taking one of these journeys home in the coming week:

- You're in rush-hour traffic. The highway has become a parking lot. You turn off the music and the traffic report and speak God's name over and over until you hear his voice replying with your name.

- Instead of going out for lunch with the gang, you bring your lunch to work, find a bench outside somewhere, and invite Christ to join you. You take in the sun, watch the trees move in the breeze, and listen for the songbird, all the while contemplating how God sees even a bird that falls to the ground.

- You stop by to visit a chapel or church after work and sit and read a couple of great hymns out loud until the truth of their lyrics becomes like water to the depths of your soul.

After doing this a few times, prayer will become an experience you look forward to with increasing anticipation. The wonderful thing about all this is that no matter where you are, you're never that far from home. In fact, you can be as close to home as you want to be.

∞

Lord Jesus, home is wherever you are. Help me to find my way home every day. I know that my time there will become more cherished as I learn to behold you face to face and as I come to you as a child, stripped of every hint of pride and self-righteousness.

Life Needs an Intermission

It is a sign between me and the children of Israel for ever: for in six days the Lord made heaven and earth, and on the seventh day he rested, and was refreshed.—Exodus 31:17 KJV

If God rested on the Sabbath, why don't we? Do we think we are exempt from the need for rest?

I love one of the Hebrew meanings behind the word *Sabbath*. It means "intermission." An intermission in a concert or play gives us a physical and emotional break. It lets us stand up, stretch, take care of physical needs—and also think about and assimilate what we have just heard and seen. Life needs intermissions too. Life needs a Sabbath.

When I was in the third grade, one weekend my dad took me out to the area we were attempting to turn into a vegetable garden. Dad got on the tractor and set me on the seat with him as he did the plowing. I felt proud that I had helped, and Monday morning I went right up to my third-grade teacher and proudly announced that I had learned to plow a field. She drew in a quick breath and said, "You mean you worked on the Sabbath?" I remember standing there sort of dumbfounded, not knowing quite what to say, and then quietly making my way back to my seat.

Times have certainly changed. I doubt that any child in recent years has had a conversation with his or her teacher like I had with mine. Of course, what my teacher did not know was that Dad was an accountant and getting on the tractor was not work to him at all. It was actually quite the opposite. However, I never forgot that conversation with my teacher and through the years have attempted to look carefully at what I do on the Sabbath.

We need the Sabbath. Jesus himself said, "The Sabbath was made for man, not man for the Sabbath" (Mark 2:27). We are not exempt because we are busy executives, full-time moms, or sports-addicted teenagers. There needs to be a time to rest, a time to review, a time to reflect before moving on.

∞

Yes, God. I get too busy with life and neglect to set aside time for rest. You have given us an example to follow. Thank you for the Sabbath.

spiritual rest

Weekend Reflections

John Bunyan said in his immortal *Pilgrim's Progress*, "I saw in my dream that just as Christian came up to the cross, his burden loosed from his shoulders and fell from his back and began to tumble till it came to the mouth of the sepulcher, where it fell in and I saw it no more. Then was Christian glad and lightsome and said with a merry heart, 'He has given me rest by his sorrow, and life by his death.'" When we rest, we relinquish our burdens, refresh our bodies, and nurture our spirits. How do you rest? You do rest, don't you?

1 If Almighty God rested on the Sabbath, why don't you?

_____

_____

_____

_____

_____

2. Life needs an intermission. When was your last intermission?

_____

_____

_____

_____

_____

3. Read Hebrews 3:19–4:11. What work is the writer referring to in verse 10?

_____

_____

_____

_____

_____

Wings and Chariots

For he has rescued us from the dominion of darkness and brought us into the kingdom of the Son he loves.—Colossians 1:13

Although God himself is never rushed to perform his will on earth, there is one thing he does rush to. He rushes to the aid of his children. Often he does not intervene, however, until that lost child cries out for help. He rushes to answer the appeals for mercy from those who have walked their own way and suddenly find themselves trapped in their own snares. He is not willing that any should perish, but he waits for us to use our wills to turn to him (see 2 Pet. 3:9).

When we do, God mobilizes the fastest imaginable rescue. "He makes the clouds his chariot and rides on the wings of the wind" (Ps. 104:3). No one can rescue like God can. As the apostle Peter said, "The Lord knows how to rescue godly men from trials" (2 Pet. 2:9).

Not only has God rescued us from the dominion of darkness, but he also delivers us from excessive temptation, providing a way of escape from every threat (1 Cor. 10:13). In Romans 7, Paul described the constant battle between flesh and spirit and then exclaimed, "What a wretched man I am! Who will rescue me from this body of death? Thanks be to God—through Jesus Christ our Lord!" (vv. 24–25).

Like Paul, do you find yourself struggling to conquer the temptations that plague your daily life? Have you veered off God's path and now find yourself backed into a corner surrounded by your attackers? Cry out to God, and don't be surprised if you hear the rustle of wings and the rumble of chariots.

∞

God, you are never too late. What an awesome God you are that you ride the wings of the wind!

Take Your Time; God Is in No Hurry

Do you not know? Have you not heard? The Lord is the everlasting God, the Creator of the ends of the earth. He will not grow tired or weary, and his understanding no one can fathom.—Isaiah 40:28

God is never impatient for us to finish our prayers. Never does he say, "Hurry up and say what you have to say!" Since time is relative and God is not confined to it, we can take as much time as we want to say what we need to say, to formulate our inmost desires and thoughts into words. Even if we were the best orators in the world and could formulate our thoughts into concise, articulate phrases and express ourselves quickly and thoroughly, it would still seem slow to him. God can take in data faster than any man-made computer. His computations and speed are infinitely beyond any known scale. Comparing our communication speed to his is like comparing today's fastest computer processor chip to an ancient monk laboriously transcribing Scripture in calligraphy using a quill pen dipped in an inkwell!

On the other hand, our Father does desire for us to develop our prayer skills. Jesus taught his disciples how to pray, saying, "After this manner therefore pray ye: Our Father which art in heaven…" (Matt. 6:9 KJV). But when we try our best and still feel as though our prayers are weak and trite, that's when it's time to step back, forget about trying to be eloquent, and simply pour out our hearts to him. He doesn't judge us on our oratory skills. He doesn't tap his toes and, with arms folded over his chest, prod us to hurry. He holds time in his hands. He has all day and all night to listen.

∞

"How precious to me are your thoughts, O God! How vast is the sum of them! Were I to count them, they would outnumber the grains of sand. When I awake, I am still with you" (Ps. 139:17–18). Your capacity to hear and to know all things is too marvelous to comprehend. All glory to you!

Must We Love Prayer?

These people draw near to Me with their mouth, and honor Me with their lips, but their heart is far from Me.—Matthew 15:8 NKJV

Prayer is the means God has designed for us to communicate with him. It is our direct channel to the other world. (In saying this, I do not mean to trivialize the great value and importance of prayer but to emphasize the importance of having our hearts engaged in what we are praying.) To lift up prayer as a holy thing in and of itself is somehow out of balance. Only when our prayers are *conversation* with the Holy One do they become holy.

My friend, we can pray all day every day without really "praying." We can spend hours with the words pouring out of us while our minds are stuck in "park," never really listening to his voice, thinking only of ourselves. In true prayer, we commune with God at a level deeper than mere words. At some point, the mindless words cease and the heart starts speaking. This is prayer! We become transparent before God and wait for his words of life.

In the parable of the Pharisee and the publican, one man prayed a prayer of honest humility while the other boasted so that others around could hear about his good deeds. Jesus said both were praying but God only heard the prayer of the one who was honest (see Luke 18:10–14 KJV).

God is not impressed with our goodness; he is only impressed with our dependence on him, which is measured by our faith in Jesus Christ and him crucified. We can be so committed to the ritual of prayer that we miss the relationship of communion; we can become so bogged down in the tradition that we miss the transfiguration. His presence may be revealed around us, but because we are so committed to the form, we don't recognize the One we are supposedly seeking.

I love to pray, not because I love prayer, but because I love the One I am praying to. And it is in that time of laying out my heart in his presence that he reveals himself to me. That is what I love about prayer that I talk and he listens. And even greater than that, he often speaks when I listen.

∞

Lord Jesus, may I never let the form take the place of friendship with you. Let my soul yearn for you, the Person, and not just the practice.

Learning with Christ

Lord, teach us to pray.
—Luke 11:1

How it must have thrilled Jesus to hear his disciples ask him for this lesson! Nothing thrills the heart of a teacher more than a student who is eager to learn. Then the heart is most teachable. Then the words sink deeper than the level of logic.

Lessons are so much harder to learn when we don't listen! Consider Martha, working in the kitchen while her sister, Mary, sat at the Savior's feet drinking in every word. The teacher was teaching, but only the eager student was privileged to hear.

Today the Teacher is teaching: "But the Helper, the Holy Spirit, whom the Father will send in My name, He will teach you all things, and bring to your remembrance all things that I said to you" (John 14:26 NKJV). Are we listening? Do you want to learn? Is the cry of your heart, "Teach me to pray"? Only those who have "ears to hear" (Luke 8:8) will hear what the Spirit is teaching.

∞

Yes, Lord. I want you to teach me to pray. I don't want to go through the motions of prayer without engaging my heart in the process. My heart is open. I want to hear what the Holy Spirit is saying.

The Foolishness of Prayer

*The man without the Spirit does not accept the things that come from
the Spirit of God, for they are foolishness to him, and he cannot
understand them, because they are spiritually discerned.*
—1 Corinthians 2:14

Either prayer is real or it is one of the craziest things a person can do.
For us to spend time talking to someone we can't see is not normal,
according to human reasoning.

But it is the normal thing for the spiritual person. The real me, the
real you, the part of us that cannot be seen with natural eyes, understands
and knows that prayer is a real thing. Our spirits long for supernatural
contact with the Holy Spirit that birthed them into existence. They yearn
for time spent with the Source of life. They dream of resting at home in
his presence.

In 1934 a man named Vernon Patterson, along with twenty-nine
other businessmen, gathered on a pasture to spend the day in prayer for
their city, Charlotte, North Carolina. One of the prayers Vernon prayed
that day was that God would raise up someone from there to "preach the
gospel to the ends of the earth." Later that year during an eleven-week
revival with Mordecai Ham, a young man named Billy Graham walked to
the altar and gave his life to the Lord. Prayer makes a difference!

It doesn't always take masses of praying people to have God intercede.
God has said he will respond to one person's earnest prayer: "I looked for
a man among them who would build up the wall and stand before me in
the gap on behalf of the land so I would not have to destroy it, but I
found none" (Ezek. 22:30).

Yes, to ordinary people, prayer may seem foolish, but believers understand the power of prayer. The world says prayer is a crutch for the
simpleminded and needy, but that is because the world cannot comprehend spiritual things (see Rom. 8:7). How about you? Are you a man or
woman who will stand in the gap today and pray?

✎

Lord, I will be one who believes your Word. I reject the lie that prayer is foolish and that you will not answer. Oh, Lord Almighty, your Word is faithful, and
powerful things happen when your people pray in faith.

communion with God

Weekend Reflections

Prayer without faith is ineffective, but the "prayer offered in faith" makes the sick whole again (James 5:15). We must believe that prayer does change things. As Richard Foster said, "It is easy for us to be defeated at the outset because we have been taught that everything in the universe is already set, and so things cannot be changed. We may gloomily feel this way, but the Bible does not teach that. The Bible pray-ers prayed as if their prayers could and would make an objective difference" *(Celebration of Discipline)*.

1. What really big dreams have you failed to present to God because of your unbelief?

   _____

   _____

   _____

   _____

2. Describe any area of your life that you are not praying about and explain why you are not praying about it?

   _____

   _____

   _____

   _____

3. The disciples asked Jesus to teach them to pray (see Luke 11:1). Ask Jesus to teach you to pray, and write down what he shows you.

   _____

   _____

   _____

   _____

   _____

What You See Is What You Get

Now faith is...the evidence of things not seen.—Hebrews 11:1 KJV

What do you see ahead? Are you excited about what is on the horizon, or are you frightened by what looks like certain defeat? When you pray about some discouraging thing that's confronting you and there is no visible change in your situation, do you question God's purposes? It's okay to answer yes. Be honest. We all wonder about God's purposes when we're in dire circumstances.

I believe there is much God would like to reveal to us but doesn't because of the danger the knowledge would bring to us. And sometimes our limited vision prevents us from seeing what he is willing to reveal. Often, just beyond our present difficulties lies the fulfilled promise we have been hoping for. Yet our present predicament forms blinders over our eyes. That's when we must close our eyes and see our future with the eyes of faith. If we wait until we have hard evidence to believe, we are believing with "Thomas faith." Jesus said, "Blessed are those who have not seen and yet have believed" (John 20:29).

Sooner or later, we all find ourselves in the dilemma Elisha's servant faced when he saw the enemy's armies surrounding the city. "Oh, my lord, what shall we do?" the terrified man cried (2 Kings 6:15).

Elisha, who had been looking through the eyes of faith, calmly prayed, "O Lord, open his eyes so he may see" (v. 17). Elisha wanted his servant to be able to see what he could already see. When the Lord opened the servant's eyes, he saw the hills full of horses and chariots of fire all around Elisha. God's heavenly army had been there all along, but it was only visible to those with eyes of faith.

The situation you are facing cannot be judged correctly simply by what you can see with your human eyes. Only with the eyes of the Spirit can you begin to comprehend God's purpose in your circumstances. So take heart. Learn to look through different eyes...his eyes. Then, just maybe, you will see God's heavenly army poised around you, ready to carry out God's will.

☙

Lord, open my eyes. Let me see things clearly the way you would have me see them...to remember that things are not always as they appear to be...that the fulfillment of your promises may be closer than I realize.

121

faith

Speaking Life...to the Dead

He is...the God who gives life to the dead and calls things that are not as though they were.—Romans 4:17

When we think of God giving life to the dead, the first image that usually comes to mind is that of Jesus standing at the grave of Lazarus, shouting, "Come forth!" But God also rejoices in giving life to those who are spiritually dead, emotionally drained, and totally hopeless.

There are countless people today who are only a shadow of what God created them to be. Their purpose in life is unknown. They are dead because the life-giving light of God has not shined into their hearts. But God loves to speak his word into the darkness and bring forth life.

Kim Clement lived in that kind of darkness. He was lying in the street, dying, in Johannesburg, South Africa, when the light of God began to shine upon his life. Against all odds, he happened to wander into a meeting where he heard the Good News. That night God spoke purpose and meaning into a life that was as good as dead, and today Kim travels the globe bringing God's life to others (*The Sounds of His Voice,* by Kim Clement).

Thousands of years before he gave new life to Kim, God spoke to Abraham, an old man whose body was as good as dead, and told him he would become the father of countless descendants (see Gen. 22:17). Later God spoke new life to common fishermen and told them, "Don't be afraid; from now on you will catch men" (see Matt. 4:19). He reassured the condemned thief dying on a cross beside him, "Today you will be with me in paradise" (Luke 23:43).

And today he still speaks. He says to the hopeless, "You have a future!" He says to those overwhelmed with guilt, "Your sins are forgiven!" And he says to the unloved, "You are my cherished one, my beloved child. You belong to me." He still is calling "things that are not as though they were."

⚬⚬⚬

Lord Jesus, thank you for looking beyond our surface appearance to speak to that higher purpose you have placed within us. You alone speak light into darkness; you alone bring life where death has been. Right now, I receive the truth of your words of life. I choose to believe what you say above all else.

When God's Voice Is Unreasonable

So she said to Abram, "The Lord has kept me from having children.
Go, sleep with my maidservant; perhaps I can build a family through
her." Abram agreed to what Sarai said.—Genesis 16:2

God made Abraham a promise: "'Look up at the heavens and count the stars—if indeed you can count them.' Then he said to him, 'So shall your offspring be'" (Gen. 15:5). "Abraham, I will make of you a great nation. Your offspring shall be as the sands of the sea" (see Gen. 12:2 and 22:17). And for a while Abraham believed. But eventually the reality of the facts of life set in, and Abraham started to doubt what God had told him. He started to think, "I am an old man. Perhaps God wants me to do something to make things happen."

You know the rest of the story—how Abraham heeded his wife's advice and fathered a son by her servant Hagar. Today when we see the strife between Israel and the Arab nations, we are seeing the result of Abraham's impatience. We are seeing the enmity between Hagar's son Ishamael and Sarah's son Isaac. Thousands of years later, the world still pays a price because one man lost hope for a moment and yielded to the voice of reason instead of to the voice of God. Paul's words are so true: "The carnal mind is enmity against God" (Rom. 8:7 KJV). Let's face it. God's ways often do not make sense to our earthly minds. It just didn't make any sense for God to wait until Abraham was in his nineties to make the kind of promise to him that he made. But we need to let God be God!

When God plants something in our heart—a promise, a vision, a dream—we must simply believe it and wait. In his own time he will bring the promise to pass. Let's think twice before we try to help God carry out his plan. Let's not try to reason everything out. Some things our Creator promises don't seem to make good sense, but they always make God-sense.

∞

Father, give me wisdom to know when to work and when to wait. I know your timing is perfect. Give me an undivided heart to do your will, to have the courage to wait for your promise without wavering, and to consider your voice above the voice of reason, even when your way doesn't make any sense to me.

faith

The Blessing of Not Seeing

Blessed are those who have not seen and yet have believed.
— John 20:29

Sometimes it just isn't enough to know that God is with us. We've been taught that his very name, Emmanuel, means that he is. And we know the verse that proclaims, "Christ in you, the hope of glory" (Col. 1:27). So why do we sometimes have trouble believing it? Why do we sometimes long for face-to-face communication with Jesus? Why, sometimes, do we feel so much like Thomas, the doubting apostle?

Certainly, Thomas's doubting was not a sin. But what did Jesus mean when he told Thomas that those who believe yet do not see him are blessed? Could it be that Jesus was saying that those who have faith to believe without seeing are blessed because there is no war within themselves? We Thomases always have to have a sign. We're always looking, always reaching for one more piece of evidence. When do our hearts get quiet in simple acceptance? When do our minds stop their endless searching and rest in the blessed assurance of believing what we have heard is the truth? Can we believe that the Holy Bible is true?

When we are convinced in our own minds and when our hearts are settled, then we are, indeed, blessed. We are blessed with peace, knowing we need nothing more—no signs, no physical manifestations—except "Christ in us, the hope of glory."

∞

*L*ord, I want to be one who believes without a sign. Create in me a heart that believes what you say more than what I see with natural eyes.

Tell the Story Again

That you may tell in the hearing of your son and your son's son the mighty things I have done in Egypt, and My signs which I have done among them, that you may know that I am the Lord.
— Exodus 10:2 NKJV

When my friend reads a bedtime story to his daughter each night, she always asks for a "Once upon a time" story. No matter what he is reading to her, he has to begin with "Once upon a time," or he hears loud protests. Somehow, "once upon a time" promises her a good story and a good ending.

In the book of Exodus, God said to Moses, "I am going to do these things so you can tell your children and grandchildren about it, so they will know of my power and that I am your God" (10:2, my paraphrase). God was giving parents for generations to come a "once upon a time" story to end all stories!

All of us love hearing this story because recounting what God has done in the past gives us hope for the future. Because he saved those people in the "once upon a time" story from so long ago, we believe he will bring us through the "wilderness" of our lives today.

David knew the power of this kind of faith. When he faced Goliath, he reached back in his own past for the confidence he had gained in God's power during previous challenges. "The Lord who delivered me from the paw of the lion and the paw of the bear will deliver me from the hand of this Philistine," he assured the cowering soldiers (1 Sam. 17:37).

Is your faith weak? Do you wonder if God will do what he promised? Tell the story again. Remember how God brought you through the midnight hour of your life? Tell the story to somebody now. Remember when you had just about given up and God suddenly rescued you? Tell it again. Remember when you were in desperate financial straits and couldn't see how you would survive another week, and somehow, some way, God provided? Tell it to your children and to their children. That is how you nurture your children's faith in God and rekindle your own.

❧

Lord, I will not forget what you have done. I will tell the story again. When I look back, I see the work of your hand. Glory to your name! To you be the glory, oh God, for the great things you have done.

faith

Weekend Reflections

To live by faith is to live by what we cannot see. Hopeful believers are not discouraged by what they see, because their hopes are fixed on what is unseen. Though they can only see the physical realm with their natural eyes, they know there is another realm that is unseen.

Often we look at circumstances we have prayed about and despair because on the surface nothing seems to change. However, we must remember that in that distinctly separate spiritual realm, unseen to the natural eye, a host of unimaginable activity continues on our behalf whether or not we are aware of it.

1. How does your certainty about what you can't see compare to your certainty about what you can see?

   _____

   _____

   _____

   _____

2. What do you place the most trust in, what people say or what God says?

   _____

   _____

   _____

   _____

3. Faith is being "certain of what we do not see" (Heb. 11:1). How certain are you about what you believe?

   _____

   _____

   _____

   _____

Keep Rowing

And he saw them toiling in rowing; for the wind was contrary unto them: and about the fourth watch of the night he cometh unto them, walking upon the sea, and would have passed by them.
—Mark 6:48 KJV

Obedience to God's will does not mean everything will go smoothly, that the wind will always be at our backs, and that the journey will be easy. Jesus told his disciples to cross to the other side of the lake, even though he knew the wind would be working against them. Despite the wind's contrariness, they struggled on, because they knew they were doing his will.

Do not doubt that you are doing his will when you meet with resistance in your mission. God has a higher purpose than what you see from your limited view. Let your motivation come from the joy of being in his service and from your complete abandonment to his will.

We do not know why Jesus waited to respond to his disciples' need for help. Perhaps he knew they were safe for the moment while he needed to pray concerning matters that were of utmost urgency. Don't despair if God does not respond when you would like him to. He sees you. He knows exactly where you are.

The writer said Jesus "would have passed by them" had the disciples not cried out to him. He must have wanted them to see him; otherwise, he would have crossed the lake at a different point, out of their sight. Perhaps he was passing by them so they would cry out to him. Or maybe he wanted them to have faith as they saw him walking on the raging water, believing if he could walk through the storm he would surely see them through to the other side, where he had told them to go in the first place.

Is your life stormy? Keep rowing. He sees you toiling, struggling against the resistance. Keep watching. Any moment now you may see him walking toward you through that lifestorm, and as you cry out, he'll stop and come onboard, and your storm will end.

❧

Oh, Father, you always know where I am, and you are always concerned about my well-being. Give me the strength to keep on rowing and to do what I know is your will. Come onboard my ship, Lord. Ride with me until the storm passes over.

persistence

Daily Winnings

Let us run with patient endurance and steady and active persistence
the appointed course of the race that is set before us.
—Hebrews 12:1 AMPLIFIED

If success is going to be achieved, often it will be achieved through many small victories—victories that in themselves may seem minuscule. Usually, it is not the flashy feat but a systematic "punch after punch" routine that cinches the win. A fighter who can make the right moves round after round, consistently confronting his opponent, will overcome him and win the match.

Several times in the New Testament, we are exhorted to "stand firm" to the end. This means we must not waver in the daily fight. We must remain strong in our faith—believing that we *are* overcoming, not just that we *will* overcome; that we *are* winning; not just that we *will* win. God is able to do more than we can imagine "according to his power that is *at work within us*" (emphasis added). Today, right now, his power *is working* within us.

I believe the "patient endurance" that the writer to the Hebrews spoke of calls for gratefulness when it comes to victories and perseverance when it comes to defeats. Think about it. To patiently endure speaks of resolve and tenacity as well as long-suffering and tolerance.

Stop and thank God for today's victories, today's achievements, no matter how small they seem to you. It is the culmination of a long line of those seemingly small conquests that will bring about the final triumphant win.

∞

Father, is there a victory you and I have won that I have not been thankful for? Help me not to overlook daily successes while pressing on toward the prize that is waiting.

Drop the Anchor and Batten the Hatches

We have this hope as an anchor for the soul, firm and secure.
—Hebrews 6:19

We're often urged to keep moving, to always press onward. But there are circumstances when the right thing to do is not to move on but to stand our ground, to not back down. In this posture of resistance, we need a foundation to anchor ourselves to. Just any old support will not do. We must fasten ourselves to a hope that is larger than life.

An anchor keeps a vessel in a desired area. An anchored boat may rock in the tempest and push toward the end of the anchor line, but the anchor brings it back to center. Our anchor is the hope we have in Jesus Christ. Our faith may waver a little from time to time, we may be pounded by the waves of uncertainty and fear, but our anchor of hope always pulls us back to a center of confidence and rest.

Sometimes we may feel like we are standing alone atop Mount Everest, holding on for dear life as the windy gusts make us shiver and shudder. Perhaps our faith feels weak during gales of difficulties. Our trust seems to be tottering on the edge. That's when we grasp for that anchor of hope and hold on with all our strength.

He is a hope bigger than all our fears and problems. He is our anchor.

∞

Father, I thank you for the security I find in knowing that you are my foundation. I am never alone in this battle. Since I trusted you for the power to save me, I will trust you now for the power to keep me saved.

persistence

Press On

*The Lord had said to Abram, "Leave your country, your people and
your father's household and go to the land I will show you."*
—Genesis 12:1

One of the things runners learn early in their training is not to constantly look back to check on the competitors. Winners concentrate on the race that is before them, not the challenges that are trailing their every step.

When God rained down destruction on the cities of Sodom and Gomorrah, the angel told Lot and his wife, "Don't look back, and don't stop anywhere in the plain!" (Gen. 19:17). We all know the rest of the story, how Lot's wife looked back and was turned into a pillar of salt. What we don't know is exactly why God sent this command. Perhaps it was because he was looking for unreserved obedience.

Pressing on under the guidance of the Holy Spirit requires total trust. We trust that God knows the best path for us, that where he is leading us is the best place to be. Looking back with a longing for what was behind us is futile. It steals from us the energy needed for the road ahead. It robs us of the "the joy that is set before us" (see Heb. 12:2).

God says to us as he did to Abraham, "Go to the land I will show you." Lift up your eyes to the joy ahead, the journey before you. What lies in the future can be much greater than anything we have ever experienced.

❧

Father, I praise you for your good purpose that you have ordained for my life. I believe that greater things lie before me than what is behind me. I am thankful for the victories and success of the past and for the lessons I have learned, but I am more thankful for where you are taking me and the good work you are doing in my life today.

No Big Deal!

None of these things move me.—Acts 20:24 KJV

Not everything in our lives needs to be intense. Sometimes a nonchalant attitude is acceptable—even called for. To say "No big deal" in the face of adversity can be a healthy approach.

It is a pleasant thing to be around people who struggle bravely, who refuse to cry over spilled milk. It's not so pleasant to be around people who, at the least indication of a ripple in their existence, throw up their hands and are ready to quit—and they aren't the least bit hesitant to let the whole world know about their "tragedy."

This is not to say, however, that spiritual warfare is not a serious matter. There are aspects of the Christian life that cannot be approached frivolously. But even in war, there is a place for calm composure. We must not become overly distressed at the sight of our enemies. Dick Eastman, in his series *The Hour That Changes the World,* tells how Joy Dawson was praying fervently when she suddenly shouted, "Satan, I'm not the least bit impressed with you!" Yes, as vigilant soldiers we should beware of our enemy, but should we be impressed with him? Absolutely not!

The dramatic soul who wants to lament and wail for months or years after personal failure must recognize that the root of such a reaction is often pride. True humility accepts one's own weakness as well as the grace and power of our Lord. Yes, we continue to persevere, but we remember that we are loved and accepted by God in spite of our deficiencies. And so we learn to be gracious to ourselves as well.

❦

Father, I choose to walk the walk of faith. I will not be overly shaken by circumstances but will seek to persist under pressure, endeavoring to see things in the light of the Holy Spirit.

persistence

Weekend Reflections

The path of least resistance is not always the path of success. To move onward, one must break through what is comfortable and easy. The boundaries we accept as normal are often chains that hold us back from progress.

To lead others to a higher place, we must walk there first. The uncharted regions of spirituality where the power and grace of God will be revealed in greater measure will take some effort on our part to find.

God told Israel that the land of Canaan was promised to them. Prosperity awaited them there. The goodness of the land would belong to them and their children. God would go before them, be their strength, fight for them and protect them. Still, they had a responsibility: They had to go in and possess it. If they didn't go and possess the land, they would remain in the Wilderness Inn.

1. There are some things worth fighting for. What is holding you back from moving forward in what God has called you to do?

   _____

   _____

   _____

2. Are you willing to do what you are asking those who follow you to do? How have you already walked there before them?

   _____

   _____

   _____

   _____

3. When you feel resistance that keeps you from moving forward, how often do you recognize that it could be Satan's efforts to keep you from moving on?

   _____

   _____

   _____

Patiently Awaiting a New Perspective

Trust in the Lord with all your heart and lean not on your own understanding.—Proverbs 3:5

The old saying is so true: Hindsight is 20/20. Often, when we look behind us, things that once perplexed us begin to make sense. From our new perspective, we can see a higher purpose in something that at the time was beyond our comprehension. And it's not just *situations* that come into focus when we view them from this different angle. It's people too. As the young man said, "It was remarkable how much smarter my parents became after I left home."

So often in our lives, we search for reasons why. We try to sort out and analyze our circumstances so they make sense. It's easy to trust God as long as we can understand why something is happening—as long as we can see the outcome.

But God longs for us to trust him *all* the time—even when things don't seem to make sense, even when we have no idea how things are going to come out or why they've taken a particular turn. He wants us to abandon this need to lean on our own understanding.

It's not always an easy thing to do, perhaps because there is no middle ground. Either we are trusting him with all of our heart, or we are holding back, reserving a portion of ourselves that still needs carnal reasoning or understanding. We may not always be able to see or understand God's purpose for us in perplexing circumstances. But we must choose to trust him anyway. He has told us his plans for us will give us "hope and a future" (Jer. 29:11). And we may have to wait until that future unfolds before our new perspective allows us to understand his purposes for our trials.

∞

Father, you have unlimited sight and vision. You know the number of my days and see my plans. I commit my plans to you and pray that you will lead me in the right way.

trust

In God We Trust

He will have no fear of bad news; his heart is steadfast, trusting in the Lord. His heart is secure, he will have no fear; in the end he will look in triumph on his foes.—Psalm 112:7–8

We put our trust in God. That is how our hearts can be at rest in a tumultuous society. Our trust is not in a nation, a national economy, or a politician. It is in God. If our trust is in people, things, or circumstances, it will surely fail. But trust that is placed in God will not fail.

Relationships are based on trust. How much we trust someone—how much he or she trusts us—determines the depth of our relationship. When we come to know God, we learn that we can trust him; therefore, our relationship grows and is strengthened in the process. Trust can only develop through time and struggle. It does not come instantaneously but through repeated dependence on God's faithfulness.

Do you really trust God? Are you confident that he is working in your life, that the center of his will is the perfect place to be? If not, maybe you aren't really trusting in God but in your ability to recognize a bad situation and get out of it before it's too late.

∞

Lord, I have said I trusted you when it wasn't really true. But I am learning. Thank you for your patience with me as I learn to relinquish my concern over things that are beyond my control.

It's Time to Look Up

Let us fix our eyes on Jesus, the author and perfecter of our faith.
—Hebrews 12:2

We gain maturity by learning from life experiences and applying what we have learned. Real learning often begins at a "life experience" we think of as failure. It is here, however, that we may learn the most, because it is here that our choice for growth or hopelessness becomes apparent. We can give up (and probably never grow up!), or we can search through and reflect on the experience to discover in it the seeds for success. This is a difficult thing to do, to be sure, yet for continued progress it is a must.

At the point of failure, what causes the most frustration? Often it is the loss of our independence and the realization that now we must look outside ourselves for help. At the bottom of the heap, we find where our dependence lies. We discover where we have placed our trust. And only then do we realize our true foundation—whether it is the sand of self-sufficiency or the rock of revelation knowledge.

Before Saul the persecutor could become Paul the apostle, he had to get "knocked off his high horse." Then, in his helplessness, he had to look up and say, "Who are you, Lord?" He was forced to turn away from total self-reliance and toward absolute God-reliance. This set the scene for the miraculous (see Acts 9).

As long as we are relying entirely on our expertise and strength, we have no need for God. But at the point of giving up, we can look up and hear our Father say, "This is what I've been waiting for!" Here we find peace; here is joy. We learn the blessing of total reliance on God's abilities, not our own. As the beautiful old hymn proclaims:

> What a fellowship, what a joy divine,
> Leaning on the everlasting arms;
> What a blessedness, what a peace is mine,
> Leaning on the everlasting arms.

❧

Lord, please forgive me for the times I have relied on my own abilities and strength when I should have depended on you. As the psalmist wrote, "Some trust in chariots and some in horses, but we trust in the name of the Lord our God" (20:7).

THURSDAY

No Other Foundation

Who can stand in the presence of the Lord, this holy God?
—1 Samuel 6:20

We must never forget how holy our God is. The Old Testament gives many accounts that reveal this to us, including the scene at Beth Shemesh, where seventy men died because they looked into the ark of the Lord. Here the mourning people cried, "Who can stand in the presence of the Lord, this holy God?"

It is foolish for us to think that through our "doing" we can measure up to the holiness of our mighty and sacred God! Our only hope of being holy is by his declaring us holy as we become partakers of Christ's divine nature. As Paul explained, "He has reconciled you by Christ's physical body through death to present you holy in his sight, without blemish and free from accusation" (Col. 1:22).

The grace of our Lord Jesus Christ is the only hope we have of being holy and attaining true righteousness. We can't do enough good deeds to make us holy. It's just a matter of grace. The Bible says, "He saved us, not because of righteous things we had done, but because of his mercy. He saved us through the washing of rebirth and renewal by the Holy Spirit" (Titus 3:5). If this righteousness could be attained through doing the right things, the apostle Paul could have done it. But he couldn't. After he listed all his accomplishments in Philippians 3, look what he said about them: "I regard them as rubbish, in order that I may gain Christ and be found in him, not having a righteousness of my own that comes from the law, but one that comes through faith in Christ" (Phil. 3:8–9 NRSV).

Are you putting all your trust in your own ability to do the right things? Are you the foundation of your own hope? Is your past the cornerstone of your experience? Remember: There is no other foundation, no other cornerstone, but Jesus. As Paul wrote to the Corinthians, "No one can lay any foundation other than the one already laid, which is Jesus Christ" (1 Cor. 3:11). The building of our spiritual house begins here, with the flesh and blood of Jesus Christ, the One who makes us truly holy.

❧

Jesus, you alone are my hope, my righteousness. You have sanctified me and made me a joint heir in your kingdom. Thank you for this wonderful hope.

The Opposing One

God opposes the proud but gives grace to the humble. Humble your-
selves, therefore, under God's mighty hand, that he may lift you up in
due time. Cast all your anxiety on him because he cares for you.
—1 Peter 5:5–7

God opposes the proud. What a heavy thought! We certainly need to have God working with us, not against us, so we must yield our need to be in control. We must invite him to become the Leader, Guide, and Shepherd while we become the followers, the students, the lambs.

Humility comes from a sense of total dependence on God, a complete trust in his faithfulness and care. In contrast, when we feel anxious we are taking control. We're being bossy. Proud. We are saying, in effect, "God, hurry! It's going to be too late! Please hurry!" We are wishing a situation would change from its present state to what it could be—from God's timing to our timing.

On the other hand, if we are humble we recognize that God is in control and that he is greater than we are. Then ours is a faith that acknowledges a bigger picture, a higher realm, than the one we may presently see.

So we boldly cast our anxiety and worry onto the greater One. We declare our dependence on him and fling away our independence. What a joy it is to do so, to place ourselves "under God's mighty hand" and to fix our eyes on Jesus, as he lifts us up—in his time, not ours.

Lord Jesus, right now I throw my anxiety, my worry, and my pointless concern onto you. I humble myself under your mighty hand. I declare my total dependence on you. Send your grace that you have promised. I receive it now.

137

Weekend Reflections

This favorite acronym speaks powerfully about what trust really is:

To
Rest
Upon
Sure
*Th*ings

When we say we trust Christ, we are resting upon the surety of who he is and what he has done. Any other foundation is sinking sand.

1. Lies destroy trust. Describe the importance of truth in a relationship with God.

   _____

   _____

   _____

   _____

2. What are the sure things of Christ that we can rest upon?

   _____

   _____

   _____

   _____

3. How was mistrust involved in the initial sin of disobedience in the Garden of Eden?

   _____

   _____

   _____

   _____

   _____

If You're Happy...

Let the righteous be glad; let them rejoice before God; yes, let them rejoice exceedingly.—Psalm 68:3 NKJV

I have heard it said, "If you are happy, notify your face." Unbelievers sometimes use a comment like this one to jab at those who do believe, often adding, "I thought Christians were always supposed to be happy!"

Must Christians always wear a smile? Are we always supposed to be happy? To answer those questions, we first have to understand what it means to "be happy." And we also need to understand the difference between happiness and joy, because Jesus didn't say we would always be *happy*. Instead he said, "I have told you this so that my joy may be in you and that your joy may be complete" (John 15:11).

Happiness speaks of a condition determined by present events. Joy, on the other hand, is a fruit of the Spirit that is not contingent on our circumstances. When the cares of the day would dictate to us that we should not be happy, we can still be joyful. Was the apostle Paul happy in the dungeon where there was not room enough for him to even sit up or to lie down? Happy? Probably, not. Joyful? Yes! Because his joy was not really his own. He said, "I have learned, in whatsoever state I am, therewith to be content" (Phil. 4:11 KJV). Contentment and joy work hand in hand.

Christians aren't always happy. But, like Paul, we can be joyful in all circumstances, because "the God of hope fills us with all joy and peace as we trust in him, so that we may overflow with hope by the power of the Holy Spirit" (Rom. 15:13, my paraphrase).

❧

Lord Jesus, thank you for your joy. Even though I may not always be happy, I believe your joy is still alive in me.

Joy for the Journey

The fruit of the Spirit is love, joy, peace, patience, kindness, goodness,
faithfulness, gentleness and self-control. Against such things
there is no law.—Galatians 5:22–23

The Christian experience is not one continual, ecstatic high but a series of victories and struggles. This is why joy is so essential for our progress. We need joy to sustain us on the journey, to help us see the victory on the other side of the struggle, and to have courage to accept the rain along with the sunshine that God allows.

Joy, as part of the fruit of the Spirit, sometimes surprises us. It may come when we least expect it. It may appear in the heat of a spiritual conflict when we suddenly find ourselves rejoicing because of what we see beyond the battle. Or it may come out of a painful experience with such power that it overshadows the pain. Jesus described this kind of joy when he said, "A woman giving birth to a child has pain because her time has come; but when her baby is born she forgets the anguish because of her joy that a child is born into the world" (John 16:21). It is incredible to think that a woman could actually forget so much anguish, but such is the power of this kind of joy.

Christ exemplified the strength of this joy by persevering through the agony of the cross to "the joy that was set before him" (Heb. 12:2 KJV). What was this joy? It was his vision of the day when he would present us blameless and faultless "before the presence of His glory in triumphant joy and exultation [with unspeakable, ecstatic delight]" (Jude 24 AMPLIFIED). Just as a mother endures the pain so that she will have the joy of holding her newborn child, Jesus endured the cross so he could escort us into God's presence with great joy and delight.

My friend, if you are enduring grief or trial, focus on the joy to come. Something wonderful is being birthed within you or through you. Let the joy of the prize that awaits you cause you to walk in God's power and might with renewed vigor and the Spirit's immeasurable energy.

∞

Lord Jesus, I open my heart to receive your joy. Though trials beset me, I boldly press on with a joyful heart at what I see, by faith, beyond each adversity and distress. Thank you for being my source of joy without measure.

The Joy of His Presence

You will show me the path of life; in Your presence is fullness of joy;
at your right hand are pleasures forevermore.
—Psalm 16:11 NKJV

Just as there's a difference between joy and happiness, there's also a difference between joy and enjoyment.

The word *enjoyment* symbolizes limited joy—joy while you have something. When that something is gone, so is your joy. On the other hand, true, sustained joy—spiritual joy—is the outward expression of what is abiding within you. The apostle Paul described it as part of the fruit of the Spirit (see Gal. 5:22). This "fruit" is harvested by those who have died to self and have been raised to life through Jesus Christ. As the apostle Peter wrote, "Even though you do not see him now, you believe in him and are filled with an inexpressible and glorious joy, for you are receiving the goal of your faith, the salvation of your souls" (1 Pet. 1:8–9).

Christ Jesus is our joy—right now and for all eternity. There's no limit on how long this joy will last. It's eternal. Nothing can take it away from us, for the Scriptures tell us, "We will be with the Lord forever" (1 Thess. 4:17).

∞

Father, sometimes I think joy is found in things. Forgive me. The real joy I long for can only be found in your presence. I will "joy in God through our Lord Jesus Christ" (Rom. 5:11 KJV).

joy

Take Time to Dance

There is a time for everything, and a season for every activity under heaven…a time to weep and a time to laugh, a time to mourn and a time to dance.—Ecclesiastes 3:1, 4

The Christian walk constantly moves forward. We're always pressing on "toward the goal to win the prize for which God has called [us] heavenward in Christ Jesus" (Phil. 3:14). But as we steadily continue on God's pathway, we can be looking ahead so much that we do not enjoy the moment. As soon as we climb over one roadblock, we say, "All right, where's the next stop?"

Think of the Israelites as they reached the far shore of the Red Sea. They had just crossed through the waters on dry ground and then watched as God released the sea to swallow up the enemy. Surely this had been a miraculous experience that brought awe to everyone involved. But if people back then were anything like they are now (and I feel certain they were), there had to be those "do-it-by-the-book" killjoys who peered over the schedule at that point and argued, "But Moses, we really need to keep moving. According to my schedule, we need to reach Elim by evening!" To quote George Burns, "Certain folks feel bad when they feel good for fear they'll feel worse when they feel better."

While these people fussed and fumed, Miriam stopped the march. She "took a tambourine in her hand" (Exod. 15:20) and said, "This calls for a party!" Then she and the other women led a celebration of dancing and singing before the assembled masses.

Hard work and steady progress are important, but we have to take time to dance, to stop and celebrate the joy of the moment, to consider the significance of each success. Then, when we face the mighty Jordan and the walls of Jericho that life will bring, we will remember those moments of celebrated successes and be inspired not to give up.

The Christian walk is long and challenging. There will be setbacks and difficulties. But there will be victories to celebrate too. Don't forget to bring along your dancing shoes!

∞

Lord, thank you for today, for the little joys you give us along the way. I don't want to forget to say thanks, Lord, for every good gift you bless me with.

Rejoice Evermore!

Through [Christ] we have gained access by faith into this grace in which we now stand. And we rejoice in the hope of the glory of God.
—Romans 5:2

Our joy does not rest in our abilities or our accomplishments of the day. Our joy comes from knowing that every day we are accepted and loved by God, not on the merit of what we have done, but because he loves us and has extended his grace to mere mortals.

I was made aware of this one morning as I considered my accomplishments of the previous day. After a rigorous schedule that began at 5:30 A.M. and continued until late evening, I was able to get quite a few things marked off my to-do list: prayer, exercise, proper nutrition, and ministry deadlines. The next morning I was feeling more than a little pleased with myself, marveling at the joy I felt, when I was prompted by the Holy Spirit to recall the scripture, "We rejoice in the hope of the glory of God." Soon I was even more joyful, but this time it was not because of what I had done but because I had been reminded of his grace.

Every day there is reason to rejoice because of grace. But will we rejoice even on that great day before his throne? Even on that day when, as one woman nervously asked, "God will read openly everything I've ever done in secret?" (see Rom. 2:16)? Will we be able to say even then, "This is the day the Lord has made, let us rejoice and be glad in it" (Ps. 118:24)? I say unequivocally, *Yes!* So what if he reads every wrong deed we've ever done? Do you actually think there will be anything we can be proud of on that day besides the grace of God?

Make no mistake; no one will be able to stand before his presence except by the grace of God. In fact, because we will know all the "dirt" on each other, we will all rejoice together in seeing how God revealed his strength in us in spite of our weaknesses! Just as today, so it will be on that great day: "We rejoice in the hope of the glory of God!"

∞

Father, I choose to rejoice today! Not because of my accomplishments or success, nor for my possessions, but for the work of grace that is so evident in my life. I am joyful at the thought that you know all of my ways, my weaknesses, and my abilities, yet you love me. I rejoice in your mercies that are new every morning!

Weekend Reflections

To attempt to endure life without joy is a draining experience. As Nehemiah recorded, it is the joy of the Lord that gives us strength (see 8:10). How can we press on without becoming exhausted, dull, and sour? By fixing our eyes on the joy that awaits us...the dreams of celebration and the thrill of victory that glimmer in the distance. Without joy we are destined for burnout.

1. Think of one of your greatest goals. Describe in detail the celebration you will have when you reach that goal.

_____

_____

_____

_____

_____

2. God rejoices too. Search a concordance for the word *rejoice,* and find what God rejoices about. How do you have joy in the same things he does.

_____

_____

_____

_____

3. God commanded his covenant people to have times of rejoicing (see Deut. 16:13). When was the last time you set aside some time for joy?

_____

_____

_____

_____

Little Foxes

A little yeast works through the whole batch of dough.—Galatians 5:9

"I just don't know what my problem is. I've tried to do my best but can't seem to live the victorious life." Have you heard statements like this? Have you said them yourself?

Often the reason for such an attitude is not a single problem but several problems. A person may point to one particular area of struggle and say, "There is my problem!" when there are many contributing factors. Could there be a bundle of little issues contributing to one major problem in your life? If we work at identifying all the little foxes, we can usually, at the same time, eliminate the lion!

The writer to the Hebrews advised us to "throw off everything that hinders and the sin that so easily entangles, and let us run with perseverance the race marked out for us" (Heb. 12:1). When we get rid of all the little hindrances that hold us back from Christlike behavior, it will be easier to throw off the bigger sin that tangles us up.

One way to overcome "everything that hinders" is to begin our day with thankful hearts. The first step of our day should be to "enter his gates with thanksgiving" (Ps. 100:4). Then, throughout the day, we must be mindful of our attitudes. The little positive decisions we make can have a domino effect on us just as much as the negative thoughts and decisions that can snowball into an avalanche of problems. We need to keep our thankful hearts beating all day long, thinking of everything we can be thankful for, no matter how trivial it may seem.

Then, from that first positive step, "let us run with perseverance." As we replace bitterness and fear with thankfulness, as we throw off those things that hinder, the sin or problem that "so easily entangles" us will fall away, and we will once again enjoy the victorious life God wants us to have.

❧

Lord Jesus, send your Spirit to reveal the little things I have allowed to creep in and choke the life of the Word in my life. I know your power will become greater in my life as I cast off the entangling vines of problems that distract me from what matters most.

discipline

Maintenance and Preservation

Until I come, devote yourself to the public reading of Scripture, to preaching and to teaching. Do not neglect your gift, which was given you.—1 Timothy 4:13–14

With a gift comes responsibility, whether it be spiritual or physical. The more valuable something is, the more maintenance, protection, and preservation it needs. We are wrong to think that because of God's grace we bear no responsibility for spiritual gifts, that God will simply take care of everything with no effort required on our parts. He certainly is there to assist us, but he will not do what we are able to do—in this case, to devote ourselves to study, prayer, and worship.

"Do not neglect your gift," the apostle said. The opposite of _neglect_ is _maintain_. Thus, the instructions might be understood as "Maintain the gift that is in you." Paul was reminding Timothy that he was to be a steward of what had been placed in him by God. Now it was his own responsibility to care for this spiritual heirloom.

Like Timothy, you have been entrusted with precious gifts. These gifts will not be used to their fullest unless you fulfill your responsibility to give them the proper maintenance and care. Listen to God; he will tell you what to do. After all, he's the manufacturer. He wrote the owner's manual.

❧

Lord, you have authorized me to care for some valuable gifts. Help me to be aware of my responsibilities in caring for them and using them. I am listening now for your instructions.

In Training

Train yourself to be godly.—1 Timothy 4:7

Ask those who are training for major athletic competitions if they enjoy all the discipline of practice and preparing, and most of them will answer with an unequivocal *No!* The daily regimen these athletes must go through gets dull and boring. But the anticipated joy of winning keeps them pressing forward, giving them the stamina they need to persevere.

The same is true in the spiritual realm. As Paul said, "No discipline seems pleasant at the time, but painful" (Heb. 12:11). But somewhere along the way Christians have been misled into thinking that all spiritual exercise should be delightful when in fact much of it is fairly ordinary. Not all prayer feels anointed. Not all worship seems heavenly. But does that mean it is not effective? No. Often the heavenly and anointed feelings come later as the result of our prayer and worship. "Later on," Paul continued, "it produces a harvest of righteousness and peace" (12:11).

In those times when we find our spiritual disciplines are not dynamic, we don't give up and declare them useless. We should make every effort to keep them spontaneous and spirited, but when they're not we must remember that "godliness has value for all things, holding promise for both the present life and the life to come" (1 Tim. 4:8). Even when the results are not readily seen, we hold on to the promise of our glorious life to come, and we continue our training so that we might rule and reign with him someday in his heavenly kingdom.

∞

Lord, I'm glad that you hear me even when I don't feel anything. I'm grateful that your Word is working in me even if I don't always see the evidence. I know I shall someday see the value in this present life and the life to come.

THURSDAY

From the Natural to the Supernatural

God can do what men can't!—Luke 18:27 LB

God has given us many abilities, and we should not ask him to do for us what he has given us the ability to do for ourselves. For example, we should not ask him to keep poverty away from us if we are not trying to make an honest living. And we shouldn't expect God to miraculously keep our marriages together if we do not treat our spouses with respect and follow the commands of Ephesians 5:25–28. God expects us to do what we know to do first, then he steps in and does what we cannot do.

The supernatural comes into operation only when the natural is functioning properly: obedience first, then unleash the supernatural. It works the way Paul described his ministering to the Corinthian church: "I planted the seed, Apollos watered it, but God made it grow" (1 Cor. 3:6). Paul acknowledged that he could not make the church grow; he had just planted the seed. It was God who activated the miracle of growth. If we want God to activate the miraculous, we must activate the natural.

The prayer of faith is the trigger that releases God's power. We pray, and God does the work. Sometimes we pray about a need, and then we despair because on the surface nothing seems to change. However, we must remember there is a distinctly separate realm that is unseen to the natural eye. Just a step away from where we are, there is a host of unimaginable activity, and all these workings of the spiritual realm continue whether or not we notice an immediate change.

We do what we are able to do, and then we turn the rest over to God. Even when we do not see him working, we have faith that he is. Faith, after all, is being "certain of what we do not see" (Heb. 11:1).

❧

Lord, help me to recognize where I have not accepted my own responsibility. I will not live as a victim the rest of my life but will do what I can do and wait for you to do the impossible.

The Right Place at the Right Time

And he trembling and astonished said, Lord, what wilt thou have me to do? And the Lord said unto him, Arise, and go into the city, and it shall be told thee what thou must do.—Acts 9:6 KJV

To be able to hear God's voice, we may have to take a step of obedience first to get to the place where God can speak to us—or rather where we can truly listen to him. In the verse quoted above, Saul heard God's voice from heaven telling him to arise and go into the city for further instructions. Maybe Saul wondered why God didn't just go ahead and tell him what he needed to know right then and there while he had Saul's attention.

I think Paul's repositioning—and ours—is part of our spiritual growth. God does not tell us everything we need to know right here and now. He knows there is a proper place and a proper time for revelation, for instruction.

And how do we find that perfect place and time? Speaking of the spiritual disciplines, Richard Foster wrote in his book *The Celebration of Discipline*, "God has ordained the Disciplines of the spiritual life as the means by which we place ourselves where he can bless us." In other words, our obedience, in itself, does not bring the blessing, but it brings us to the position where God can bless us and revolutionize us.

If sometimes your spiritual growth seems to have slowed down, don't stop praying. Remain in obedience. God may be waiting for you to reposition yourself to that right place at the right time so that he can bring about a radical change in your life.

∞

Father, is there a place you want me to be where I can hear and obey? Teach me to act quickly, to position myself where you can move and work in me to transform me into your likeness.

discipline

Weekend Reflections

Often, it's the little things that are done consistently that make the greatest impact. As Samuel Smiles said, "Sow a thought, reap an action. Sow an action, reap a habit. Sow a habit, reap a character." What a principle! Thought leads to action, action leads to habit, and habit leads to character. There is nothing that replaces consistent discipline.

1. A child without discipline will not mature properly. Describe the similarities between the balanced discipline of a child and the disciplines of the believer.

   _____

   _____

   _____

   _____

   _____

2. A tried-and-true saying is "Change the behavior, and the feelings will follow." You can't change your feelings by force. What habits are you willing to change?

   _____

   _____

   _____

   _____

   _____

3. When and how will you begin?

   _____

   _____

   _____

   _____

   _____

The Supreme Purpose

*What is more, I consider everything a loss compared to the surpassing
greatness of knowing Christ Jesus my Lord, for whose sake I have lost
all things. I consider them rubbish, that I may gain Christ.*
—Philippians 3:8

Maybe you have heard a comment like this: "It's so sad about the
Smith boy. He's not serving the Lord anymore. It seems God called him
to preach, but he doesn't want to. He's running from the call of God."

It may be true that someone called "the Smith boy" to preach, but
most likely it wasn't God. The enemy uses all sorts of trickery to pull us
out of a right relationship with our heavenly Father—yes, even calling
someone to the ministry. But *anything that's detrimental to your supreme
purpose, anything that keeps you from being a child in proper relationship with
the Father, is not a purpose from God.* "For he chose us in him before the
creation of the world to be holy and blameless in his sight. In love he pre-
destined us to be adopted as his sons through Jesus Christ, in accordance
with his pleasure and will" (Eph. 1:4–5). It was God's pleasure and his will
(his purpose) from the beginning that we could stand before him "holy
and blameless." And he gave us a destiny—that we would be his sons and
daughters through Jesus Christ. This is the supreme purpose of man.

Yes, there will be times in our lives when God asks us to do something
that we find uncomfortable. But never will he demand something of us
that will destroy our relationship with him. When we find ourselves
responding to an urge that simultaneously seems to pull us away from our
closeness to the Father, we can be assured that the "call" we sense is not
from God but from the enemy. In contrast, God is able to make even the
heaviest burdens feel light because of his perfect timing and because he
knows what we are able to bear. He tells us, "Take my yoke upon you and
learn from me, for I am gentle and humble in heart, and you will find rest
for your souls. For my yoke is easy and my burden is light" (Matt.
11:29–30).

Father, I lay down every purpose that is man-made, anything that tears me
away from you. I confess that my supreme purpose is to know you, to realize
that I am your child and you are my Father. This is my destiny, and I receive it
now.

A New Name

*She gave birth to a son, and they named him Solomon. The Lord
loved him; and because the Lord loved him, he sent word through
Nathan the prophet to name him Jedidiah.*
—2 Samuel 12:24–25

From Abram to Abraham, from Jacob to Israel, from Solomon to
Jedidiah, from Saul to Paul, God has always changed names. Since God's
plans are often different from the plans of men, God frequently sends a
new name to fit his purpose.

David and Bathsheba named their boy Solomon, a name that has its
root in the word shalom, meaning "blessed, happy, prosperous." This was
a name that Solomon definitely lived and fulfilled; there was possibly
never a man who prospered like Solomon. But above this, the Lord had
his own name for the boy: Jedidiah, meaning "praised of Jah," because
"the Lord loved him."

What name does God have for you? Are you living out God's
ordained purpose for your life? Just as God loved Solomon and sent his
word to him, so also he loves you and is speaking words into your life,
into your heart, into your being. Are you listening?

This new name, this new life, is part of the joy of being born again.
God sends his word into us, and we become a new creation, a brand-new
person. We start over.

God wants you to be reborn into the person he planned you to be
from the start. He has said, "You should not be surprised at my saying,
'You must be born again'" (John 3:7).

∞

Lord Jesus, send your word, send a revelation of my destiny. Show me who
you have created me to be. Change me daily that I may become the person
you planned for me to be from before my birth.

purpose

Moving On

*So Elisha left him and went back. He took his yoke of oxen and
slaughtered them. He burned the plowing equipment to cook the meat
and gave it to the people, and they ate. Then he set out to follow
Elijah and became his attendant.*—1 Kings 19:21

When Elisha received his call to assist Elijah in doing God's work, he
went back home to kiss his parents, showing his love for them and his
thankfulness for their nurturing, then he left. His actions remind us that
our call to God's purpose for our lives is a call forward. There must be a
thankfulness for the past and then a time of letting go. But this letting go
does not mean abandonment. In fact, our moving forward into our own
purpose is the greatest validation of our parents' competence.

Elisha's actions also illustrate another principle. By burning his plowing equipment, he taught us to see that the tools of our past may not be
practical for the future. God will give us new tools for the mission he is
appointing us to.

When we are born again, we are reborn as new creations. The old has
passed away. It served us well, but God is not into remodeling; he creates
us as entirely new beings. We express thankfulness for the past, but our
purpose as new creations is to move forward, continually dying to the old
self and letting the new creation live and move through Jesus Christ. As
we allow this rebirth to take place, our old natures will have less and less
power, and we will become more and more like Jesus...until we see him
face to face.

∞

God, I want to move onward and upward toward the prize of knowing you.
Forgive me for the times I have thought that I have somehow "arrived" and
that I can "coast" on yesterday's experiences. I will press on!

purpose

Where Is Your Legacy?

You show that you are a letter from Christ, the result of our ministry,
written not with ink but with the Spirit of the living God, not on
tablets of stone but on tablets of human hearts.—2 Corinthians 3:3

When we celebrated my father's sixty-fifth and my mother's sixtieth birthdays, we surprised them by hosting a dinner for them with family and church members. During the reception, guests stood up to say how their lives had been touched by the Gospel as shared by my parents. It was a gospel, these friends said, that was revealed by my parents' love, compassion, and generosity much more than through mere words.

As I listened to the heartwarming, sometimes tearful, remarks, I thought how great a treasure it is for any of us to know we have impacted another life! When it comes to lifetime achievements, the ones that will endure will not be the financial or material accomplishments but the living memorials—men, women, and children whose lives are better because of what we have done. Maybe we taught someone to read or showed a neighbor how to grow things. Maybe we held them when they were broken with grief; maybe we showed them how to laugh at themselves. In one way or another, we showed the person our love for him or her. This is what the apostle Paul was saying in his letter to the Corinthians: You are my testimony. You are my living legacy. Not a memorial of marble, not a granite monument but a living, breathing letter of remembrance.

This reminds me of the eloquent words of Charles H. Spurgeon: "Those who loved you, and were helped by you, will remember you when forget-me-nots are withered. Carve your name on hearts, and not on marble" (Jon Johnston, *Courage: You Can Be Strong in the Face of Fear*).

Where is your legacy? Will it be written only on a tombstone—or on the hearts of men and women?

∞

Lord Jesus, I want to leave a legacy that will not pass away. I want to lay up treasures in heaven where they will never become moth-eaten or rusty.

Proper Acknowledgment

*In all your ways acknowledge him, and he will make your
paths straight.*—Proverbs 3:6

A perfectionist always seeks to do things the right way. But the ideal is to do the *right thing* the right way. God has a wonderful plan for each one of us. He is at work in us right now to bring about a divine purpose and destiny in our lives. Our job is to discover that purpose and work with the Holy Spirit to see it accomplished (see Phil. 2:25).

I suspect that one of our problems in discovering God's purpose for our lives is that we seek him only in moments of great decision such as a job change, relocation, or marriage. This habit is contrary to the spiritual principle. The wise man said, "In *all* your ways acknowledge him." This means that in everyday circumstances we must realize the presence of Jesus. We must recognize that he is with us.

If an honored guest joins us at a meeting, we usually acknowledge him or her publicly. We announce, "We are honored to have Mr. or Ms. A with us today." In the same way we are to acknowledge God in all our ways. We recognize and acknowledge that he is with us in every decision, no matter how small.

∞

Jesus, I declare you Lord of this day and every day, Lord of my next decision and every decision I make. I pray that I will see you, know and recognize you, in the routine and in the extraordinary and that, as a result, my future will be directed and steered by you, as you have promised in your Word.

Weekend Reflections

What is the whole purpose of mankind? Is it to acquire wealth? (Can you name the five wealthiest people in the world?) Is it to acquire fame? (Who can remember who won the Academy Award for "Best Actor" just three years ago?)

Money is not an end unto itself, and fame is fleeting. Our real purpose is to know God. Everything else flows from that one goal.

1. What are you doing in your efforts to reach your supreme purpose of knowing God more intimately?

_____

_____

_____

_____

2. How are you, as Charles Spurgeon said, carving "your name on hearts and not on marble"? What lives are you pouring yourself into?

_____

_____

_____

_____

3. They say you can discover people's values by looking at their calendars and their checkbooks. What do yours say about how you are fulfilling your purpose?

_____

_____

_____

_____

_____

Hope Building

Those who hope in the Lord will renew their strength. They will soar on wings like eagles; they will run and not grow weary, they will walk and not be faint.—Isaiah 40:31

There is a hope beyond understanding, a hope that has its source in the Spirit of God. This is the kind of hope that catches the attention of others. They watch in wonderment and say, "I can't figure it out. How can she persevere under such a load?"

Such hope is conceived by the Spirit working within us, but it cannot be birthed in a vacuum. In his letter to the Romans, Paul made clear the prerequisites for this kind of hope when he wrote, "We also rejoice in our sufferings, because we know that suffering produces perseverance; perseverance, character; and character, hope" (Rom. 5:3–4).

It might seem strange to most people to hear that hope is produced by suffering, which most people would assume is counterproductive to hope. But the truth is that there is no reason to hope if there is not some level of suffering. As Paul explained, "Hope that is seen is no hope at all. Who hopes for what he already has?" (Rom. 8:24).

Without weakening in his faith, Abraham, when he was about a hundred years old, faced the fact that his body was as good as dead and that Sarah's womb was also dead. Yet against all odds, Abraham held on to the hope that he would become, as God had promised, the "father of many nations" (Gen. 17:4). He could not summon up this kind of hope from his own psyche; instead, it was birthed from suffering, perseverance, and character.

This is why we can rejoice in sufferings. We do not rejoice for suffering itself, but its result; what is being formed through suffering. We are thankful because on the other side of the suffering we will be better men and women.

∞

God, I thank you for hope. As long as I live in you, there is hope for tomorrow, for you are the source of hope. I rejoice in the supernatural hope of your power, which is at work in me.

Don't Move Your Hope

He has reconciled you by Christ's physical body through death to pres-ent you holy in his sight, without blemish and free from accusation—if you continue in your faith, established and firm, not moved from the hope held out in the gospel. This is the gospel that you heard and that has been proclaimed to every creature under heaven, and of which I, Paul, have become a servant.—Colossians 1:22–23

Is it possible to be saved and still see yourself as God's enemy? Absolutely! This is what happens when we place our hope in our per-formance rather than in the hope of the gospel. When this happens, we've forgotten that one of the miracles of salvation is the complete change in how God sees us. When we step through the veil of Christ's body, God then sees us holy and blameless. He sees us in love as his dear and beloved children. This change happens immediately through the supernatural work of salvation. But our self-portrait, the way we believe God sees us, may not change instantly, or it may become distorted from time to time due to our wavering faith.

Paul described this possibility when he said, "*If* you continue in your faith...not moved from the hope held out in the gospel" (emphasis added). If our hope is anywhere but in the Gospel, in knowing the life of Jesus is working in and through us, we cannot be "free from accusation," especially the enemy's. When he comes to accuse us, we will believe him unless we are totally relying on the power of Jesus Christ, who has raised us to life everlasting.

Where is your hope? Is it in Jesus, or is it in something else? Only his death and resurrection has the power to change God's view of you. Only a steady hope in the Gospel has the power to tear down the false self-image you may have of yourself, an image of being an enemy of God. Only a testimony like that so aptly expressed in the words of this old hymn shows that you know you are an esteemed child of God: "My hope is built on nothing less than Jesus' blood and righteousness."

❧

Father, I repent now of placing my hope anywhere but in the Gospel of Jesus Christ. I boldly confess now that my only hope is Jesus. Give me clear vision to see myself as you see me, blameless and free from accusation. Thank you for the miracle of salvation that is working in me now.

Words of Life

Simon Peter answered him, "Lord, to whom shall we go? You have the words of eternal life."—John 6:68

The words that carry eternal life can only be found in one place—at the feet of Jesus. We urgently need those life-giving, power-packed words, and they only come when we spend time listening with our hearts to our heavenly Father's voice.

Every day we are bombarded with words that impart everything but life: gloom, doom, and pessimism; futility, despair, and negativism. In contrast to such life-draining messages, how refreshing it is, then, to hear God's words of promise! They revive us spiritually, the same way words of rescue encourage us physically when all seems lost.

Tell a dying man on a battlefield that a medevac helicopter is on the way, and he can hang on until help arrives. Give a sinking ship's fearful crew word that a rescue ship is on its way, and watch them strengthen their resolve to keep their vessel afloat just a little longer. Let a wanderer lost in the wilderness hear the sound of searchers calling her name, and watch her make it safely down the mountain, following the sound of their voices.

Just as God spoke the earth and all its riches into being, he also speaks life into our hearts just when we need it most. Are you dying in despair? Lost in a sea of doubt? Wandering through spiritual wilderness? Listen! God is speaking a word of hope that brings new life to your heart.

Oh Father! Help me to hear the words of hope and life you speak into my heart. I will seek at Jesus' feet the words that bring eternal life. Thank you, Lord, for sending your word into my life and saving me from a life of despair and wandering!

THURSDAY

hope

Don't Close the Book Just Yet!

He will renew your life and sustain you in your old age. For your daughter-in-law, who loves you and who is better to you than seven sons, has given him birth.—Ruth 4:15

It was January 3, 1993. The Houston Oilers were leading the Buffalo Bills 28-3 at the half. Then, with a little under seven minutes left in the third quarter, Buffalo's second-string quarterback, Frank Reich, began to lead the charge down the field. By the close of the quarter he had brought the Bills within three points of tying Houston.

Being a Houston fan at the time, I turned off the game sometime during the third quarter, frustrated with "my" team's sudden collapse. As a result, I missed seeing the greatest comeback in NFL history as Buffalo went on to win the game in overtime, 41-38.

I'm reminded of how I missed seeing that incredible comeback when I read again the story of a woman named Naomi in the book of Ruth. When Naomi returned to her hometown of Bethlehem late in her years, she told her friends, "Don't call me Naomi.... Call me Mara, because the Almighty has made my life very bitter" (Ruth 1:20). As far as she could see, the best days of her life had long since passed because she had lost her husband and both of her sons in the space of ten years.

But God had something else in mind for Naomi. Her daughter-in-law Ruth would marry a wealthy businessman named Boaz, who would redeem the family estate and provide much-needed income for Naomi. Ruth and Boaz would have a son named Obed, whom Naomi would consider her own grandson, teaching and caring for him devotedly in her later years. This grandson of Naomi would be the grandfather of the great King David, whose descendant would be the Messiah.

Have you closed the book on your life? Do you have the feeling it's just about over? Your best days may well be in front of you. You don't know the ending of your "story." Only God does. Place your hope in him and be faithful. As long as you're living, God is still writing.

∞

Lord, you are the author and the finisher of my story. I will place my trust in you. I am looking with great anticipation toward the future, knowing you alone are in control of my life.

Life Is Not Permanent, But Our Hope in Christ Is

If in this life only we have hope in Christ, we are of all men most miserable.—1 Corinthians 15:19 KJV

I remember exactly where I was when I heard the horrifying news: "The *Challenger* has exploded." And I vividly remember the moments after hearing about the bombing of the federal building in Oklahoma City.

Such cataclysmic events have a way of bringing the world to a halt for a moment and uniting us as one fragile community. We are shaken once again by the realization that life is not as predictable as we thought.

This must have been how the disciples felt when they first heard the news that Jesus had been condemned for blasphemy and would be crucified."

Horrified thoughts and questions must have swirled through their minds: *No! It can't be! It wasn't supposed to end like this! What about the kingdom of Israel? I thought he was the Messiah. Is this the end?*

For those awful moments, time surely stood still, and the earth held its breath. But God had a bigger plan—a plan that would cause the kingdom of darkness to shudder, a plan that would turn his disciples' tears to shouts of joy. Yes, it was a different ending than the disciples predicted, but it was a much better ending, a conclusion that far exceeded their wildest dreams!

Remember, friend, our hope does not lie in the permanence of life. Much of life is unpredictable. Our only hope is in the permanence of God's purpose for mankind. It lies in the symbol of an empty grave! It rests in a risen, triumphant, and glorified Christ.

∞

Oh God, I praise you because your plan is bigger and better than mine! You always win. I place my hope in you, my security and my faith in your power to do immeasurably more than I can ask or imagine (see Eph. 3:20).

hope

Weekend Reflections

Jim Wallis wrote, "Hope is the very dynamic of history. Hope is the engine of change. Hope is the energy of transformation. Hope is the door from one reality to another" ("The Door of Hope," *Sojourners,* April 1988). Hope lifts our eyes from the present grief to the promise of tomorrow and causes us to look upward instead of inward, to trust in God and his delivering power. It empowers us to look past the present darkness to a brighter place. It gives us strength in times of weakness to press on a little further, a little longer, a little higher.

1. Describe a picture of a person who has little hope.

_____

_____

_____

_____

2. Have there been times when hope carried you through a seemingly impossible situation to a better place? Describe those times.

_____

_____

_____

_____

_____

3. Some people scoff at the hope of eternity. Why is this hope so important?

_____

_____

_____

_____

_____

This Too Shall Pass

Momentary, light affliction is producing for us an eternal weight of glory far beyond all comparison.—2 Corinthians 4:17 NASB

Life brings change—sometimes for the better, sometimes for what seems to be the worse. I have a friend who says her favorite phrase in Scripture is "And it came to pass." She rejoices in the knowledge that nothing on earth is permanent, including whatever troubles beset us. The worst calamity is a passing thing; new possibilities lie on the horizon.

King David understood this principle. In the most famous of the psalms he wrote, "Even though I *walk through* the valley of the shadow of death, I fear no evil" (23:4 NASB, emphasis added). We may walk through the valley of death, but we do not dwell there. Instead we dwell in Jesus.

Knowing what *is* permanent—our promise of eternal life with God in heaven—gives us the grace to endure the "momentary affliction." Christ is permanent—"the same yesterday, and to day, and for ever" (Heb. 13:8 KJV). His faithfulness is permanent; even "if we are faithless, he will remain faithful, for he cannot disown himself" (2 Tim. 2:13). And our hope of his coming kingdom is permanent because he "set his seal of ownership on us, and put his Spirit in our hearts as a deposit, guaranteeing what is to come" (2 Cor. 1:22).

For you, it may seem that your "affliction" is permanent. But it, too, will pass. There will come a time when your present trouble will be just a memory. Then you may look back and wonder how things fell into place the way they did. And beyond that, when his kingdom comes, even those painful memories will be erased.

∞

Lord, I am thankful to know that even though trouble may come, it is "achieving an eternal glory." Thank you for the permanence of your love, your faithfulness, and your kingdom, which means that when affliction is just a memory…you will remain.

Morning Will Come

From the rising of the sun to its going down, the Lord's name is to be praised.—Psalm 113:3 NKJV

There will always be moments of darkness in our lives. Midnight always comes…with all its shadows, worries, and fears. We find ourselves tossing and turning on those long, lonely nights, our minds obsessively sorting through possible solutions to life's dilemmas. Or the telephone rings in the darkness, a harbinger of bad news.

But here is good news: The night will pass. It is a temporary state. And once morning has broken, the darkness is dispelled.

The shadows are overcome by the brilliance of the sun. There is no turning back. Night may come again, but for now it is morning. As the psalmist wrote, "Weeping may remain for a night, but rejoicing comes in the morning" (Ps. 30:5).

No night can last forever. The sun will shine again. The birds will sing, and creation will blush beneath the radiance of heavenly beams.

My friend, rejoice with me. We know another kind of morning. The Son has risen! He is no longer in the cold grave. The gloom of midnight has been vanquished by resurrection morning's light! As Isaiah urged us long ago, "Arise, shine, for your light has come!" (Isa. 60:1).

∞

Jesus, thank you for the promise of a new day—for your mercies that are new every morning. No night can overcome your everlasting light, for you are the true Light, the Light of the world.

A Harvest of Godly Feelings

Remain in me, and I will remain in you. No branch can bear fruit by itself; it must remain in the vine. Neither can you bear fruit unless you remain in me.—John 15:4

Feelings are the fruit of what is going on inside us. Perhaps they are better described as evidence of the condition of our hearts. When we hear a negative report, a feeling of fear, shame, or regret may arise from within us. This is evidence of the condition of our hearts. When we have thankful hearts, even in the face of bad news, we react differently than if our hearts are darkened with pride.

When we can see our feelings as nothing more than the fruit of our hearts, we can begin to control them instead of allowing them to control us. As someone so wisely said, "We don't do what we do because of the way we feel, but we feel the way we feel because we do what we do." By changing what we do, it is possible to change the way we feel. When we change what we allow into our spirits, our feelings change. But it is futile to try to change our feelings by working on the feeling itself—as futile as trying to make an orange out of an apple.

The work of the Spirit in our lives will be shown by the fruit that follows: feelings of love, joy, and peace. Don't think you can simply say, "I have to start being less discouraged," and cause changes in your feelings. Instead, allow the Spirit to work in your life by being grateful, by carrying out Christ's love in giving and sharing, and you will reap a bountiful harvest of good feelings.

∞

Spirit of the living God, fall fresh on my heart today. I give you full authority over my life. Create in me a clean heart and give me a willingness to do your work in the earth. I know that as my heart is refreshed by your love and refilled with your will, it will become confident and hopeful of the new possibilities you can work in me.

possibilities

Don't Forget the Benefits

Bless the Lord, O my soul, and forget not all His benefits.
—Psalm 103:2 NKJV

Don't forget! We have all heard those words countless times. Sometimes they help you remember. Other times you still forget—until it's too late: You're on your way to work and realize you left that important report at home on the kitchen table. Or it's 1 P.M. and you just finished lunch when you remember you were supposed to meet a friend across town for lunch. What you feel as you berate yourself for forgetting does not evoke a pleasant image. Pond scum comes to mind!

Being able to remember important matters is an essential element of our success in our career and in our relationships. But in our Christian walk, one of the keys to success is actually learning to forget some things while remembering what is important. The apostle Paul taught us the importance of forgetting those things that are behind us and of pressing on toward the goal (see Phil. 3:13), and the psalmist told us what to remember: "all his benefits" (Ps. 103:2).

It is important to remember the benefits of serving Christ, because the time may come when we are faced with trying circumstances that will bring voices of doubt whispering in our hearts, "Where is God? Does he care?" It is at those times we must not forget "all his benefits."

And just what *are* some of those benefits? David offered us reminders: "He forgives all my sins and heals all my diseases. He ransoms me from death and surrounds me with love and tender mercies. He fills my life with good things. My youth is renewed like the eagle's!" (Ps. 103:3–5 NLT).

It may be that in times of doubt we should talk to ourselves as David did. He wrote, "Praise the Lord, I tell myself, and never forget the good things he does for me" (103:2 NLT).

Do a little mental housecleaning today. Throw away the things you need to discard, but don't forget the benefits.

∞

Lord, I will remember your goodness. When I realize where I am today and where you brought me from, I know my progress is a symbol of your loving kindness to me. Thank you for the future I have in you, but thank you also for the benefits of serving you today.

Why Are You Sad?

"Woman," he said, "why are you crying? Who is it you are looking for?"—John 20:15

Peter and John had come to the tomb at Mary's request. Seeing that his body was not there and thinking that it had been stolen, they hurriedly went back into hiding. Mary, however, lingered at the tomb.

The word translated here as *crying* doesn't mean to weep quietly but to sob or wail. Mary was so overcome with grief she began to cry aloud. Then she heard, "Woman, why are you crying?"

Mary started to explain. Her torrents of anguish may have kept her from hearing the voice clearly. Apparently, she couldn't even lift her head as she poured out the problem to the one she thought was the gardener.

Then the voice came again: "Mary."

Jesus stood before her. He arose from the dead and appeared first to Mary as she wept beside his empty tomb. Not on Main Street in Jerusalem, not in the temple, not to the disciples in hiding, but first to a sobbing woman who had collapsed in anguish as she mourned her great loss.

Even today Jesus appears to us in our anguish. It is then, when we are at our most vulnerable point, that he is nearest to us. I have a friend who talks freely about the day her husband died unexpectedly while he was having minor surgery. She tells how immediately after his death she experienced a peace and love so real she couldn't believe how secure she felt. Looking back, she knows it was Jesus holding her in her anguish. It was his peace, the peace that transcends understanding, that comforted her in her darkest moment. The psalmist wrote, "The Lord is nigh unto them that are of a broken heart; and saveth such as be of a contrite spirit" (34:18 KJV). Though God sometimes seems further away when our hearts are broken, he is actually closer than ever. Look up. Listen. Seek him, and you will sense his presence in you.

❧

Lord, I love you for your faithfulness. You always know when we are at our weakest point. When we hurt the most, you are nearer than ever because you identify with our grief and adversity.

167

possibilities

Weekend Reflections

Summer has arrived. This is the season of vacations, sunshine, and recreation. It would be great if there were spiritual seasons, too, wouldn't it? Think how we could prepare if we knew when we were entering the temptation season or the blessing season. But there is usually no warning. Living with Jesus means adventure and a bright future filled with never-before-explored possibilities. If you find yourself in a season of temptation, sorrow, or suffering, look to the future God has in store for you and know that no season lasts forever—at least here on earth.

1. What benefits does God have in store for you beyond your present circumstances?

   _____

   _____

   _____

   _____

2. Your faith in future possibilities may seem unreasonable to others. What is your hope based on? (What does the Bible say regarding your circumstances?)

   _____

   _____

   _____

   _____

3. Take a moment to consider what season you might be in right now. Write about it now, then reflect on it six months from now and see if your perceptions were on target.

   _____

   _____

   _____

Enemies of Intimacy

The Lord says: "These people come near to me with their mouth and honor me with their lips, but their hearts are far from me. Their worship of me is made up only of rules taught by men."—Isaiah 29:13

Religiosity will drive intimacy with God right out of your life. People who focus on the religion rather than the reality of worship never really become transparent before God; they simply get caught up in the recitation of familiar prayers and pleasing music. They may speak in tongues and sing dozens of hymns and repeat many prayers, but they never pour their hearts out to God in a real way.

Look at the contrast between the prayers of the Pharisee and the tax collector in Jesus' parable. "The Pharisee stood up and prayed about himself: 'God, I thank you that I am not like other men—robbers, evildoers, adulterers—or even like this tax collector. I fast twice a week and give a tenth of all I get'" (Luke 18:11–12).

Meanwhile, said Jesus, the tax collector "would not even look up to heaven, but beat his breast and said, 'God, have mercy on me, a sinner'" (v. 13). The Pharisee's prayer focused on his fulfillment of spiritual duties while the publican humbled himself before God, focusing on his neediness rather than his accomplishments.

Surprised God by changing your spiritual routine. Study new ways to make your relationship with the Lord fresh! Work hard to develop intimacy with him!

Every moment spent in communion with God may not be an ecstatic high, but you should not be content to remain at status quo with an empty spiritual devotion. Enter your worship time as if you were spending time alone with God…with no one else watching.

⚭

Father, what are the enemies of intimacy that I have allowed in my life? Reveal them to me by your Holy Spirit. I want to be close to you, to hear your voice and know your heart.

A God Far Away?

*A large crowd followed and pressed around [Jesus]. And a woman was
there who had been subject to bleeding for twelve years....When she
heard about Jesus, she came up behind him in the crowd and touched
his cloak, because she thought, "If I just touch his clothes,
I will be healed."—Mark 5:24–25, 27–28*

I've been thinking lately about a song I often sang as a child sitting in
the church pew. It said, "Reach out and touch the Lord as He goes
by...He's passing by this moment..." While it was an inspiring song,
offering hope in one sense, I wonder now if it might have imparted a sub-
liminal message that implied, "You'd better catch Jesus while he's here
because he may not be back for awhile."

The erroneous concept that God is far removed from us can sneak
into our thinking before we're aware of it. There was a time when Jesus
did literally walk on earth, and to let him walk by without reaching out
to him was to miss a golden opportunity. But now we don't have to wait
beside the road or climb a tree to see the Lord passing by. He has told us,
"I will not leave you comfortless: I will come to you" (John 14:18 KJV).

And he does. His being with us is not a matter of condition but of
relationship. He is not just the God of crises, but he's also the God of
calmness. Not only does he walk the waves of the tempest, but he leads
us beside the still waters. He is Yahweh-Rohi, the shepherd of our souls.
He has promised to be with us "always, to the very end of the age" (Matt.
28:20). He is here. He is "Immanuel—which means, 'God with us'"
(Matt. 1:23).

⚯

Lord, there is not a time when you cannot hear me. Your eyes are ever on the
righteous (see Ps. 34:15). Even if I walk through a time when I don't feel you
near me, I know your promises are true.

The Deep, Deep Heart of Man

Deep calls to deep in the roar of your waterfalls; all your waves and breakers have swept over me.—Psalm 42:7

Scientists tell us there are areas of the ocean so deep that even though the temperature is below freezing, ice will not form. The pressure above is too great. Yet living things exist in those depths that can exist nowhere else.

The same God who created these great depths of the sea also created human beings, and like the oceans, he gave us mysterious depths. The Bible says, "The purposes of a man's heart are deep waters" (Prov. 20:5). This deepest part of our hearts is something we have only begun to understand, yet it is a familiar place to God, our Creator. For him, there is no such thing as unexplored territory. This is his dwelling place in us.

Our friends and loved ones only scratch the surface of who we are, even after years of knowing us, but in an instant God reaches the very core of us. He is not looking for a surface relationship but one of depth and intimacy. Paul prayed that we might someday "grasp how wide and long and high and deep is the love of Christ, and to know this love that surpasses knowledge" (Eph. 3:18–19).

We are not meant to skim along the surface of God's love. Whether or not we admit it, there is a cry from deep within us that reaches for something more than a shallow affinity: "Deep calls to deep." Our innermost beings cry out, "Take me deeper. Don't give me the superficial!"

God has given us hearts deep enough to know him (see Jer. 24:7). We invite him in to our depths by accepting his love for us, loving him in return, and by obeying his commands (see 1 John 2:3).

❧

God, I have heard your call to the deep places. I don't want to become content in the mundane and the shallow. The deeper life awaits me, and I will follow you there.

171

THURSDAY

Everyday Christianity

Talk about them when you sit at home and when you walk along the road, when you lie down and when you get up.—Deuteronomy 6:7

Being a Christian is more than enduring a Sunday-morning ritual and catching a few midweek services. It is a way of life. Jesus is meant to be an everyday experience.

Why are we so reluctant to allow this to happen? I am convinced that one of the problems is that we think God is so busy and preoccupied with other things that he does not have time to get involved in our personal lives. A related reason may be that we are afraid to let God see just how pitiful we are as we wallow in our weaknesses.

It is inaccurate to believe God is too busy for personal involvement. God is all-knowing. He reveals his infinite capacity time and again. God sees every knee that bows. He collects every tear that falls.

And when it comes to trying to hide our weaknesses from God, remember that Scripture tells us Jesus himself is our advocate, able to sympathize with our feelings of weakness (see Heb. 4:15). Real change begins in us when we acknowledge Jesus' strength in our weakness (see 2 Cor. 12:10). To push him out of our moments of weakness is not the answer. For if we could change by our own strength, there would be no need for salvation. The power of the Cross and the Resurrection are most powerfully revealed through their working in our lives—right there in our weaknesses, our struggle with carnality.

Let us acknowledge right now God's perpetual presence beside us—when we sit down at home, when we walk along the road, when we lie down, when we get up. He is not too busy; nor is he offended by our weakness. Remember how Jesus walked and talked with the two disciples on their way to Emmaus? Though they were unaware that he had risen from the dead and though they were filled with doubt, Jesus was there with them. Right in the middle of their unbelief. And so he is with you.

∞

Father, I want to be one who acknowledges you in all things—not just in time of triumph but in the hour of temptation. Not only in Sunday morning worship but in mowing the grass or in doing the laundry. I want to know what it means to abide in you and live in your presence.

Knowledge with Experience

[That you may really come] to know [practically, through experience for yourselves] the love of Christ, which far surpasses mere knowledge [without experience].—Ephesians 3:19 AMPLIFIED

How do we know something that "surpasses mere knowledge"? This statement implies something impossible—to comprehend something that is incomprehensible. Yet that is exactly what the apostle Paul prayed for the Ephesians: that they would "know this love that surpasses knowledge" (NIV).

We know that faith comes by hearing the Word of God, and we know that Christ dwells in our hearts "through faith." But we cannot really know God's love by faith, not in the sense the apostle Paul spoke of. We know God's love by experience and revelation. We can believe in God's love, but to know God's love is something much more. It takes an enlightening of our understanding, an empowering of our spiritual senses, to know what is beyond knowledge.

This kind of "knowing" is not something mystical. It is not weird or spooky, but it is supernatural. It is what happens when we really come into communion with our heavenly Father, when we hear his voice and listen to his heart. In this position we are experiencing God's love, not "just" believing in it.

Knowing God's love sustains us when our faith is challenged. We not only say, "I believe," but we say as well, "I know *whom* I have believed." Though circumstances would dictate to us otherwise, because of our experience in the love of Christ and the step-by-step revelation, we stand strong "rooted and established in love" (Eph. 3:17).

∞

Oh Father, according to your Word, I pray that I, being rooted and established in love, may have power together with all the saints to grasp how wide and long and high and deep is the love of Christ and to know this love that surpasses knowledge—that I may be filled to the measure of all the fullness of God (see Eph. 3:17–19).

Weekend Reflections

It's difficult to fathom how and why Almighty God desires to befriend us. Friendship is usually based on trust and common interests, and knowing ourselves as we do, it may be difficult to see how God could find either in us. But he has proven his love for us by the Cross and seeks to have an intimate relationship with us.

1. How does an intimate friendship develop? How do these steps apply to developing our intimacy with God?

   _____

   _____

   _____

   _____

   _____

   _____

2. Does intimacy with God frighten you? If so, why?

   _____

   _____

   _____

   _____

   _____

3. While God loves the whole world, he does have a closer relationship with some of his children, and he reveals himself in a greater way to those people. Who do you know who seems to have this kind of relationship? What do you see in that person that makes his or her close relationship with God obvious?

   _____

   _____

   _____

   _____

   _____

In the Steps of Jesus

Whoever claims to live in him must walk as Jesus did. —1 John 2:6

As a child, did you try to walk in your father's footsteps? Do you remember how you had to stretch your short legs to plant your foot squarely on your dad's footprint without taking extra steps? Or maybe you recall trying to keep up with your mother's quick pace, exhausting yourself in the attempt. As human children, it wasn't easy for us to follow in our parents' footsteps. We had to wait until our legs grew longer and our stamina increased before we could walk the way our parents walked.

As children of God, it seems even harder to walk the path that Jesus modeled for us. In fact, it may seem like climbing Mount Everest. But Scripture teaches us that our love for Christ is revealed when we walk as he walked. That is the goal we strive for.

But how can we be like such a man—a man who prayed for those who crucified him and who called his betrayer his friend?

The answer is we can't—not by ourselves. The power to walk as Jesus walked is simply not in us. It is the Spirit who gives us this ability. It is the Spirit who instructs us and leads us in the way of truth. As Paul wrote to the Galatians, "Since we live by the Spirit, let us keep in step with the Spirit" (5:25). If we are open to its guidance, the Spirit will teach us how to take those first small steps toward Christlikeness. But we must walk according to our own level of maturity.

The Spirit sets our pace, not other Christians. We must be content to take small steps, patiently waiting as our spiritual growth lengthens our legs and increases our stamina and understanding. When we attempt to keep in step with other believers, trying to walk as they walk, we are no longer in step with the Spirit. Their walk is not my walk. Their pace is not mine. Only the Spirit can teach us to walk as Jesus walked. The Spirit patiently walks with us, guiding our steps, giving us strength to get up when we fall...until we find ourselves walking in the footsteps of Jesus.

∞

Father, I yield now to your Spirit as he teaches me to walk as you walk. Forgive me for the times I have tried to walk as others walk. Thank you for your patience with my small steps as I grow.

Abiding in Christ

Look to Jesus

Therefore, holy brothers, who share in the heavenly calling, fix your
thoughts on Jesus, the apostle and high priest whom we confess.
—Hebrews 3:1

Are you troubled when you see the failures of those who call themselves believers? Rather than focusing on others' shortcomings, "fix your
thoughts on Jesus," who was faithful on every account, fulfilling the mission the Father created him to do. It is Jesus—not our human brothers
and sisters—who serves as our role model. To live a victorious life, we
must keep our gaze fixed solidly on him.

We see how he was faithful and obedient to his purpose while he
walked here on earth, and we are encouraged, knowing that he will be
faithful to complete what he has begun and that he will not give up on us
until his purpose in us has come to maturity. By clinging to this promise
and fixing our eyes on him, we can have peace when the world around us
is in turmoil and when daily stresses unsettle us. We make a conscious
decision to turn our thoughts from the problem to the problem solver. As
Isaiah said, "Thou wilt keep him in perfect peace, whose mind is stayed
on thee: because he trusteth in thee" (Isa. 26:3 KJV).

We make a decision to turn our eyes away from people and to look to
God, completely trusting him. We deliberately choose to trust in his wisdom and providence and not lean on our own understanding.

∞

Lord, help me to fix my thoughts on you, to turn away from the things that are
beyond my control, and to trust completely in your omnipotence. I receive
your peace now as my mind comes into the obedience of your Word. You
know what is best. You are in control. I place my life in your hands.

Your Life or His?

*For as the Father has life in himself, so he has granted the Son
to have life in himself.*—John 5:26

None of us have life in ourselves alone. Oh, we are alive, and everything on the surface may appear to be fine, but we have no life, no spark, in and of ourselves. The only life we find in ourselves is a cheap imitation at best. In contrast, the life Christ offers is abundant and full of passion; it is a conduit carrying the limitless love of God to an empty world of brokenness.

This is why, as Christians, we must stand at the Cross, taking fellowship with his suffering and emptying ourselves of the counterfeit. Then and only then can we receive what is authentic. There at the Cross, his life will come pouring into us so that, as he said, "Streams of living water will flow from within" (John 7:38).

There at the Cross the voice of God is heard, and the dead can experience life. Jesus said, "A time is coming and has now come when the dead will hear the voice of the Son of God and those who hear will live" (John 5:25).

What is your source of life? Are you trying to find life from within yourself? If so, you will soon find that you're "running on empty." A richer, more rewarding, more gloriously abundant life than you've ever dreamed of is available to you. And Jesus wants you to have it. In fact, he came to earth, suffered a cruel death, and arose from the grave to give it to you. All this so you could "have life, and have it to the full" (John 10:10). So which do you want? Your narrow, empty, self-focused life...or eternity with him?

∞

Jesus, by faith I believe you are living in me, that your abundant life is working and flowing in me. I don't want to settle for anything less than real life—your life. Fill me up and let your love overflow to any heart that I may touch today.

Daily Bread

Then Jesus declared, "I am the bread of life. He who comes to me will never go hungry, and he who believes in me will never be thirsty."—John 6:35

There is never a moment when we do not need Jesus, never a time when we don't depend totally on him. If such a moment comes, we cease in that instant to be God-dependent and instead become self-reliant. We stop looking to Jesus for life, and instead, we seek it from within ourselves.

Jesus taught us to pray, "Give us this day our daily bread" (Matt. 6:11 KJV), and he declared, "I am the bread of life," while assuring us, "He who comes to me will never go hungry" (John 6:35). We come to him for life itself, and there is so much more to this coming to him than the form and ritual of worship. We must come to him crying, "I look to you and you alone, Jesus! My help comes from you!" If we do, he will never send us away hungry.

But if we are full of ourselves, we say to him, in effect, "I have no need," even though the emptiness of our hearts is oh so apparent to the One who created us. Sadly, when we come to him in that state, he does not share the bread with us. He does not force-feed us. Only when we come to him humbly, acknowledging our needy state, does he become our daily provision, our all-sustaining source of life.

∞

Father, I cry to you, "Give me the bread I need for today. I am hungry and needy apart from you, the Bread of Life."

In the Garden

Whoever does not love does not know God, because God is love.
—1 John 4:8

Why did God create mankind? He knew what the outcome would be. He knew that creating a being in his own image and granting it the power to choose would be risky at best. Yet nothing short of this could fulfill God's desire to love a creation that could choose to love him back.

God is all-sufficient. He has no needs in the true sense. But God is love (see 1 John 4:8), and love in and of itself is virtually meaningless until it is given away. Therefore, if God does have a need or desire, it is to love. And oh, how he loves us!

He loves us so much that he left heaven and came to earth to dwell among us sinners. He loves us so much that he stood in our place—hung in our place on the cross—and suffered the cruelest punishment for our sins. *Our* sins! Yet he himself is without sin. He did it all for love—his love for us.

To need love is human; to give love unselfishly is Christ. To love as he loved, not basing the love we show on what we receive in return, is to exhibit a small part of the substance of God himself that he has placed within us. His Word tells us, "We know and rely on the love God has for us. God is love. Whoever lives in love lives in God, and God in him. In this way, love is made complete among us so that we will have confidence on the day of judgment, because in this world we are like him" (1 John 4:16–17).

We are loved, and we are like him. So what are we going to do?

∞

Jesus, am I abiding in you? Show me what that means. Teach me to abide so that I will bear much fruit to your glory—that I will be an expression of your everlasting life in a lifeless world.

Weekend Reflections

"Abide in me," Jesus said (John 15:4 NKJV). The word *abide* is rich with meaning. In most cases in Scripture it means "to stay or to remain." This understanding points us to the reality that Christ is not someone we visit on Sundays but someone we live in, between Sundays.

1. How can we abide, or remain, in Christ and still continue our regular work and play?

   _____

   _____

   _____

   _____

   _____

   _____

2. Name someone you know who abides in the Father's love. What is the evidence of his or her abiding there?

   _____

   _____

   _____

   _____

   _____

3. Practice abiding in Christ when you are tempted. What happens when you do?

   _____

   _____

   _____

   _____

   _____

Hands That Bless

*When he had led them out to the vicinity of Bethany, he lifted up his
hands and blessed them.*—Luke 24:50

What a thrill it must have been for the disciples to stand near
Bethany as Jesus lifted up his hands and blessed them and then was carried away. Imagine what it would be like to literally stand before God in
the flesh and have his hands lifted over you as he declared a blessing.

While God no longer walks this earth as a man, he sent the "Com-
forter," the Holy Spirit, so that we could constantly walk with him and
know he did not abandon us (see John 14:16, 26 KJV). And although we
cannot literally stand beneath his uplifted hands of flesh and blood, we
still feel his blessings each time we enter his presence. God no longer
walks this earth in a man's body, but he has raised up another body here
on earth to do his work. In a glorious mystery, his church has come
together as a spiritual body, unseen with the natural eye (see Eph.
5:30–32), as well as a body of believers representing Christ to the world.

As his body, we have the power to bless one another as Jesus did when
he walked the earth. We can be the salt of the earth, the light of the world
(see Matt. 5:13–14). We can speak words that heal and encourage, affirm-
ing words that literally strengthen and lift the human spirit. The apostle
Paul instructed us to speak "only what is helpful for building others up
according to their needs, that it may benefit those who listen" (Eph. 4:29).

Whose life have you blessed today?

∞

Lord, I want to follow your example and bless those around me. Let my hands
and the words of my mouth be a blessing and not a curse. Help me remember the great power of words to minister grace and hands to bless.

Remember Your Prison

Remember those in prison as if you were their fellow prisoners.
—Hebrews 13:3

Once we leave the prison of self and sin, it doesn't take long to forget the misery we suffered there. Living happily in the land of promise, where freedom is an everyday experience, prison can fade into nothing more than a forgotten memory. To appreciate freedom, every now and then we must have a vivid reminder of prison.

We must remember what that old, dark, musty prison was like. We must see it. Smell it. Feel it. And then, remembering how good it feels to be free, we must declare this freedom to those who need to hear it, those who are still imprisoned. Only then will we see God "confirming the word with signs following" (Mark 16:20 KJV).

In making these "prison visits," we must not take out of context the verse that says, "Friendship with the world is enmity with God" (James 4:4 NKJV). Christians who argue that this verse says believers are not to extend friendship to those in the world would also seem to indicate that Jesus was in error when he befriended Zacchaeus or any of the other publicans! Yet Jesus made it clear: He was not *entangled* with the world. He touched the world, but the world never "had" him. "The prince of this world...has no hold on me," he said (John 14:30). Christ is our model. His life is our example.

We must bring freedom to the prisoners. As long as we talk about freedom only to those who are free, the Gospel doesn't have room to work. There is no need for God to display his might and freedom until the Good News is declared to all who are held captive in the prison of self and sin. Jesus was not afraid to do this work. He went right into the depths of the prison of all prisons and preached freedom to the captives. The end result was the confirmation of his word: He "led captivity captive" (Ps. 68:18 KJV).

Jesus reached out to the imprisoned, and so must we.

∞

Father, may I never forget the chains that once held me. Thank you for freedom. Thank you for the glory of knowing that by you I am free.

Light Up!

That was the true Light, which lighteth every man that cometh into the world.—John 1:9 KJV

Why is it some people light up the room wherever they go and others are like the Peanuts comic-strip character who has a little dark cloud that follows him around?

I had a friend who always brought life to any party—or any other gathering—she attended. Though she is now with the Lord, I still cherish her wonderful way of bringing out the best in people. She knew how to make you feel like you had something to contribute when it was really her own conversation skills that kept the communication flowing.

I believe she was so likeable because she was a builder of people, a female version of Barnabas, the "Son of Encouragement" (Acts 4:36). It seemed to come so naturally to her. Her encouragement was never forced or coercive. She had learned that the key to loving people was knowing first that she was loved by Christ. Then, knowing that fact, she could tap into the glorious and enduring love Jesus has for those around us.

Jesus was loved by people because his love was not self-seeking. People like Mary of Bethany loved hanging out with him because he brought out the best in them. He saw their potential and called it forth. His was a love that was always directed outward.

How do some people light up the room wherever they go? They know how to ignite the light in others.

∞

Lord Jesus, you are the Light of the world. Please ignite the light in me so that I can shine on others and bring out the good in them.

183

loving others

Still Water Runs Deep

Now there are different kinds of spiritual gifts, but it is the same Holy Spirit who is the source of them all.—1 Corinthians 12:4 NLT

How deep is your river of belief? The strength we show in the toughest of times shows the depth of our rivers. God said he would "give unto him that is athirst of the fountain of the water of life freely" (Rev. 21:6 KJV). Yet many believers exhibit a life that seems shallow, a faith that seems easily exhausted. How can we share Christ's love with others if our own reservoirs are dry?

As Oswald Chambers wrote in *My Utmost for His Highest,* "Whether or not you are exhausted will depend on where you get your supplies." If the life you offer to others is of yourself, it will not be enough. The people you touch will walk away having had only a sip of refreshment; their thirst will still be unquenched, and you will soon be depleted, yourself. Only God, "the fountain of life," can offer living water. The water we provide from ourselves is at best an imitation with God's residue in it. To get the living water—and to give it to others—you have to go back to the Source: Jesus, the fountain from which all our rivers flow.

When you see believers who show courage when you would expect them to be fearful, who glow with peace when their hearts should be in turmoil, you can know that their rivers run deep—and that the source of their strength is the fountain of abundant life.

∽

Father, thank you for the gift of abundant life, the nourishment of living water. At your right hand are pleasures forevermore.

Have You Mocked His Face?

We curse men, who have been made in God's likeness.
—James 3:9

I have been with people who claimed to know Christ and yet would mock those of different cultures, openly displaying their preconceived notions and ugly prejudice gained through legend and gossip. What fools we are to think that we are somehow better than others because we have a different upbringing, different skin pigmentation, or were born in a different state or country! What fools we are to think we have any significance at all—except in God's eyes!

How can we who were dead and spiritually impoverished before God found us mock and prejudge those who are different from us and yet so much like us? More importantly, they were created in the "likeness of God." So when we ridicule others, we are, in essence, laughing at God's image. Laughing at something he created and died for. "My brothers, this should not be," James said (3:10).

How can we, insignificant as we ourselves are, ridicule anyone or anything? Our insignificance must be what the psalmist had in mind when he wrote in Psalm 2 that God laughs in derision as "the heathen rage, and the people imagine a vain thing...[and] the kings...and the rulers take counsel together, against the Lord" (vv. 1–4 KJV). God laughs at those who lift up their heads with arrogance as he asks them, "Where were *you* when I laid the earth's foundation?" (Job 38:4, emphasis added).

Considering the way God scoffed at those of ancient times who "put on airs," we might shift from arrogance to humility and begin to wonder about our real self-worth today. Just how much *are* we worth? To God, we are priceless! We're so valuable, in fact, that God gave his only Son to die for our transgressions. Why? Because of his immeasurable love for us. Because when he looks at us he sees his image, and it is impossible for God to hate something that looks like himself.

❧

Lord, forgive me for the times I have not seen others through your eyes of love. I have rejected people because of their differences instead of celebrating the diversity of your creation. I "will" to love.

loving others

Weekend Reflections

The love Christ has placed in our hearts is for sharing; the grace he has covered us with is to be extended to others. As Christians, we are the hands and feet of Jesus on earth. It is our privilege and responsibility to represent him lovingly.

1. Do you know people who "light up the room" when they enter? Most likely they are people who love other people. How do they demonstrate it?

   _____

   _____

   _____

   _____

2. If there is to be long-lasting fruit from our ministry, then the ministry must be motivated by love. Why do you do what you do?

   _____

   _____

   _____

   _____

3. We can literally love Jesus by loving others. He said so (see Matt. 25:38–40). What will you do for others that will demonstrate your love for Jesus?

   _____

   _____

   _____

   _____

Seize the Day!

This is the day the Lord has made; let us rejoice and be glad in it.
—Psalm 118:24

There has never been a day just like today. Nor will there ever be again. The exact combination of today's people, ages, weather, and places cannot be duplicated. For you—and for all of us—today is unique.

There is a Latin phrase, *carpe diem,* that means "seize the day." How often we let days go by, wasting precious opportunities that will never come again. When we're always waiting for that "someday" to begin a new challenge or adventure, wasted days turn into weeks and years, and eventually we lose sight of dreams and goals.

What is the thing you have always dreamed of doing or being? Begin today! Each day can bring you one step closer to your goal as you use every moment to its fullest. How long have you been saying, "One of these days I'm going to start a consistent daily devotion of prayer and time in the Word. I'll even spend some time just waiting in God's presence"? Friend, let me ask you: If not today, when? As the apostle Paul told the Romans, "The hour has come for you to wake up from your slumber, because our salvation is nearer now than when we first believed. The night is nearly over; the day is almost here" (Rom. 13:11–12).

Let us not lose sight of our long-range and eternal goals while working through the routines of the day at hand. Instead, let us awake each morning with ambition and discipline to live each day to its fullest, using each moment to further the kingdom of God.

Lord, thank you for this day. Open my understanding so that I may see the opportunities of today—the people I can touch and the things I can accomplish for the sake of your kingdom. Where do you want me to begin? Point the way, and I will be obedient to your holy will.

Is Your Life in a Holding Pattern?

Ye have compassed this mountain long enough: turn you northward.
—Deuteronomy 2:3 KJV

Have you ever felt like your spiritual walk was going in circles? Do you have dreams and visions for the future that seem to stay beyond your reach while again and again you do the same thing you've been doing? You probably feel like pilots do when air-traffic control puts them in a "holding pattern," causing them to fly in circles until the weather or traffic are resolved and they can land. Several planes may be directed to "hold" at a certain altitude, circling until instructions are given to move down to another altitude and continue circling, until finally the pilot works his or her way down through the stack and is given final clearance to land. If you have done much flying, I am sure you have found yourself in one of these holding patterns at one time or another.

The book of Hebrews describes how God put the Israelites in a "holding pattern" in the wilderness because of their disobedience. They were not allowed to enter the Promised Land but were forced to wander in the desert for forty years. Today, when we find ourselves in a holding pattern, doing the same thing we've done before, falling short of our hopes and dreams for the future, perhaps we need to look back and consider where we may have disobeyed. I believe God puts us in these holding patterns, not to punish us, but to give us time to learn and mature before he allows us to enter the next "altitude." He waits for us to act in obedience before we can break out of the pattern and finally move on.

Is there something you have been refusing to do or give up or act on? Perhaps God is waiting for you to obey at point one before he allows you to move to point two. Then he will say to you, as he said, in effect, to the children of Israel, "You have circled this mountain long enough. Step out in obedience. Act upon your faith. Just beyond this mountain there is a promise waiting for you!"

∽

Lord, empower me to always choose the path of obedience, no matter the cost. You have shown me that obedience leads to true fulfillment and that there is no other way to success in your kingdom. Reveal to me anything that has impeded my progress. I want to move forward in your power.

The Flower of Life

As for man, his days are like grass, he flourishes like a flower of the field; the wind blows over it and it is gone.—Psalm 103:15–16

God compares our life on earth to a flower. Like a flower, life is a thing of beauty, something to be enjoyed. But no matter what we do for the flower—even if we put it in a vase with plenty of water, even if we pamper it, care for it, and love it, we cannot hold on to its beauty.

We pamper our bodies, trying to hold on to youth. But no matter what we do, youth smugly escapes our tight grip. The book of James compares our life to a vapor: "For what is your life? It is even a vapour, that appeareth for a little time, and then vanisheth away" (James 4:14 KJV). A vapor is impossible to grasp; it slips right through our fingers.

That's why the Lord taught us not to worry about tomorrow or to say, "Next year I will go here, do this and that" (see James 4:13). We are not promised tomorrow. All we have is the here and now. So don't say, "On my friend's next birthday I'm going to really show her how much I appreciate her." Your friend may not be here on her next birthday. Go tell her now! What's wrong with exuberantly celebrating a forty-seventh wedding anniversary instead of waiting for the fiftieth? Why put off the big party until age forty? Celebrate thirty-nine!

Today is the flower of our lives. Its radiant, velvet petals shimmer in the light of life that God has granted. Bloom now! Let the beauty of his grace shout out to the world, "I'm loved! I'm free! I'm alive!" Tomorrow may be too late.

❧

Lord, thank you for today. I want to live now, this moment. I will open my eyes and seek to know what you are doing in and around me on this day you have given me.

THURSDAY

Is Your Head in the Clouds?

carpe diem

*Whoever watches the wind will not plant; whoever looks at the clouds
will not reap.*—Ecclesiastes 11:4

If you're waiting for perfect conditions before you do anything, you
will never do anything! Or maybe you're honest enough to admit the
truth. You're not really waiting for the perfect time or the perfect circumstances. You're daydreaming. Wasting time.

Sometimes the work of God can seem mundane and unproductive.
We lose our commitment; our enthusiasm fades, especially when people
ask, "Why even bother preaching [or witnessing or praying]? People get
saved, but then they don't walk the Christian walk. What's the use?"

In those moments we must not let our attention wander. We must
not fall into periods of reverie where we do nothing but watch the wind
and study the clouds. For, as the wise man said, "As you do not know the
path of the wind, or how the body is formed in a mother's womb, so you
cannot understand the work of God, the Maker of all things. Sow your
seed in the morning, and at evening let not your hands be idle, for you
do not know which will succeed, whether this or that, or whether both
will do equally well" (Eccles. 11:5–6).

We cannot understand the ways of God, at least not while we're here
on earth. But while we are working in God's field, we will have greater
peace if we remember that our job is to sow the seed while God is the one
who causes it to grow (see 1 Cor. 3:7). Sow your energy into your job. Sow
yourself into your children. Sow wherever the path leads you. The law of
the harvest says that some of those seeds are going to fall on good ground
and bring a great harvest. God knows which ones. He's working in them.
Don't be frustrated about the others. Keep your eye on the path, not on the
clouds and the wind. Look to Jesus and start planting!

∞

Lord, help me to rid my life of idle daydreaming and procrastination. I confess
that sometimes I wait for perfect conditions instead of following you in obedience. I believe your Word that declares, "He who continually goes forth
weeping, bearing seed for sowing, shall doubtless come again with rejoicing,
bringing his sheaves with him" (Ps. 126:6 NKJV).

Is It Time to Laugh or Cry...
or Neither?

carpe diem

*A time to cry and a time to laugh. A time to grieve and a time
to dance.*—Ecclesiastes 3:4 LB

There is a time for every emotion. Sooner or later we're all probably
going to experience every feeling that can be felt. Why, exactly, do our
feelings change? Who can predict how any of us are going to feel on a particular day?

Sometimes we try to have a feeling we enjoyed at another time—a
feeling of intimacy or affection or enthusiasm, perhaps—and we just can't
quite recapture it. The truth is, the harder we try to get a particular feeling, the more it seems to escape us. It's like chasing the wind. And the
wind is unpredictable. "The wind blows where it wishes, and you hear the
sound of it, but cannot tell where it comes from and where it goes" (John
3:8 NKJV).

Have you ever felt down and didn't know why? King David must have
wondered the same thing when he wrote, "Why am I discouraged? Why
so sad? I will put my hope in God! I will praise him again—my Savior and
my God!" (Ps. 43:5 NLT).

David knew the solution. He exerted his will to do the right thing.
He told himself, *Even when you don't feel like it, do the right thing anyway!*

David willed himself to "put [his] hope in God...[and] praise him
again." For your situation, you might need to will yourself to love or to
care or to attack a job eagerly. David's advice was: Just do the right thing,
and the time will come when you'll feel like dancing again. Don't spend
your time chasing the wind. Chase after God's will for your life instead!

∞

Lord, I will praise you with my whole heart. Not because of the feelings there
but because you will remain faithful when I am faithless, when there are no
feelings. I will myself to love and cherish those you have placed in my life
because you love me.

carpe diem

Weekend Reflections

Tomorrow is fleeting and the past is out of reach. Today is a fresh gift from God. The psalmic writer triumphantly declared, "This is the day the Lord has made; let us rejoice and be glad in it" (Ps. 118:24). Each day brings new opportunities, and each day holds the promise of mended relationships, deeds of kindness, or thoughtful expressions of love. Don't let this day go by without seizing the opportunity to touch someone's life for good or deepen your relationship with your Creator.

1. What have you always dreamed of being or doing? What can you do today to take a first step toward making that dream a reality?

_____

_____

_____

_____

_____

2. Is there something you have been refusing to do or give up or act on? What step of obedience can you take today?

_____

_____

_____

_____

3. Do you have your head in the clouds? Are you daydreaming instead of sowing seeds of love, kindness, and the Good News of Jesus? Where can you sow God's seed today?

_____

_____

_____

_____

The Way to Abundant Life

His divine power has given us everything we need for life and godliness
through our knowledge of him who called us by his own glory
and goodness.—2 Peter 1:3

In the business world, often it is whom you know more than what you know that brings success. Relationships become all-important, and we work hard to maintain a network of friends and colleagues we can turn to in time of need. That's the real motivation for relationships in the workplace: *need.*

In contrast, God called us into relationship with himself for no other reason except that he loves us. He doesn't value us because of our own goodness but simply because of his loving kindness. And he gives us everything we need to maintain this relationship with him as well as the ability to live a life full of true joy and abiding happiness.

We achieve this fulfilling life as a result of our personal knowledge of God—not so that we can sit and relish his gifts, but to escape the prison of carnal vices and so that we can be "partakers of [his] divine nature" (2 Pet. 1:4 KJV) and expressions of a loving God to his creation.

Only by knowing God can we be transported out of the dungeon of hopelessness, out of spiritual poverty, and into the abounding riches of his glory. There, in his riches—in relationship with him—we find the essentials for an exhilarating life as well as the power to be free to grow into his likeness.

∞

Father, you have called us from darkness to life—a life of godliness. I know that true godliness comes from a right relationship with you. From that I find everything I need to live a godly and abundant life.

If You Remain in Me

If anyone does not remain in me, he is like a branch that is thrown away and withers; such branches are picked up, thrown into the fire and burned.—John 15:6

To remain in Christ as a permanent state is a challenge, even for the most devoted believers. To be in the world yet not a part of it is a constant struggle. Yet to survive, our reliance on him must become perpetual, not conditional. We must learn to abide in him in times of strength as well as in times of need.

The abundant life we have as believers doesn't come from something outside of us but from Christ's presence within us. He remains in us, and we abide in him, finding there the very source of our existence. While the external demonstrations of Christianity—the fellowship with believers, the blessing by the laying on of hands, and the receiving of exhortation— can bring temporary life, the enduring, abundant life that comes from within us is a result of our remaining in Christ.

He is the vine; we are the branches. Just as branches get their sustenance from the vine, so we draw sustenance from Christ. The branch separated from the vine withers, becomes brittle, and is easily destroyed. Those who do not remain connected to Christ become "brittle" in their spirits. They are susceptible to the enemy's assault, and they burn easily. Those who remain in the vine, however, are full of the sweetness of its sap, the lifeblood that gives them strength to withstand hard times. They cannot be burned, for they are alive with the love of God and have become a channel of this love to others.

Who is the source of your life? When you are in despair, who do you draw your strength from? Get connected to the Vine. Realize Christ in you. He is the source of powerful, abundant life.

❧

Lord, I thank you for giving me all things that pertain to life and godliness. Teach me to remain in you wherever I am, wherever I go, always keeping you as my real source of life.

Knowledge Is Power

I want to know Christ and the power of his resurrection and the fellowship of sharing in his sufferings, becoming like him in his death.—Philippians 3:10

Why can one church sing a song of worship and generate a great sense of the glory of God while another congregation sings the same song and there is only hollowness? It's not just a matter of whether the orchestra and the singers are on key (though that can certainly enhance the worship experience!); it's a matter of knowledge. Not a book knowledge but the knowledge that Paul referred to when he said, "I know whom I have believed."

One church *believes* what it is singing while the other actually *knows the Lord* and sings about that experience. To realize the power of God in our lives and in our churches we must move from believing to knowing. Knowing whom you are singing about and praying to puts fire in your worship and passion in your prayer.

Think of the difference of these two statements: I believe in Jesus. I know Jesus.

I am not trivializing the power of the first statement, for certainly that is the foundation of our relationship with God. But to grow in knowledge is to build on the foundation of faith.

In this sense, knowledge *is* power. Not self-power but power through Christ.

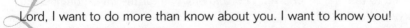

Lord, I want to do more than know about you. I want to know you!

At the Table with God

*And the third day there was a marriage in Cana of Galilee; and the mother of Jesus was there: And both Jesus was called, and his disciples, to the marriage.—*John 2:1–2 KJV

Your close friend is getting married. You make the trip from Jerusalem to the village of Cana. Friends and family you have not seen for some time are there for the celebration. There is joy, laughter, and plenty of food, but the wine runs out.

A friend of the family, Mary, is there along with her son. You have not met, but you have heard that he is quite knowledgeable, a man of understanding. Mary whispers something to him. The stranger speaks softly to his mother then stands alone, silently meditating as if trying to decide what to do. Then he turns to you and asks you to fill six of the stone water pots with water. It's a strange request, but you do it. Now he asks you to take a cup of it to your cousin, who's serving as emcee at the party. He drinks it and says, "It's the best wine I've ever tasted!"

Mary's son is smiling. He is seated off to the side with a few of his friends. You must find out more about this man! You walk over, introduce yourself, sit down, and look into a kind face with eyes that peer into the depths of your soul. His undivided attention is focused on *you.* I'm not wanting, here, to address the controversy of wine versus grape juice but to present the man Christ Jesus. Though he was fully God, he was a man who smiled, rejoiced, conversed, and celebrated life. And this same man Jesus has invited you to come sit beside him at his table. He smiles at you and pulls out a chair beside him. Will you come and sit down by him, talk with him, listen to him—or will you simply watch from afar?

∞

Oh Jesus, I want to sit at the table with you! I want to look into your eyes, hear your voice, and know you as my Lord and as my friend. I hear you saying, "Come to me," and I answer, "Lord, thank you for the invitation! Behold your servant. I am here!"

Life Infinity

And this is life eternal, that they might know thee the only true God,
and Jesus Christ, whom thou hast sent.
—John 17:3 KJV

The concept of the eternal is beyond my comprehension most of the time. I regularly try to stretch my mental faculties to understand that the life of the soul surpasses the life of the body, but words like *infinity, forever,* and *eternity* defy my rational course of reasoning.

One illustration describes eternity like this: "If a bird flew around the world once a year and brushed its wing against the top of the tallest mountain, when the mountain has become level ground, eternity has just begun."

Jesus said eternal life is found in knowing the "only true God, and Jesus Christ." No one else can bring us this kind of rich reward. To know him—not just to know *about* him—is our highest aim as Christians. Certainly, knowing about him is a worthy goal, but it is not life eternal.

Saint Augustine said, "Thou hast made us for thyself, O Lord, and our hearts are restless until they find their rest in thee." That's why real life does not begin for us until we know God by experience and not just by "head knowledge."

God has offered us the way out of this limiting and confining rat race. To know God through Jesus Christ is to know the way out! In him is life infinity (see John 1:4).

∞

Lord Jesus, I don't want to just exist; I want to live by knowing you in experience, in fellowship, and in friendship—not just in theology. You have set eternity in my heart. Though I cannot fathom it, I know it is real, and I want to experience it through intimacy with you.

Weekend Reflections

The kingdom of God has many principles, from the principle of sowing and reaping to the principle of confession and forgiveness. While all of God's principles and laws are important, some are more consequential.

While God wants us to be successful and to supply our needs, his higher purpose is to bring us into a more intimate relationship with him. That why "the first and greatest commandment" is "Love the Lord your God with all your heart and with all your soul and with all your mind" (Matt. 22:37–38). God is committed to loving us regardless of our success, our popularity, or our spiritual achievements.

1. God's first priority for you—above your ministry success, your reputation, and your prosperity—is your relationship with him. How should this affect your priorities?

   _____

   _____

   _____

2. Consider what it takes to really get to know someone. How does this relate to your getting to know God?

   _____

   _____

   _____

   _____

3. God loves all the world, but Jesus did have an inner circle of friends. Why did Jesus reveal more to them than he did to the rest?

   _____

   _____

   _____

   _____

The Aroma of Christ

*Thanks be to God, who…through us spreads everywhere the fragrance
of the knowledge of him. For we are to God the aroma of Christ
among those who are being saved and those who are perishing.*
—2 Corinthians 2:14–15

Have you noticed that when you are around people with a heavy, negative spirit their pessimism seems to cling to you after they are gone, while others seem to brighten your day and deposit some of their zest for living into your life? I find it difficult to understand how people can be such fountains of gloom and doom—and then wonder why no one wants to be around them.

God wants to anoint us with the oil of gladness and the "fragrance of the knowledge of him" so that everything and everyone we encounter is blessed by the smooth touch of the Holy Spirit. Everywhere we go, we as believers should be leaving with others the fragrance of Christ, the residue of the oil of his Spirit.

The words we say should minister grace and excellence, not doubt and depravity. We should edify, or build up, the hearer. God's Word tells us, "Let no corrupt communication proceed out of your mouth, but that which is good to the use of edifying, that it may minister grace unto the hearers" (Eph. 4:29 KJV). Our words, our actions, should leave behind a fragrant spiritual reminder of the Rose of Sharon.

What will you leave with the ones whose lives you touch today? Are your family members, your coworkers, your fellow worshipers, or the strangers you meet going to be better people for having been with you today? Will you bless them with the fragrance of Christ, the grace you have been freely given?

Lord, I pray that the aroma of Christ will flow from me. Let the words of my mouth be as a pleasing fragrance to you so that I can minister grace and life to those around me.

conversation

The Blessing of Godly Counsel

*In every matter of wisdom and understanding about which the king
questioned [Daniel, Hananiah, Mishael and Azariah], he found them
ten times better than all the magicians and enchanters in his
whole kingdom.*—Daniel 1:19–20

It has been said that a woman often resolves problems through dialogue while a man resolves difficulties by retreat and thought. A woman often finds the answer to a problem by talking things out while a man may need to go for a drive or a walk alone to find a solution.

While both methods can achieve the desired results, depending on the circumstances, Scripture commends seeking good counsel from godly people (see Prov. 11:14). When a problem is consuming our thoughts it may be beneficial to confide in a trusted comrade and pore over the dilemma together. Godly men or women are plugged in to supernatural wisdom and insight. Avail yourself of their connection and wisdom.

When Jerusalem was besieged by Nebuchadnezzar, Daniel and his three friends were summoned to the Babylonian king's palace for three years of instruction in "the language and literature of the Babylonians" (Dan. 1:4). At the end of three years, the Bible says they were ten times wiser than the wise men of Babylon! The king retained them in his courts to advise him in his royal affairs.

You see, God's wisdom exceeds the wisdom of man. Though the Babylonian training certainly helped Daniel, he obviously received heavenly wisdom that was above and beyond his palace training.

How do you know if the wisdom you are getting is heavenly? Consider the words of James: "The wisdom that comes from heaven is first of all pure; then peace-loving, considerate, submissive, full of mercy and good fruit, impartial and sincere" (3:17).

Is the wisdom that's being shared with you full of mercy and peace? Is it submitted to Christ's Lordship? If it is, count yourself blessed.

∞

Father, I bless your name for your supernatural wisdom with which you have blessed your sons and daughters. As your Word instructs me to do, I ask you for wisdom (James 1:5). I choose to abandon my pride and seek out godly counsel when it is needed.

Ministering to the Heart

*For I wrote you out of great distress and anguish of heart and with
many tears, not to grieve you but to let you know the depth of my love
for you.*—2 Corinthians 2:4

The words with which we minister are meaningful only if our motive
is love. Without love our words are noise—nothing more. Whether we're
ministering to someone who has experienced some great loss, or teaching
a youth Bible class, or sharing the gospel, our motive must be love. If we
are not being effective, we must check our motive. What do you stand to
gain by your words? Are you speaking for your own gratification or for a
greater cause?

Truth spoken without love is noisy and bothersome. It is "as sounding brass, or a tinkling cymbal" (1 Cor. 13:1 KJV). No real ministry takes
place; there is no distinct message. Without love our message is cluttered
with the clamor of selfish ambition and personal desire. Truth spoken in
love, however, is like "apples of gold in settings of silver" (Prov. 25:11). It
goes straight to the heart because the message is clear, unencumbered with
the weight of avarice or self-indulgence.

You may say, "I pray, I fast, and I study, but nothing is happening."
But do you love? Is it religion or is it relationship you seek? Is compassion
at the core of your service? Love is the missing ingredient. As we cultivate
our intimacy with Jesus, his love will be the source of our ministry. It will
be the catalyst for the words we speak and the gospel we must share.

⸎

Lord, send your Spirit to check my motives, my ambitions. Let it be love that
moves me to speak, to minister, to serve. When I speak, let it be to minister
grace to the hearer, hope to the hopeless, life to the helpless. And in all
things, may Christ be exalted and magnified.

conversation

Beautiful Feet?

_How beautiful upon the mountains are the feet of him that bringeth
good tidings, that publisheth peace; that bringeth good tidings of good,
that publisheth salvation; that saith unto Zion,
Thy God reigneth!_—Isaiah 52:7 KJV

Sister Hawks would often stop me in the aisle of the sanctuary and quiz me briefly about my family. Then she would share with me how yet again God had come through and supplied her needs in the nick of time. "Let me tell you how God answered my prayer," she would begin.

Sometimes I would get lost in the details of her story, but I always carried away from our encounter some good news about the faithfulness of God. I think of Sister Hawks when I read the beautiful passage from Isaiah: "How beautiful on the mountains are the feet…"

I must admit that I have seen very few "beautiful feet" in my lifetime. I mean, why didn't Isaiah talk about a beautiful mouth or beautiful hands! But beautiful feet? Especially feet that cross a mountain to carry a message. I picture rugged, callused, blistered, and swollen feet that ache at the end of the journey. Why did Isaiah describe them as beautiful?

Perhaps he knew that when your soul is starved for good news and God sends his messenger swiftly to you, every part of that letter carrier seems beautiful to you, even his or her feet!

Sister Hawks's feet were certainly not beautiful. She struggled with diabetes and poor circulation, so her ankles were usually swollen and her toes were discolored. But in heaven's eyes they were as beautiful as the message of God's faithfulness that she brought to me.

∞

Father, with your help I will be one who brings good news, one who proclaims, "God reigns!"

Guard Your Well

Above all else, guard your heart, for it is the wellspring of life.
—Proverbs 4:23

Inside each one of us is a well from which we draw our life, our conversation, our hopes, and our dreams. If we would speak life-giving words, we must allow life-giving words to fill our hearts. If we want to nourish our dreams and live in hope, we must fill our well with water from above. We cannot draw from what is not there.

We have all been surprised from time to time when in frustration or anger we speak words that do not bring life but hurt feelings or carnality. Upon examining our lifestyle, we may find that we have been feeding on similar conversation. Or there may be a deeper cause—a root of fear or insecurity that becomes a breeding ground for low self-esteem and negative thoughts. Either way, the words come from the "overflow of the heart."

We must stand guard at the door of our heart. We must protect what goes into our well. Inside is a wealth of good or evil. "A good man's speech reveals the rich treasures within him" (Matt. 12.35 LB). In the world of finances, most treasure increases in value over time. This is why we must deal with evil treasure swiftly, removing what is impure and holding on to what is lovely, pure, just, and honest.

∞

Father, I lift up to you all that is impure and unholy in me. Send the fire of your Holy Spirit to search my well and burn out the impurities until all that remains are the golden riches of your kingdom living and working in me.

conversation

Weekend Reflections

Singer Karen Carpenter died of heart failure at age thirty-two after years of self-abuse from the eating disorder anorexia nervosa. What brought on Karen's fatal obsession with her weight? Three little words. It seems a music reviewer had once dubbed her "Richard's chubby sister." "The tongue has the power of life and death," the proverbs tell us (18:21). What message are you sharing when you speak?

1. Why is it important to choose our words carefully? (See Matt. 12:36–37.)

_____

_____

_____

_____

_____

2. Words bring life or destruction. Which way do your words balance out?

_____

_____

_____

_____

_____

3. Speak a word of praise or say something positive to everyone you meet today and the note the way your comment impacts them.

_____

_____

_____

_____

_____

Out of the Gate and Winning!

This is the day the Lord has made; let us rejoice and be glad in it.
—Psalm 118:24

Our attitudes in beginning the day have a great deal to do with how things will go for us later that afternoon and evening. In the same way, how we live today—-our attitudes and sense of purpose—will help determine our tomorrows.

As a boy, David exhibited a winning attitude when he faced Goliath. While the armies of Israel cowered in the shadows, David stepped out boldly and said, "The Lord who delivered me from the paw of the lion and the paw of the bear will deliver me from the hand of this Philistine" (1 Sam. 17:37). His experiences as a young shepherd boy gave him the courage he needed to face Goliath. This same confident attitude caused the apostle Paul to say, "Forgetting what is behind and straining toward what is ahead, I press on toward the goal to *win*" (Phil. 3:13–14, emphasis added). He did not set out to lose, but to win! His attitude of confidence in Christ carried him forward.

Do whatever it takes to start your day with the right attitude. Get up on the right side of the bed. Start out on the right foot. Your determination to get started right will go a long way toward making the rest of your day flow smoothly. And just as you start each day with a winning attitude, start your future—right here, right now—with a confident attitude and a sense of God's purpose for your life. Each confident *today* will lead toward a future of confident *tomorrows*.

∞

Lord, thank you for renewed courage to face the day. I will be successful today because you empower me to triumph over all discouragement. I have utmost confidence in your ability that is alive in me. I am a winner because of you.

attitude

Living in the Light
of the Long Tomorrow

*But do not forget this one thing, dear friends: With the Lord a day is
like a thousand years, and a thousand years are like a day.*
—2 Peter 3:8

"When will it be tomorrow?" the little boy asked.

"Well, tomorrow is the day after today," his mother replied.

"When tomorrow comes, will it still be tomorrow?"

"No. When tomorrow comes, it will be today, and the day after that
will be tomorrow."

"I guess it will never be tomorrow, will it?"

Like this little boy, many people seem to have difficulty seeing beyond
today. They "live today like there is no tomorrow." I think it would be
wiser to do as A.W. Tozer advised, "We would do well to think of the long
tomorrow."

What would our todays be like if we lived them all in the light of the
eternity—that long tomorrow Tozer mentioned? If we made every decision today based on the weight of eternity, what would our lives look like
right now? How would we spend our hours and our money? Would our
prized possessions still hold their same attraction?

If you live to be eighty, you will have lived 29,200 days. If you're
thirty-five now, you only have 16,425 days left. Then the long tomorrow
begins. Where will *you* spend forever? The little boy decided that tomorrow never comes, but if you think about it, tomorrow has already begun.

∞

Father, I pray as your servant Moses did, "Teach us to number our days, that
we may gain a heart of wisdom" (Ps. 90:12 NKJV).

Lift Up Your Voice

When he came near the place where the road goes down the Mount of Olives, the whole crowd of disciples began joyfully to praise God in loud voices for all the miracles they had seen.—Luke 19:37

What kind of passion do you put into your prayers? Do you enthusiastically praise God for the blessings of your life? Or do you wait until the last few minutes of the day, mumble a few words from the Lord's Prayer, then fall into bed?

Maybe a good way to improve our prayer time is to raise our voices and speak our thoughts out loud. The Gospel of Luke reports that when Jesus entered Jerusalem riding on a colt, the people joyfully praised God in "loud voices." So disturbing was this to the religious Pharisees that they told Jesus to rebuke them. But Jesus refused. "I tell you," he replied, "if they keep quiet, the stones will cry out" (Luke 19:40).

When John received a vision of the angels worshiping around the throne, he described them as singing in a loud voice (see Rev. 5:11–12). In fact, there are more than a dozen references to loud voices in John's vision—and only one reference to silence.

Prayers and praise spoken aloud reveal our passion and help us heed "the first and greatest commandment" to love God with all of our hearts, minds, and souls (see Matt. 22:37–38). There is certainly a time when we should be quiet in solemn worship. But there is also a time when it's appropriate to lift up our voices to God in prayer and worship.

So go ahead. Raise your voice to God. Show your passion for God. Join the worshiper David and sing, "Awake, my soul! Awake, harp and lyre! I will awaken the dawn" (Ps. 57:8).

∞

Lord, I will lift my voice in praise to you. I love to call on your name. I love to worship you. With my whole heart I will bless your name.

attitude

God Sent You a Gift Today

Therefore God again set a certain day, calling it Today.
—Hebrews 4:7

Today I saw a friend I had not seen in a long time. After a brief greeting, he had to go his way, and I had to go mine. Later, I reflected on our friendship, on laughs we had shared and even tears we had cried together—all the stuff life is made of. I thought, *We really need to get together soon. It's been too long since we really got to visit.* But time marches on, and the visit never occurs.

I have a closet I've been wanting to clean out for years. I'll bet you have one too—a closet filled with the remnants of good intentions. Maybe you have a stationary bike in there along with a dusty tennis racket, a rusty fishing reel, and a book you never read. There may be brochures for the cruise you never took, postcards you never mailed, and the baseball mitt you bought so you and your kids could play catch. We buy such things with high hopes and vivid dreams. But we wait too long for the circumstances to be just right to carry out our plans. We save the good dishes for special occasions, the skates for a day when the weather is perfect, the Bible study project for a time when we aren't quite so busy. We save our good intentions, store them away in a closet of our house or a corner of our minds, and as a result, words go unsaid, prayers go unprayed, and loved ones pass through our lives not knowing how we feel about them.

God has given us this moment to live, to breathe, to love. We are not promised tomorrow, and we can't hold to yesterday. What God offers us is the here and now. As a wise man once said, "Yesterday is history, tomorrow is a mystery, but today is a gift. That's why it's called the present."

❦

Father, "order my steps in thy word" (Ps. 119:133 KJV). Open my eyes to see the things that are most important. Teach me to number my days. Thank you for this day you have given me. I choose to rejoice and be glad in it.

Your Today Impacts Your Tomorrow

Go to the ant, you lazybones; consider its ways, and be wise. Without having any chief or officer or ruler, it prepares its food in summer, and gathers its sustenance in harvest.—Proverbs 6:6–8 NRSV

At one time or another, we've all thought, *I just don't feel like praying. I don't feel like reading the Bible.* When such feelings occur, we're caught in a struggle between the physical and the spiritual. We know what we should do, but somehow we just can't muster the energy or enthusiasm to do it.

What we do in spite of such feelings shows our maturity. Think of the child who says, "I don't feel like going to school today." Let's face it. If most of us had gone to school only when we felt like it, the teacher would have never learned our names! Part of growing up is learning that we will be rewarded later for doing today what we don't really feel like doing. We learn that if we go to school today, we can be more selective in our vocational pursuit later. We learn that if we skip football practice today, we pay a price on game day.

The same is true when it comes to prayer and praise. Even when you don't feel like it, go for it! Lay aside the temporary feelings and fix your eyes on the goal. Keep on praying. Keep on studying God's Word. The reward will come. As Charles Swindoll wrote in his book *Strengthening Your Grip,* "Even though yesterday's actions are irreversible, tomorrow's are not. We can dramatically affect our future by the decisions we make today."

∞

Lord Jesus, I choose to do your will regardless of how I feel. I know the truth, "The just shall live by his faith" (Hab. 2:4 KJV). I will not live by how I feel but by my faith. I am not a captive to my emotions; you have freed me to do your will, oh God.

attitude

Weekend Reflections

"We cannot change the past....We cannot change the fact that people will act in a certain way. We cannot change the inevitable. The only thing we can do is play on the string we have, and that is our attitude.... I am convinced that life is 10 percent what happens to me and 90 percent how I react to it" (Charles Swindoll, *Strengthening Your Grip*). On what "string" are you playing the music of your life? How are you reacting to the things that happen to you? Attitude makes a difference!

1. Describe two incidents that happened in the last week where attitude had a great impact on your relationship with someone.

   _____

   _____

   _____

   _____

2. Considering the words of A.W. Tozer, "We would do well to think of the long tomorrow," what things will you do differently today? How can your attitude affect the conflicts and decisions you are facing?

   _____

   _____

   _____

   _____

3. Zig Ziglar says that the first greeting you have in the morning is the most important one of the day. What can *you* do to start the day with a better attitude—and help others to do the same?

   _____

   _____

   _____

The Wings of the Wind

The wind blows wherever it pleases. You hear its sound, but you cannot tell where it comes from or where it is going. So it is with everyone born of the Spirit.—John 3:8

Who knows how the wind will blow today? Weather experts take a look at satellite images and atmospheric data and give their educated predictions, but at any time the wind may shift directions unexpectedly. It "blows wherever it pleases." So it is with the Spirit.

The apostle Paul rode the wind of the Holy Spirit as it initiated his first missionary journey and directed him along the way, moving him constantly forward. When the change in the wind came, Paul changed with it. Scripture says, "They tried to enter Bithynia, but the Spirit of Jesus would not allow them to" (Acts 16:7).

God is sovereign. He alone decides where and when the Spirit will blow. We cannot control the wind of the Spirit, but we can fly on his wings, soaring as the Spirit empowers us.

God sets the course of the wind of the Spirit. We can't change his direction or slow it down, and we shouldn't try to. Instead, our responsibility is to raise our sails, batten down the hatches if we must, and prepare ourselves for the ride of our lives as we carry God's Word to the world.

∞

Come, Holy Spirit. I give you full authority in my life to lead, direct, and empower me as you will. Oh, that I may be sensitive to your every bidding!

Are You a Kindler?

Do not put out the Spirit's fire.—1 Thessalonians 5:19

It was John the Baptist who said Jesus would baptize us with the Holy Spirit and with fire. And even today, nearly two thousand years later, God's church should be a church on fire. But too many religious people are like buckets of water. Probably without meaning to, they threaten to put out the fire before it can spread.

God wants his fire to burn in our hearts, cleansing and purging us of everything that is not like Christ and igniting a fire in those around us. We can't do that unless we let his truth blaze within us. As Phillip Brooks said, "Nothing but the fire kindles fire."

I was a firsthand witness to this phenomenon from a physical standpoint when I was a child. I ran an errand for Mom on my bicycle and was returning home when an electric line about three hundred yards away from me suddenly snapped loose from the pole and began flailing about wildly. Sparks from the broken wire ignited some dry brush, which then ignited some nearby pine trees that were loaded with sticky sap. I watched in disbelief as one whole tree after another burst into flames from the bottom up and was completely consumed by flames in a matter of seconds. One tree, afire, kindled the next one.

As Christians we can either ignite God's fire in one another—or we can put it out. We are either fire kindlers or fire quenchers. We're either fanning the flames or we're dousing the live embers of those around us.

The apostle Paul would not have said, "Do not put out the Spirit's fire," if it were not possible to do. You *can* quench the fire, or you can stir it up. Our goal should be "to fan into flame the gift of God" (2 Tim. 1:6).

∞

Lord, I want to be one who keeps your fire burning in my heart and in the heart of everyone I know. Forgive me for the times I have discouraged others in their passion for you.

By Him, Through Him, and in Him

For by him all things were created: things in heaven and on earth, visible and invisible, whether thrones or powers or rulers or authorities; all things were created by him and for him. He is before all things, and in him all things hold together.—Colossians 1:16–17

All that is good originated in God. He is the source of all that is beautiful, all that is wonderful. In creation we get a glimpse of the imagination and artistry of his being. The intricate design of a maple leaf, a snowflake, or a rose all reveal to us the spectacular originality of God.

As Christians, we see ourselves as channels of God's life and love. We set about doing his work with one hand in God's hand and the other free to minister to others. God's beauty and goodness continue to flow through us as long as we stay "plugged in" to the Source. "Every good and perfect gift is from above" (James 1:17). There is a danger, though, for those who minister, or for those who are creative. If we're not careful, we may come to believe we are ministering out of ourselves. Paul knew this danger. He described it when he wrote, "Not that we are competent in ourselves to claim anything for ourselves, but our competence comes from God" (2 Cor. 3:5). When we start believing we're "competent in ourselves," our focus turns toward the blessing and away from the Blesser. This path, if continually pursued, eventually inhibits the flow of creativity and life.

God has a way of pulling the rug out from under us when we begin to revel in the glory of our gifts, not because he desires to make fools of us, but because he wants to be our sufficiency. He wants us to always declare him as the Giver of Life. He wants us always to need him, to wholly trust and rely on his power within us that he may be glorified in our need. And he wants to flow through us to become a blessing to others.

∞

Father, I recognize my insufficiencies, my needs; I look to you for help. I know that everything I am comes from you. Forgive me for the times I have taken credit for what is solely you. I wholly and unreservedly ascribe to you all glory, all honor, and all praise.

213

Becoming Yes-People

And the Spirit and the bride say, Come. And let him that
heareth say, Come.—Revelation 22:17 KJV

A family, friendship, or church can be stifled by one person with a "no" attitude. This is the person who, when something new is introduced, quickly responds, "But we've never done it that way before!" or who immediately answers, "I can't," when asked to do something that might stretch him or her socially, physically, or spiritually.

While being a yes-man or yes-woman in the corporate world is viewed as a weakness, in the kingdom of God those with a willing attitude receive the greater blessing. The man or woman of God is one who is open to challenge, freshness, and vulnerability. This is the person who quickly steps forward to heed God's will and follow his calling.

There have always been the no-people standing ready to shoot down anything new. When Jesus longed to reveal himself to his own extended Jewish family, to demonstrate God's power among them for their own good, most of them shook their heads and argued, "No, he can't be the Messiah. Isn't that the son of the carpenter? Isn't he from Nazareth?" (see Matt. 13:54–56).

Ah, but look what happened to those who said yes. They got in on the best thing that ever happened to them—and to the whole world.

The Gospel of Jesus Christ has always been a *whosoever will* gospel. It's a message for the yes-people of the world. Though God has the power to show up whether or not he is welcome, he chooses to reveal himself to those who invite him in. He longs to flow in power and might throughout the earth, but he chooses to enter by standing at the door of our hearts and knocking.

What does the sign on your heart say—"Yes" or "No"? "Come, Lord Jesus" or "No vacancy"? "Welcome Holy Spirit" or "Don't rock the boat, God"?

∞

God, I choose to say yes. I want to participate in your kingdom purposes. I want to be a part of the greatest opportunity there is: to know you and join you in the field.

Are Your Heart Eyes Open?

I pray also that the eyes of your heart may be enlightened in order that you may know the hope to which he has called you, the riches of his glorious inheritance in the saints.—Ephesians 1:18

When you are trying to find something, how many times have you stood there looking right at it but unable to see it? The working of the Spirit is often like that. Sometimes God is trying to show us something, and the lesson is so obvious we can't see it. As the saying goes, We can't see the forest for the trees! Many times we're blinded by our own personal agendas or our preconceived ideas. We're looking for one thing while God is doing another. Or we're misinterpreting the signs all around us.

When we're overlooking the obvious, it may be that we're looking for spiritual things that the carnal mind simply cannot comprehend. This is why God gave us *heart eyes,* the ability to sense what the natural eyes can't see. Paul explained this ability when he wrote, " 'No eye has seen, no ear has heard, no mind has conceived what God has prepared for those who love him'—*but God has revealed it to us by his Spirit.* The Spirit searches all things, even the deep things of God" (1 Cor. 2:9–10, emphasis added).

The psalmist asked God to "open my eyes that I might see wonderful things in your law" (Ps. 119:18). We, too, must ask God to open not only our physical eyes but our heart eyes so that we are aware of all the blessings and lessons he has for us.

∽

Lord, give me the eyes of the Spirit to walk circumspectly. Don't let me overlook the obvious while searching for some hidden meaning.

Weekend Reflections

The Bible reminds us, "As he is, so are we in this world" (1 John 4:17 KJV). The Holy Spirit gives us the power to live as Christ in this world. We must rely on the Holy Spirit to live holy. Andrew Murray made this principle clear when he said, "A man cannot live one hour of a godly life unless by the power of the Holy Spirit. He may live a proper, consistent life, an irreproachable life, a life of virtue and diligent service. But to live a life acceptable to God in the enjoyment of God's salvation and God's love, to live and walk in the power of the new life—he cannot do it unless he is guided by the Holy Spirit every day and hour" (*Absolute Surrender*).

1. The Holy Spirit guides us into all truth (see John 16:13). How is *guiding* different from *leading?*

_____

_____

_____

_____

2. It is the Spirit of God who reveals the thoughts of God (see 1 Cor. 2:9–11). Are you listening to your own mind (natural reasoning) or to the Spirit? How does listening to the Spirit change your behavior and thoughts?

_____

_____

_____

_____

3. Who is the Holy Spirit telling you to pray for this week?

_____

_____

_____

_____

Where There's a Will, There's a Way

The one who calls you is faithful and he will do it.
—1 Thessalonians 5:24

Sometimes as believers we find ourselves facing a new challenge we feel unprepared for. As God opens the door for a new assignment, we hesitate to abandon the security we have grown accustomed to in order to reach for the unknown. However, God's perfect will for us is always the safest, securest place to be. When we disobey him, we distance ourselves from the protection of his keeping. When we are not listening to his voice and obeying his will for us, we are setting ourselves up for the enemy's assault.

For every challenge we face that is truly God-directed, there will be sufficient strength to accomplish the goal. God will not thrust us into some responsibility without adequately preparing us for the work he sets before us. God makes provision for his purpose; he has the best training school imaginable.

Consider how God prepared Moses for the tasks ahead of him by dropping him in the house of Pharaoh, where he received the most elite teaching of his day. Or think of Paul, who studied under the capable teaching of Gamaliel. Neither man knew he was being prepared for a specific calling and purpose that would be presented to him at a later time. But when God laid out the challenge before these men, their training for the work became obvious.

Is God revealing some new opportunity to you? Do you fear what you have never tried? Don't hesitate! He has equipped you for this moment.

∞

Lord, give me courage to meet the challenges you have set before me and confidence to know that you have prepared me for such a time as this. I choose to lean on your strength and your power to accomplish great things for your kingdom's sake.

TUESDAY

I Am Not Who I Was

I tell you the truth, unless a kernel of wheat falls to the ground and dies, it remains only a single seed. But if it dies, it produces many seeds.—John 12:24

The simple truth of being born again can be summed up like this: We die to who we are and rise from death to live as new creations through faith in the power of Jesus Christ. We are not reformed; we are reborn. We lose our old identities and find new ones in Christ Jesus.

The new creatures we become are nothing like our old selves. Our old natures were the seeds, the shells, that died in the ground so that our new creations could spring to life. Seeds do not have the same form as the plant; the acorn is not the oak tree. The seed looks nothing like the tree. But when it is planted in the ground and dies, up springs a mighty, living thing that bears no resemblance to the seed!

In the same way, we, as new creations in Christ, do not resemble our old natures. Our faith does not depend on what we had to give Christ, which really was nothing. All he wanted from us was our willingness to die to who we were. Now we "live by faith in the Son of God" (Gal. 2:20). "In Him we live and move and have our being" (Acts 17:28). We live not in the seed that was but as a new creation that exists by the resurrection power of Jesus Christ.

Don't be bound by who you were. That old creature has no relevance to the new creation you are now. That was the seed that died so the new creature could spring to life. You are a new person with a proud heritage and a rich inheritance!

❦

Father, thank you that I am not who I was. You have made me a brand-new being. Let your Holy Spirit bring me into a greater revelation of what happened when I was born again. I have faith in your great ability to cause me to live as a new creation.

Who Is That Standing with You?

If God is for us, who can be against us?
—Romans 8:31

Have you ever stood alone? Have you ever faced something that terrified you when you had no choice but to stand there and take it?

I recall one such incident: I was about twelve years old. With two other boys from my Sunday school class, I was out on a Friday evening going from door to door in the country neighborhood where my family was living at the time. We were handing out flyers advertising our church's upcoming revival services. At one house we hopped out of the car, walked to the door, rang the bell, and waited. Suddenly, we heard the unwelcome sound of the owner's dog, who obviously felt we were trespassing on his turf. As the dog came tearing around the corner of the house, my two buddies bolted back to the car. When I realized I had been deserted, I, too, made a run for it, but being the last one back to the car (and the closest one to the dog), I was the one who fell victim to the attacker. The dog promptly took a nip at my backside. Thankfully, it was not a severe wound. The biggest injury was to my pride for having been deserted.

If we live long enough, we're going to have to face a mean dog or two, an attack of some kind. And much to our dismay, our friends may leave us stranded to face the terror alone. Oh, sure, they tell us *now* that they will back us up all the way, but when the heat is turned on—when that beast comes roaring around the corner to rip a piece out of us—we may find ourselves standing there all alone to face the attack. In those times, we must pray for the courage to never back down from doing what we know is right.

When we are doing the right thing, there is One who stands beside us—Someone human eyes can't see. My friend, if God is standing with you, that's the only One you need. When you seek first to obey, you are joining hands with God. And God always wins.

∞

Oh God, if you are for me, who can be against me? Oh Lord, you are well aware of my life. You know the things I am facing today. Thank you for being my friend who sticks closer than any brother or sister.

No Mistaken Identity

What, then, shall we say in response to this? If God is for us,
who can be against us?—Romans 8:31

I was recently in a local hospital to pray a blessing over Zina, a dear woman in the church, before and after the arrival of her tenth child, a beautiful, healthy baby girl. Immediately after the baby's birth, the family and I all held her and took pictures as each of us remarked about her distinguishing characteristics—her strong lungs and her healthy appetite.

As Zina and her newest child cuddled for a few minutes before they whisked the baby away for her first bath, Zina lifted her arm and quizzed her husband. "Did you check the numbers on our bracelets?" she asked. "Are they all the same?"

She was referring to the hospital ID bracelets that match the mothers and their babies. Zina's husband made one more security check. "Yes, honey," he replied. He then told me about the wonderful security system the hospital used. If someone tried to get on the elevator with the baby, the elevator doors wouldn't shut, he said.

As I walked out the doors of the hospital, I was reminded of the words of our heavenly Father: "Can a mother forget the baby at her breast and have no compassion on the child she has borne? Though she may forget, I will not forget you!" (Isa. 49:15). You see, God has his own security number system. He has numbered the hairs on your head! (see Matt. 10:30). There's no mistaken identity in heaven.

God will never forget us. He knows our names...and our numbers. Like the psalmist, we can take great comfort in such a thought: "How precious to me are your thoughts, O God! How vast is the sum of them! Were I to count them, they would outnumber the grains of sand. When I awake, I am still with you" (Ps. 139:17–18).

∞

"How precious to me are your thoughts, O God! How vast is the sum of them! Were I to count them, they would outnumber the grains of sand. When I awake, I am still with you" (Ps. 139:17–18).

The Life of Ease

*The Lord confides in those who fear him; he makes his covenant
known to them.*—Psalm 25:14

What do you fear? Failure? The future? Normally, it is the unknown that conjures up the most fear. We say, "If I could only know the outcome, I wouldn't worry."

Did you know there is a bypass around this blockade of fear or worry? It is a covenant relationship with our heavenly Father. It is wholly trusting and leaning on the God we worship with reverence and awe. In this kind of relationship, he teaches us to know his ways, which are higher than our ways and beyond human understanding.

As he confides these secrets in us, the covenant relationship develops, our eyes are enlightened, and our spiritual senses are finely tuned to see, to hear, and to know. Writing to the Ephesian church, the apostle Paul prayed "that the eyes of your heart may be enlightened in order that you may know the hope to which he has called you" (Eph. 1:18).

This concept of God's confiding in man is not new. Throughout history God looked for a man, a woman, even a child such as the boy Samuel, to speak his secrets to. It is part of his covenant. As we love God and show reverence for him, his ways begin to unfold before us. Soon we have exchanged fear and worry for confidence and trust. The psalmist wrote, "Who is the man who reverently fears and worships the Lord? Him shall He teach in the way that He should choose. He himself shall dwell at ease, and his offspring shall inherit the land" (25:12–13 AMPLIFIED). This doesn't sound like the life of fear and worry, does it!

Are you ready to trade your anguish and anxiety for peace of mind—for a mind that is at ease, resting confidently in the care of your Father? Place the Lord at the highest place of reverence in your life, enter into a covenant relationship with him, then listen as he shares his secrets and reveals his ways to you.

❦

Father, I confess that there are other things and people I have honored more than you. Help me to put everything in my life in proper prospective as I lift you to the highest point of reverence in my life. Let me stand in the position where you will confide in me and teach me your ways that are far above mine.

confidence

Weekend Reflections

It was 1947. Jackie Robinson, the African American in the major leagues, ran onto the field in Cincinnati. Jeers and ridicule bellowed from the stands. But when his team captain and friend Pee Wee Reese walked over and put his arm around him, the crowd grew silent. Suddenly, Jackie was no longer alone. Our confidence as believers is based on who's standing beside us. It isn't so much *self-confidence* as it is *God-confidence*.

1. What are you facing that causes you to be filled with dread? What would Christ say to you regarding this (see Heb. 13:6)?

_____

_____

_____

_____

_____

2. Timidity does not come from God (see 2 Tim. 1:7). Where does it come from?

_____

_____

_____

_____

3. Boldness comes when you fear God more than you fear man (see Prov. 29:25). Whom do you fear?

_____

_____

_____

_____

Peace in Prison

But while Joseph was there in the prison, the Lord was with him; he showed him kindness and granted him favor in the eyes of the prison warden.—Genesis 39:20–21

In prison, young Joseph had every reason to complain. Ever since his childhood dream foretelling that his brothers would someday bow down to him, his life had been one tragic event after another: from being sold as a slave by his brothers to being falsely accused by his boss's wife. Now, in prison, he surely had the opportunity to question what God had in mind for him. Yet Joseph remained faithful to God and fervent in his prayers.

There's something about godly men and women. They have a way of rising to the top no matter where they are. They may be hidden away from the public eye, but they are never out of God's sight.

God kept his hand on Joseph when the young man was locked away in prison. Before long he became a powerful official, and his brothers did, indeed, bow down to him, begging for mercy.

God never lost sight of another little shepherd boy who composed and played his songs out on the hills of Judea. No one suspected that this boy, David, would someday be king. But then no one suspected that the boy who worked in his father's carpenter shop was the Creator of the world around him.

The wonderful truth that arises in all of this is that God knows where we are—even when we land in a prison cell or an isolated pasture or a carpenter's shop along the way. His favor will rest upon us regardless of where we are as long as we are in his will, following his purposes. Our responsibility, then, is to be his godly representative in that prison house, that carpentry shop, that pasture. It is his desire that wherever we are we spread "the fragrance of the knowledge of him" (2 Cor. 2:14). We are to expect and enjoy the kindness, favor, and care of our heavenly Father, who sees us no matter where we are.

∞

Lord, you are all-knowing. Regardless of where I am, I do believe that you see me—that your eyes are ever on me. I thank you for your kindness, your favor, that you freely give.

TUESDAY

The Price of Character

But we also glory in tribulations, knowing that tribulation produces
perseverance: and perseverance, character.—Romans 5:3 NKJV

God does not entrust the riches of the kingdom to just anybody. We only receive responsibility according to the level of our character. Can he trust us? That is the question. Maturity is an absolute necessity.

Character is not formed without crisis. Every person will at some time encounter adversity. That's one of the facts of life—at least a little rain will come, and there's no umbrella big enough to shelter us from *all* of it. Character is built by the way we choose to respond to the hard times and crises.

Do you sometimes find yourself looking at the seemingly good life of others and saying, "Why not me, God? How come they seem to get all the blessing?" What you may not know is the crises they have endured, the storms they have encountered, that have brought them to that level. What trials have they faced that have caused their roots to sink deep into the true knowledge of God? How much wisdom have they gained in their pursuit of God? These are the questions that must be asked.

Jesus said those who "have not been faithful in the unrighteous mammon [money]" cannot be trusted with true spiritual riches (Luke 16:11 KJV). In other words, those who are not good stewards over what they have now, whether it is natural or spiritual, cannot be entrusted with more. Only those who show themselves faithful in the small things will find themselves "trusted with much" (16:10).

As character grows, so grows the capacity to serve. As our relationship with Christ grows, so grows our responsibility in his kingdom. As our ability to follow grows, so grows our ability to lead.

∞

Father, what can I learn from this crisis I am in? Help me to have a teachable spirit, one that says, "Yes, Lord!" I thank you for your faithfulness in my time of trouble. You hold me up, you preserve me, and you sustain me. And on the other side of the storm, I see a stronger child of God. Oh God, give me a heart that trusts you.

A Rich Welcome

And God will open wide the gates of heaven for you to enter into
the eternal kingdom of our Lord and Savior
Jesus Christ.—2 Peter 1:11 NLT

When traveling through airports, I enjoy observing the various emotions at play when travelers get off the plane. My favorite scenes feature travelers who begin craning their necks as they walk through the jetway, eagerly scanning the waiting crowd to see who is there to meet them. Children are usually the most unrestrained in showing their emotions. I love the way they run and leap into the open arms of a waiting (or arriving) parent or grandparent and allow themselves to be smothered with kisses for only a few seconds. Sweethearts, on the other hand, may linger for several moments, locked in an embrace that releases just enough to let them walk down the corridor.

I love going home for the holidays and walking through the doorway to find that Mom has the table set and the candles lit. Fresh loaves of pumpkin bread, still warm from the oven, are usually waiting on the counter. Warmth, love, smiles, hugs, and food welcome me; it's a reception anyone would look forward to.

It's wonderful to be welcomed. But even the warmest welcome here on earth cannot compare with the exuberant greeting the Lord himself will extend to us someday. For his faithful servants, God will open wide the pearly gates and say, "You have done well. Welcome to the joy of heaven!" (Matt. 25:21, my paraphrase).

The apostle Peter reminded us that this anticipated reception is why we should "be all the more eager to make [our] calling and election sure" (2 Pet. 1:10).

Jesus is now preparing a glorious reception for you. The table is being set, and the heavenly band is warming up.

ॐ

Lord Jesus, help me to live in the light of eternity. I look forward with great anticipation to the time that we sit together in the new kingdom. I want to live so that I can hear you say, "Well done, good and faithful servant!" (Matt. 25:21, 23).

THURSDAY

"But It Doesn't Look Dead"

These men are those who are hidden reefs in your love-feasts when they feast with you without fear, caring for themselves; clouds without water, carried along by winds; autumn trees without fruit, doubly dead, uprooted.—Jude 1:12 NASB

Jesus was hungry, but when he scanned a fig tree, looking for fruit, it had none. Jesus cursed the tree, and it withered (see Matt. 21:19). One principle revealed in this story is that fruit trees are not planted to just stand there and look good but to bear fruit. Jesus plainly spoke of this when he said, "By this My Father is glorified, that you bear much fruit; so you will be My disciples" (John 15:8 NKJV).

You may have heard the saying, "The proof is in the pudding." Jesus said it a different way: The evidence of the disciple is in the fruit, not in how good the tree looks.

Jude wrote about some people who apparently were making the rounds. In twentieth-century lingo, they were "doing lunch" with various churches. In an effort to promote themselves for selfish gain, they were apparently making great promises. But when it came time to deliver, they produced no fruit.

In modern times, their spiel might go something like this: "If you'll give to this ministry, you will get a hundredfold return." Like an investment company, they promise, "If you'll invest in my firm, I'll see to it that you get more bang for your buck." Likewise, the hucksters Jude described were promising what they could not deliver. There is only one Lord of the harvest. Ultimately, how much fruit we bear depends on the One who said, "Without Me you can do nothing" (John 15:5 NKJV).

Beware! Some trees look good, but they bear no fruit. Some people may look the part and even say some of the right things, *but inside they are dead.* No power, no life, no fruit. "They are like clouds blowing over dry land without giving rain, promising much but producing nothing. They are like trees without fruit at harvesttime" (Jude 12 NLT).

∞

Father, your watchful eye is on your garden. You are the husbandman in your vineyard, the One who prunes us so that we are more fruitful. Apart from you, Lord Jesus, I can do nothing. I will bear no fruit if I do not abide in you.

So You Want to Lead?

At my first defense, no one came to my support, but everyone deserted me. May it not be held against them.
—2 Timothy 4:16

The picture of a man such as Paul standing alone is both inspiring and discouraging. A man who risked his life for others now found no one to stand beside him in the crucial hour of testing. When his life was hanging in the balance, none of his earthly friends were there to comfort him. Still, Paul, a man of character, stood firm for what he believed.

The willingness to stand alone is what being a leader is all about. To lead others is to point the way and do the right thing, even when no one else has enough courage to stand with you. Being a Christian leader means boldly sounding the clarion call that points men and women to the way of holiness when everyone else is calling for compromise.

How often do we turn our heads and close our eyes to sin? How often do we allow ourselves to be bowled over when we should be standing tall? For the sake of so-called unity, do we allow ourselves to be persuaded to abandon the principles that were forged in us by a praying mother, a God-fearing father, or a faithful teacher? Or do we have the character to stand firm in what we believe? Harry Truman liked to quote Horace Greeley's words: "Fame is a vapor, popularity an accident, riches take wings, those who cheer today may curse tomorrow, only one thing endures—character."

To do the right thing when it's popular takes excellence. To do the right thing when no one cares takes integrity. But to do the right thing when peers forsake you and others say you're being dogmatic, now that takes character!

∞

Father, your Word says "There is a way that seems right to a man, but in the end it leads to death" (Prov. 14:12). I pray that you will lead me in the right way, not the way that seems right. You know my heart and the choices before me. Give me unfailing courage to choose the high way, not the low path of destruction. Thank you, Lord, for standing with me when otherwise I would be standing alone.

excellence

Weekend Reflections

"Daniel distinguished himself above the governors and satraps, because an excellent spirit was in him; and the king gave thought to setting him over the whole realm" (Dan. 6:3 NKJV). Daniel was in the midst of a godless nation and political structure, yet he kept "an excellent spirit." Since we are representatives of God's heavenly kingdom, we should be committed to excellence no matter where we find ourselves stationed and no matter that we stand alone except for God.

1. Are you committed to excellence on your job? Are you doing what you're getting paid to do?

   _____

   _____

   _____

   _____

2. Excellence means "extraordinary." It's a mark above the rest. What do you do that is excellent?

   _____

   _____

   _____

   _____

3. If we are faithful stewards with what God has given, God often gives us more (see Luke. 16:10). What evidence do you see of this promise in your own life?

   _____

   _____

   _____

   _____

   _____

patience

At the Proper Time...

Let us not become weary in doing good, for at the proper time we will reap a harvest if we do not give up.—Galatians 6:9

Are you weary of doing good? The work God has called us to will not always be glorious. In fact it can be quite ordinary. Tedious. More like a yoke than a gift. Certainly, there may be glorious times—those Mount of Transfiguration experiences when we want to stop and build a temple. There may even be days when we think we can hear the rushing wind of Pentecost and we're so inspired that we're ready to head off into the mission field. But eventually we have to come down off the mountain and carry on with our everyday activities. The rushing wind moves on, and so must we, back into those narrow, breezeless trenches of ordinariness.

Later, perhaps, we may realize that it was those joyful moments of inspiration that prepared us for the stormy nights when we felt adrift in a sea of trials that otherwise would have drowned our hope, extinguished our zeal, and crippled our weary bodies. Clinging to the lifeline of faith, we wait for God to hear our cries…and then the sun comes up again, and we toil on.

God's plan for us unfolds according to his time frame, not ours; he lives outside of time and is not governed by it. Before our lives had even begun, he already knew how our work would progress and how our lives would end. He sees us working…sometimes wearily. He knows the seeds we have faithfully sown in earnest prayer, and only he knows when the harvest will come. Only he knows the *proper* time for our prayers to be answered.

So we cast off our weariness; we will not give up, knowing our glory lies ahead. It will come at the right time—God's time—not a second early, not a moment too late.

∞

I choose to believe, Lord, that your timing is perfect. I know that at the proper time I will receive those answers for which I am asking. Thank you, Lord, for your faithfulness, not just to hear my prayers, but to supply what I really need—when the time is right.

Patience for the Harvest

So Jesus grew both tall and wise, and was loved by God
and man.—Luke 2:52 LB

Possibly no other aspect of Jesus' life has been theorized about more than those silent years between ages twelve and thirty. Because the Bible has so little to say about this span of time, we must resist the temptation to surmise or fabricate. It would be wonderful to know more about this period, but because the Bible is silent, we must also remain silent.

The truth that *is* revealed, however, is that "Jesus grew tall and wise." There had to be time for him to experience life as a child and as a young man…to be a boy, then a teenager, so that he might "sympathize with our weaknesses" (Heb. 4:15). To state it more simply, he had to be a boy before he could be a man.

The growing season can be exasperating. Nothing expends our patience like waiting for the harvest. But in the kingdom of God, there is no instant maturity. Pastor Philip Munsey, said it like this: "God has no microwaves. There is no push-button maturity in the spiritual kingdom."

We need the Father's patience; no one suffers along with us like he does. And if he is willing to wait, should not we have the same forbearance with ourselves? James said, "See how the farmer waits for the land to yield its valuable crop and how patient he is for the autumn and spring rains. You too, be patient" (5:7–8). Like that steady farmer, God waits patiently for the fruit of our maturity.

If we dare to be mighty men and women of God, we must first learn to be his children.

❧

Lord, thank you for your patience, your mercy that endures forever. Let me first be content to sit at your feet before I go out to slay the giants in my life.

Keep on Doing It!

Do not merely listen to the word, and so deceive yourselves. Do what it says.—James 1:22

It is one thing to hear God's Word but another thing to obey. Are you doing what he has said, or have you merely listened? Obedience isn't always exciting. Sometimes it's downright monotonous. It is then that we must keep our eyes set on the joy awaiting us—the joy of the harvest. The key is to obey.

"But I have," you may say. "I have shared the Gospel, and people just reject it."

Even when our message seems ineffective, we must keep on declaring the Good News. Only God knows who will receive it. Just because someone rejects it does not mean the Word does not work. Sooner or later, the seed we sow will land on good ground and a bountiful harvest will result. Jesus said, "The seed on good soil stands for those with a noble and good heart, who hear the word, retain it, and by persevering produce a crop" (Luke 8:15).

Pray, and keep on praying. Preach, and keep on preaching. Believe, and keep on believing. You may not see immediate results every time, but you *will* see results. People did not always receive the apostle Paul's message, but he kept at it because he knew that "at the proper time we will reap a harvest if we do not give up" (Gal. 6:9).

∞

Oh Father, you are the Lord of the harvest. You have your own timetable for harvesting. Strengthen my tenacity to persevere in doing the right things despite weariness and discouragement. I know the harvest will come.

THURSDAY

Hang On to Your Future

The thief comes only to steal and kill and destroy; I have come that
they may have life, and have it to the full.—John 10:10

What vision has God placed in your heart? Has he given you a promise that seems like something impossible to fulfill? If it is a promise from God, it could very likely be unthinkable in your present circumstances. After all, God enjoys confounding human wisdom, specifically our carnal reasoning.

Even when the promise seems implausible, hold fast to it, stand firm, and keep the dream alive. These are the actions God expects us to take. When he plants a promise in our spirits, he depends on us to believe his word. Be alert to the enemy's trickery. He comes in many disguises to "steal and kill and destroy," and he may try to steal your future by destroying the vision God has planted deep in your spirit.

The book of Hebrews tells us that Moses was able to leave the security of Egypt "by faith...not fearing the king's anger; he persevered because he saw him who is invisible" (11:27). Moses had a vision of the invisible. He had faith in God's promises.

Will you take God at his word? Will you believe the vision he has placed in our hearts? Hold on to his promise. It is your future and your life.

∞

Father, you have placed dreams and visions in my heart. I know you have good plans for me. Illuminate my spiritual vision and ignite a holy fire in me so that I will remember the word of the Lord. I will hold on to what you have promised.

He Is the Author and the Finisher of Our Faith

Looking unto Jesus the author and finisher of our faith.—Hebrews 12:2 KJV

It is one thing to understand how God "begins" our faith and still another to comprehend that he also finishes it. It is easy for me to agree that he has initiated my faith but more difficult for me to agree that he is completing it day by day and glory to glory. Such agreement seems to remove me from the picture, as far as my faith is concerned. And there are times when I want to believe that I am saving my own soul.

Only Christ has the power to save me, and it is he who is saving me today and tomorrow. I cannot, by sheer will power, perfect the image of Jesus Christ in me. Only as I allow his grace to work in my life can the nature of Christ be revealed in me.

Quite frankly, it seems that it is only when I am totally helpless, realizing my powerlessness the same way the apostle Paul described in Romans 7, that I am truly aware and totally dependent on Christ in me. Paul talked about the futility of trying to do good apart from Christ and ended by saying, "What a wretched man I am! Who will rescue me from this body of death? Thanks be to God—through Jesus Christ our Lord!" (Rom. 7:24–25).

If you had the faith to believe that Christ began the work of salvation in your heart, trust him as well to complete that work in you.

∞

Lord, I realize that apart from you, I am powerless. You said, "Without Me you can do nothing" (John 15:5 NKJV), and I know your words are true. With you nothing is impossible, and that includes my becoming more like you every day.

patience

Weekend Reflections

There's only one recipe for patience: tough times. As James said, "The testing of your faith produces patience" (1:3 NKJV). Patience is a virtue that is *developed* in us, not *zapped* into us. As it grows, it produces a faith that trusts in God and waits for his timing. As Oswald Chambers said, "There are times when you cannot understand why you cannot do what you want to do. When God brings the blank space, see that you do not fill it in, but wait" *(My Utmost for His Highest).*

1. Identify some times when you have been too impatient and missed out on the ideal.

   _____

   _____

   _____

   _____

   _____

2. Do you know someone who exhibits patience? What results does patience bring this person?

   _____

   _____

   _____

   _____

3. Looking back, how has God developed patience in you?

   _____

   _____

   _____

   _____

   _____

Temptation Meets Opportunity

*Having put him to sleep on her lap, she called a man to shave off the
seven braids of his hair, and so began to subdue him. And his
strength left him.*—Judges 16:19

The story of Samson and Delilah is puzzling to me. Why couldn't he
figure out the evil scheme she was up to? After the first time he fell asleep
and she bound him up, it should have been obvious. But this is what happens when we place ourselves in "the lap" of temptation. Our spiritual
senses can become overwhelmed by the lure of what seems desirable or
pleasing to the carnal nature.

This story illustrates the two factors that are involved in committing
sin: temptation and opportunity. As my pastor friend Mike Hayes says,
"Sin usually happens when temptation and opportunity meet." Temptation is not sin, and neither is opportunity. Temptation comes to everyone,
and opportunities occur as a part of everyday life. Our responsibility as
believers is to try to prevent the two from meeting. Despite our best
intentions, they *will* meet from time to time, but there are precautionary
measures we can take to reduce the likelihood of that happening. If only
Samson had taken these steps! What a difference it would have made!

You see, there are places and moments when we are most vulnerable
to temptation. We must identify these places and situations and know
how to avoid them, for these are the circumstances in which temptation
and the opportunity to sin meet. In these situations we're vulnerable to
the sin that "easily entangles" us (Heb. 12:1).

We must take responsibility to keep ourselves as far away as we can
get from people, places, and things that can create easy opportunities for
us to sin. As the apostle Paul instructed us, "Each of you should learn to
control his own body in a way that is holy and honorable" (1 Thess. 4:4).
This means we must be alert to the situations in our lives where temptations and the opportunity to sin intermingle. And it means if you're a
Samson, don't lay your head in Delilah's lap!

∞

Shepherd of my soul, you know my ways, my thoughts. Lead me in the way
of truth, in your paths, away from temptation.

temptation

Here and Now

Surely I am with you always, to the very end of the age.
—Matthew 28:20

One of the tragedies of modern religion is that it seems to remove God from the personal. Instead of close communion between God and mankind, it becomes a detached sort of fellowship separated by ritual and formality.

We can learn some important lessons by studying Jesus' interactions with the religious leaders of his day. It might be surprising to realize that he spoke more harshly to them than to any other group—largely because they sought to elevate themselves above the common people he came to seek and to save. The Pharisees and other religious leaders could not see that he had come to build a bridge between holy God and humankind, to bring God close to his people and establish close communion with them.

Even today, it's easy for the erroneous concept of a God far removed to sneak into our thinking. Sometimes, like the psalmist, we look around us at God's spectacular creation and exclaim, "When I consider your heavens, the work of your fingers, the moon and the stars, which you have set in place, what is man that you are mindful of him, the son of man that you care for him?" (8:3–4). We seem so small, so insignificant, in light of the earth and all that is in it. *Why would the Creator of the world want to be close to us?* we wonder. And then we remember the next part of this psalm that says God "made [us] a little lower than the heavenly beings and crowned [us] with glory and honor" (v. 5).

Our God loves us and stays close to us. He has inscribed our names on his hands (see Isa. 49:16 NKJV). He shelters us in the shadow of his wings (see Ps. 17:8). He is our hiding place and our protector (see Ps. 32:7). His right hand holds us fast (see Ps. 139:10), and nothing can separate us from his love (see Rom. 8:38–39).

❧

Holy God, you are too wondrous for comprehension. The heavens cannot contain you, and yet you pursue us. I worship you because you are awesome, but I am thankful that you are closer than a brother (see Prov. 18:24).

That Happened to You Too?

No temptation has seized you except what is common to man. And God is faithful; he will not let you be tempted beyond what you can bear. But when you are tempted, he will also provide a way out so that you can stand up under it.—1 Corinthians 10:13

It wasn't too many weeks after I was born again that I was plagued with doubts about my experience. *Maybe I'm not really saved. What if this whole thing is fake?* I worried. My questions and self-doubt grew until it consumed my spiritual life. I couldn't sing with confidence. I couldn't pray. *After all,* I figured, *what's the use if I'm not really saved?*

Then during one Sunday-evening service, a woman who had served the Lord many years gave a short testimony. I was both shocked and relieved to hear her say, "You know what the devil told me today? He told me I wasn't saved! Now here I am, forty years after being saved, and he tries to tell me that. Can you believe it?"

Her words were like music to my ears. I suddenly realized that the doubt I had felt was actually the enemy of my soul feeding me lies. If someone could know the Lord as long as that sister of the faith had known him and still be tempted to doubt, then I would worry no more about my own bouts of questioning.

Getting a glimpse of another Christian's trial of faith gives us confidence to know that we are not alone in our troubles. And as we hear another's testimony of overcoming, we, too, vow to overcome!

If doubts arise in your heart from time to time, you are not alone. As Christians, we are in this struggle together. As Paul wrote, "No temptation has seized you except what is common to man." Everyone fights discouragement at one time or another. Knowing that others have struggled and prevailed gives us hope and courage. If they can remain faithful, so can we.

❧

Lord Jesus, thank you for being a high priest who understands our weaknesses. You lived and walked this same earth that I do now, and you were tempted as I am tempted. I will not fear because you have overcome and your overcoming power is alive in me.

Winning Is Everything

Our struggle is not against flesh and blood.—Ephesians 6:12

temptation

It's 6:45 A.M. As you gingerly make your way through the morning traffic, you are moving at a reasonable speed, minding your own business, when a little red sports car with tinted windows moves up behind you. We'll call it Little Red.

You are keeping a safe distance between you and the car in front of you, but Little Red tails you like you're the only thing between him and a wild ride on the autobahn. You know that if you have to stop suddenly, Little Red will be in your front seat, and his ignorance of that fact begins to get under your skin. Your adrenaline begins to rise, and thoughts come unbidden into your head: *I think I'll just tap my brakes and send Little Red a message,* or *I'll get in the next lane and match the speed of the car in front of him and block his path. Maybe that will teach Little Red a little lesson!*

In the case of you versus Little Red, the only way to win seems to be to match his aggression and teach him a lesson. To give in and move out of Little Red's way now would make you a loser, wouldn't it?

As the saying goes, "Sometimes you can win the battle and lose the war." In this case, however, you can really come out a winner. You just have to correctly identify the enemy and redirect your competitive resistance.

So who is the most dangerous enemy here? Is it Little Red? Or is it Satan working through your stinking pride? By recognizing the real enemy, you can come out on top and win the most important battle: the spiritual battle for your soul.

Instead of spending valuable time and energy trying to win a stupid battle of cat and mouse with Little Red, expose the more dangerous enemy and use that spiritual energy to put the enemy where he belongs: under your feet, not in a cloud of smoke from your tailpipe!

Remember, the enemy doesn't show up in a red suit with a pitchfork. Sometimes he shows up in your mirror.

∞

Lord, give me the insight to discern the real enemy, to walk and live as a free child of God, not as a person enslaved to the whims and wishes of my old nature. I choose to walk in the Spirit and win the war against self and the enemy of my soul.

Jesus, Our Helper

For because He Himself [in His humanity] has suffered in being tempted (tested and tried), He is able (immediately) to run to the cry of (assist, relieve) those who are being tempted and tested and tried [and who therefore are being exposed to suffering].
—Hebrews 2:18 AMPLIFIED

As believers, temptations come to us that bring mental pain as well as physical suffering. How many times have we wondered, *How can I be a Christian and be tempted in such a way?* This kind of suffering can be worse than physical suffering because it can destroy our position and relationship with Christ. We want to please him, to be loved and accepted by him, and this kind of suffering can destroy our security and confidence in Christ.

Jesus knew such trials would beset us. He knew because he endured them himself. He lived as a man and "was in all points tempted as we are" (Heb. 4:15 NKJV). Not only did he experience temptation, but he also endured the suffering that is a part of it. That's why he sent the Helper to be with us in our hour of temptation.

We are never alone in this struggle. "Because God has said, 'Never will I leave you; never will I forsake you'" (Heb. 13:5). When we are tempted, we must let his compassion sink deep within our soul "so we [can] say with confidence, 'The Lord is my helper; I will not be afraid. What can man do to me?'" (Heb. 13:6).

Be assured, my friend, Jesus is with us in our trials and in our suffering. No matter how bad the situation gets, the only direction Jesus runs is toward his children…to help us, to relieve us, to aid us. Never will he forsake us. Never will he run the other way.

∞

Lord Jesus, I know you alone are my source of help. You know my weaknesses and see me in my darkest hour. I lift up my suffering to you with a thankful heart. I know you understand what it is to suffer. I know you will hear my cry and will come.

temptation

Weekend Reflections

Sin is never satisfied. Giving in to temptation only means there will be a greater desire next time, a deeper chasm longing to be filled. Sinful desire is a bottomless pit, a black hole.

Ask Solomon. In his desire to find the goodness of life, he said, "I denied myself nothing my eyes desired; I refused my heart no pleasure.... Yet when I surveyed all that my hands had done...everything was meaningless" (Eccles. 2:10–11).

There is only One who can fill the chasm. The next time you are tempted to sin, listen. See if you don't hear the voice of God saying, "Turn to me instead." When we are tempted, we have a choice: we can turn to what is meaningless, or we can turn to God.

1. What things have you pursued only to find them meaningless?

   _____

   _____

   _____

   _____

2. In the things we desire most, we can often see the aspect that is lacking in our relationship with God. Considering this possibility, what hunger in your soul do you need God to fill?

   _____

   _____

   _____

   _____

   _____

3. In the hour of your temptation, how can you turn to Jesus in a practical way?

   _____

   _____

   _____

   _____

Does Time Fly?

One day is with the Lord as a thousand years, and a thousand years as one day.—2 Peter 3:8 KJV

We all have those days when we look at the clock and it's 2 P.M., and then we look at the clock three hours later and it's 2:05. On the other hand, we've also experienced those days when the hours seem to vaporize, and we look up at 5 P.M. and wonder where the time went. Of course time doesn't really slow down or speed up. How we perceive its passing depends on whether we're doing something we enjoy or something we dread. The psalmist said that one day in God's presence is better than a thousand days spent elsewhere (see 84:10).

On the other hand, Peter said that one day with the Lord can seem like a thousand years. While most scholars agree that 2 Peter 3:8 refers to our life in eternity, I believe the verse offers a lesson for today as well. I believe that when we get beyond the *thee*s and *thou*s and arrive at that place of intimate fellowship with God, we should agree with the singer, David, about our time spent with the Lord—it should be a time of joy and blessing. If our time seems to drag by when we're in prayer—if one day seems to drag by as if it were a thousand years long—then we need to re-examine our relationship.

Maybe we're in prayer instead of in his presence. Maybe we're in church instead of in Christ. "This is life eternal," Jesus said, to "know…God" (see John 17:3 KJV). Eternal, unending *life*—not eternal drudgery—limitless, boundless life, springing up and flowing freely.

∞

Father, I come into your presence with praise and adulation, treasuring the time I spend worshiping at your feet. Someday, Lord, you will raise the dead "in the twinkling of an eye" (1 Cor. 15:52). Someday you will come "in an instant" (Isa. 29:5). I long to be with you through eternity. Come, Lord Jesus, come!

To Open, to Hear, to Know

Behold, I stand at the door, and knock: if any man hear my voice,
and open the door, I will come in to him, and will sup with him, and
he with me.—Revelation 3:20 KJV

What a picture this text creates! It does not take a great imagination to envision the scene. Often used in sermons of evangelism, this passage reaches out to those who have never met the Lord. But I believe the context of this verse shows that it applies even more directly to believers than to nonbelievers.

There are several observations to be made here. First, Jesus is seen standing at the door and knocking. He does not force his way in. We must open the door. As believers, we know who's knocking. Perhaps we've even invited him to come into our lives. But we have to do more than give lip service. We have to take action, opening the doors of our hearts and allowing him to enter.

Second, we must be in a position to "hear [Jesus'] voice," because that is what calls us, draws us into relationship with him. Certainly as believers we often find ourselves in situations where his word—his voice—is shared.

Third, we must learn to recognize the Lord's voice in our hearts. The verse above describes total communion, complete fellowship: "I will come in to him and will sup with him, and he with me." So we not only pray to him, praising him and humbly beseeching him for our needs, but we also listen to him.

Jesus stands at the door of our hearts. Have you heard his voice today? Will you open yourself to him and seek his fellowship as he seeks yours?

∞

Lord, put me in the position to hear your voice. Come into my life and fellowship with me. Thank you for not giving up on me when I fail. Keep knocking on my door, Lord. Keep calling me into a deeper relationship with you.

Come Home!

Thou wilt keep him in perfect peace, whose mind is stayed on thee.
—Isaiah 26:3 KJV

If you have ever traveled for any length of time, you know the truth of the old cliché. Truly, when you've been away awhile, *there's no place like home.* There you can relax in your chair, sleep in your bed, and cook what you want in your own kitchen. At home you can be truly at ease, comfortable to just be yourself. There's no one to impress, no one to feign sincerity to.

In the beginning, God made a home for his creation. There, in the Garden, Adam and Eve were in perfect harmony with each other and with God. Naked, they felt no shame because there was nothing to hide from God. Then sin entered the picture. And they were driven out of the beautiful, peaceful garden God had prepared for them. Now there was no rest. No home.

We would all be "homeless" still, except that Jesus came to build a road so we could find our way home. Today the only home for our hearts is in his presence. Just as we weary travelers can never really rest until we are in our own physical homes, so our spirits cannot rest until we are in his blessed presence.

Are you tired of traveling? Go home, where you long to be. Open the door, pull up your chair, and settle in.

Is your spirit weary? Come home to his presence. There you will find peace. You can be yourself. (You couldn't impress him even if you tried!) Once you are there, you will know it's where you belong.

∞

Father, I want to be where you are, for your presence is home. Thank you for your mercy, which endures forever.

A Solitary Place

Jesus got up, left the house and went off to a solitary place, where he prayed.... When they found him, they exclaimed: "Everyone is looking for you!"—Mark 1:35, 37

Have you ever followed Jesus to a solitary place? Have you ever found yourself in a lonely, desolate place and wondered, *What am I doing here?*

Throughout the centuries, God has called those who will listen to solitary places: "The Lord had said to Abram, 'Leave your country...and go to the land I will show you'" (Gen. 12:1). It was while he was tending his sheep, alone on the far side of the desert, that Moses met God in the burning bush. John was in exile on the tiny isle of Patmos when he had the brilliant vision of the glorified Christ.

Maybe there are times when God tries to get through to us amid the clamor and hubbub of our busy lives, but we can't see or hear him. Then, suddenly, our jobs call us to a lonely place far from family and friends. Maybe it's not the island of Patmos but a town in the middle of Kansas or Arizona or Maine where we feel forsaken and long for a familiar face. Or perhaps in difficult times we find ourselves lost in a spiritual wilderness, wondering where God is and why we feel so alone. It may be that this feeling is no accident.

Have you been secretly crying out for renewal and a fresh revelation of Christ in your life? Maybe he has led you to this place to answer your prayer. Maybe this is where your heart can be quiet and you will hear his voice. Maybe later you will tell others, "I was alone in a small town in Kansas when the Lord appeared and said..."

Jesus knew where to find strength. He knew how to commune with his Father. He "got up, left the house and went off to a solitary place."

Are you looking for him? He may be waiting for you in a solitary place.

∞

Lord, I thank you for using the lonely places in my life. There is nowhere so far away that you do not know where I am and that you cannot speak to the desolation. Help me to stay tuned to your Spirit, to have the eyes to see you and the ears to hear what the Spirit would say.

Sabbath of the Soul

Then he said to them, "The Sabbath was made for man, not man for the Sabbath."—Mark 2:27

Sometimes in everyday life, we forget that God's laws are meant to protect us, not to restrict us.

The statement Jesus made regarding the Sabbath answered a question the religious people asked after Jesus had healed a man. Jesus made it clear that God did not create the law of the Sabbath and *then* create man so he would have somebody to obey that law! He made the law of the Sabbath *for* us! When we break the law of the Sabbath, we hurt ourselves more than we hurt God. God gave us the Sabbath because he knew we needed it!

We are "fearfully and wonderfully made," the psalmist said (139:14), and the complex creatures that we are need rest for the spirit, soul, and body. If we do not get enough rest, our bodies will often go on strike, and soon we find ourselves resting whether or not we want to!

It is much the same in our souls. They, too, need time to recuperate. I believe this is why our emotions run in waves and why, sometimes, after an emotional high, we suddenly find ourselves on an emotional low. Our souls need time to rest, and God has ways of bringing us to rest, even when we do not think we need it: "He makes me lie down in green pastures, he leads me beside quiet waters, he restores my soul" (Ps. 23:2–3).

∞

Jesus, you are Lord of the Sabbath. I want to know your voice and listen when you bid me to come to you and rest. Then I will come to you and find rest for my soul.

Weekend Reflections

God made a home for our spirits: the presence of God. Ever since Adam and Eve were removed from the place where they walked and talked with God (see Gen. 3), humankind has been in search of this home. As believers, we have the privilege of living in God's presence. Whether we are at school, in the car, or on the job, we can still be at home in Christ.

1. Brother Lawrence believed that "all spiritual life consists of practicing God's presence" (*The Practice of the Presence of God*). Contemplate and describe how you can practice the presence of God.

   _____

   _____

   _____

   _____

   _____

2. Adam and Eve hid from God's presence. Do you hide from his presence? If so, why?

   _____

   _____

   _____

   _____

3. The psalmist wrote that in his presence is "fullness of joy" (16:11 NKJV). What does this mean to you?

   _____

   _____

   _____

   _____

   _____

the presence of God

You Are Not Your Own

*For ye are bought with a price: therefore glorify God in your body, and
in your spirit, which are God's.*—1 Corinthians 6:20 KJV

It is an imaginary scene—and yet it is real: The auctioneer in his gibberish shouts out the bids, and slavemasters peer at the slave with discriminating eyes, wanting the most for their money. The slave stands alone before them. She wonders what her next owner will be like. She fears for her life, for now she is older. Her body cannot tolerate the long, hard hours with little rest as it used to. Maybe her next owner will be more understanding. Then she shudders as someone in the crowd shouts out a bid. She knows that one. He is known for his intolerance and his abuse. There is a long silence. No more bids. She silently prays for one more. "Going once…going twice…"

Then, just before the dreaded word *sold!* seals her fate, a strong voice shouts out a bid from the back of the crowd, and the other slavemasters gasp. No one has ever paid that much for a slave!

Hurriedly the stranger steps up to claim his newest possession. Eagerly he helps the old woman down from the auction block. Then, ever so gently, he removes the chains from her arms and legs. And he looks into her eyes and tells her, "Now. Go free."

I cannot begin to imagine the horror of actually standing on an auction block. Yet, as Christians, this is our story. We were enslaved to serve the master of sin, who abused us by his evil devices. Were we valuable? No. Strong? No. Needy? Yes. There, in our weakness and bondage, we waited. Then Christ came. He paid the highest price one could pay.

Is it any wonder why we should serve him with our very lives? We belong to him! He loved us and bought us when no one else could see our worth. We owe him everything, yet we can never earn our keep. We must continually remember it was his choice, his decision, to make us his prized possessions.

❧

Father, thank you for loving us so much that you paid the highest price and offered your Son for our sakes. Once we were slaves to a master we could not escape from. But you have set us free!

247

TUESDAY

Do You Want to Let It Go?

When Jesus saw him lying there and learned that he had been in this
condition for a long time, he asked him, "Do you want
to get well?"—John 5:6

When Jesus walked the earth, it was common to see many sick people and beggars lying beside the streets and roadways. There were no welfare programs and few resources for such as these, so most were forced to find their own way. Surprisingly, some of them found the begging lifestyle to be quite profitable, and they had no real desire to change even when the opportunity arose. Perhaps that is why Jesus asked this man beside the pool at Bethesda, "Do you want to get well?"

This story always reminds me of children who pout and become angry when they don't get their way. No matter what anybody does or says, the child is determined not to smile, laugh, or enjoy whatever might be going on around him or her. Some of us never outgrow this grudge-holding tendency. As adults, many of us still hold on to our anger and our refusal to forgive our offenders, even to the point of becoming ill. The sad thing about this is that God does not help us get well until we decide to let go of our anger. He waits for us to say, "I want to be happy. I want to forgive. I want to be well."

I am convinced that if the man at Bethesda had answered no when Jesus asked him whether he wanted to get well, Jesus would have walked on by. Instead, Jesus saw in the man a desire to let the familiar go, a willingness to stand, pick up his mat, and move on.

Do you want to get well? Do you want to be happy? Are you willing to let your anger go? Will you choose now to forgive? These are the questions you must ask yourself before God can heal you.

❦

Lord, I want to get well! Help me to release the anger that holds me in its grip and impoverishes my spirit. I choose to forgive and move on in your love.

Grace for You and from You

Be merciful, just as your Father is merciful. Do not judge, and you will not be judged. Do not condemn, and you will not be condemned. Forgive, and you will be forgiven. Give, and it will be given to you.... For with the measure you use, it will be measured to you.
—Luke 6:36–38

Here is one of God's principles that affects our lives everyday: Sow, and you will reap; give, and you will receive. And this is not just a principle of finance but of life.

Are you a generous giver, willing to share the blessings God has given you? If so, you probably find most of the people around you to be generous in return. But this biblical principle doesn't apply only to material goods. It also pertains to giving of ourselves, of our knowledge, our devotion, our love. Jesus went out among the people to share the Good News. So should we. If we isolate ourselves, tending only to our own needs, how can we follow his example?

And there's something else this principle teaches, something that may be the most difficult lesson of all. It tells us to forgive so that we will be forgiven.

Does it take a lot of effort for you to be merciful, to forgive someone for wronging you? If so, not only will you find others unforgiving, but you may also find it equally difficult to forgive yourself. Your attitude about others and their failures will also become your attitude toward yourself. It is in administering grace and forgiveness to others that we find grace for ourselves. Even when they don't deserve it, even when they don't ask for it, we forgive them, because in doing so we learn about the free gift of grace, which God applies so generously to our own failures and weaknesses.

This message is for those who have a desire to please God, to discover his nature, and to bear his image: Be merciful. Do not judge or condemn. Forgive others. Give generously. And be filled.

❧

Lord, I want to be a person who pours grace on others. Because I am forgiven, I will forgive. Because I have received so much, I will be a giver. Because I am free, I will point others to freedom.

freedom

Free Indeed!

Now a slave has no permanent place in the family, but a son belongs
to it forever. So if the Son sets you free, you will be free indeed.
—John 8:35–36

A slave cannot free another slave. The power to set a slave free is reserved for the slavemaster or a higher authority. Jesus was not a slave but a Son. He was the Creator of all of us who, through Adam, were born slaves to sin. But though we were born slaves to sin, we don't have to remain enslaved to its power. We were created in the image of God as God's property, but we have the power to choose our master. When we choose Jesus, he sets us free and makes us "free indeed"!

Only Jesus has the authority to declare you free. He said, "All authority in heaven and on earth has been given to me" (Matt. 28:18). As long as you serve sin, you remain a slave to its power over you. But once you choose Jesus as your Savior and Lord, you are free to serve him. You are no longer a slave but a son—a joint heir with Jesus Christ to all that the Father freely gives!

∞

Jesus, I declare you as not just my Savior but also my Lord. I look to you to do what I cannot do. Thank you for making me free to serve you and to leave the slavery of sin. Now sin is no longer my master. I have been set free from sin and have become a slave to righteousness (see Rom. 6:14, 18).

I Am Not Who I Was

When you sow, you do not plant the body that will be, but just a seed.... But God gives it a body as he has determined, and to each kind of seed he gives its own body.—1 Corinthians 15:37–38

The simple truth of being born again can be summed up like this: We die to who we are and rise from death to live as new creations through faith in the power of Jesus Christ. We are not reformed; we are reborn. We lose our old identities and find new ones in Christ Jesus.

The new creatures we become are nothing like our old selves. Our old natures were the seeds, the shells, that died in the ground so our new creations could spring to life. Seeds do not have the same form as the plant; the acorn is not the oak tree. The seed looks nothing like the tree. But when it is planted in the ground and dies, up springs a mighty, living thing that bears no resemblance to the seed!

In the same way, we, as new creations in Christ, do not resemble our old natures. Our faith does not depend on what we had to give Christ, which really was nothing. All he wanted from us was our willingness to die to who we were. Now we "live by faith in the Son of God" (Gal. 2:20). "In him we live and move and have our being" (Acts 17:28). We live not in the seed that was but out of a new creation that exists by the resurrection power of Jesus Christ.

Don't be bound by who you *were*. That old creature has no relevance to who you are now. That was the seed that died so the new creature could spring to life. You are a new person with a proud heritage and a rich inheritance!

Father, thank you that I am not who I was. You have made me a brand-new being. Let your Holy Spirit bring me into a greater revelation of what happened when I was born again. I have faith in your great ability to cause me to live as a new creation.

freedom

Weekend Reflections

You can't know what freedom means until you've experienced it. You can hear about it and talk about it, but freedom is best understood by living it. You especially appreciate freedom when you know how much it costs. Jesus didn't pour out his life for us so we could be half free. Instead we "were called to be free" (Gal. 5:13)—"free indeed"! (John 8:36).

1. Are you living free? Why or why not?

_____

_____

_____

_____

_____

2. Walking back into sin is like walking back into prison. What are the similarities?

_____

_____

_____

_____

_____

3. How can you best preach freedom to those imprisoned by Satan and self?

_____

_____

_____

_____

_____

_____

Do You Know Who You Are?

Now we are children of God.—1 John 3:2

Everyone struggles with insecurity at some level. While some people deal with it as a minor issue, others are held captive by its grip. They fear new situations so greatly that they are immobilized, unable to accomplish what is within their reach. They may break out in a cold sweat whenever they even think of meeting new people or going on a job interview. On the other hand, confident individuals face those same situations with hope and excitement about the adventure and challenge. Which one are you?

If you're a confident person, secure in your God-given abilities, you have been given the gift of affirmation somewhere in your lifetime. You know who you are, and you feel comfortable with that knowledge. You don't fear rejection because you know that how another might see you does not change your personal worth.

As confident Christians, secure in the promise that God loves and cherishes us, we come eagerly before the Lord, knowing he delights in our devotion. When we recognize who we are—beloved children created by a holy God—we can confidently claim the authority we have as believers, and we can face whatever lies ahead with courage and faith.

Our example of unshakable confidence is Jesus himself. Even when he was tempted with the challenge "if you are the Son of God…," he did not yield. He knew who he was. He didn't have to prove himself to Satan (see Matt. 4:3–11). And in the same way, we can know who we are: beloved children of God. Not because of our merit, not because we've earned a prize or joined an exclusive club, but by the grace of God. It is a gift. God has chosen us.

∞

Father, thank you for choosing me even before the foundation of the world. Today, I am a child of God. Today, I am a joint heir with Christ. Though others' opinions of me have some importance, your opinion of me is the only one of real value.

identity

Gene Therapy

*That which is born of the flesh is flesh; and that which is born of the
Spirit is spirit. Marvel not that I said unto thee, Ye must
be born again.*—John 3:6–7 KJV

There is a lot of talk these days about cloning, as scientists make major breakthroughs in the study of gene therapy and how it works. It is an exciting yet fearful topic, because we are playing with the very essence of life.

Most psychologists agree that we are predisposed to be outgoing, shy, bold, or sociable according to the traits that have been passed on to us, and they say that most of our personality is formed by the age of five. While our environment can affect our personality, most of who we are, they say, is "written in our genes."

It's a common thing these days to hear people use their genetic makeup as some sort of excuse. They say, "I can't help it. It's just the way I am."

Our personality is "born of the flesh." That is why we must be born again "of the Spirit," as Jesus said. If we are going to manifest the love, patience, and goodness of Christ, we are going to need a new nature. The hope for us and for every one who believes is that when we are born again we acquire a bent toward godliness instead of toward sin. It's as if God has taken our spiritual DNA and infused it with the power of the resurrected Christ! (see Gal. 2:20). We have been empowered with the traits of our heavenly Father by the blood of Christ, and we are compelled to sin no longer. Now when they ask us how we can love when there is reason to hate, forgive instead of holding a grudge, pray for our enemies instead of seeking revenge, we can say, "I can't help it. It's written in my genes."

&

Father, I thank you that the same Spirit that raised Jesus from the dead is living in me. I am obligated to sin no longer. As a child of God I have become a partaker in the divine nature of Jesus, my Lord (see 2 Pet. 1:4 KJV).

identity

When Was the Last Time You Built an Altar?

And he erected there an altar, and called it El-elohe-Israel.
—Genesis 33:20 KJV

The literal meaning of the word *altar* is "slaughter place." Not a pretty image, is it? To many people, the church altar has become a place of traditional duty, a place we go to "pay our respects to the man upstairs," as if this somehow appeases God and quenches his anger for another week. But is an altar truly an altar if nothing is offered?

After Jacob's encounter with God and his dreaded meeting with Esau, Jacob built an altar and named it El-elohe-Israel, meaning "God, the God of Israel." In effect, he was saying, "The Lord has now become the Lord of me, Israel. He is not just my father's God, he is my God! I have seen him at Peniel, and he has become my Deliverer!"

What was placed on the altar called El-elohe-Israel? In a sense it was Jacob, himself. There he said his last good-bye to the old Jacob, the supplanter, the deceiver, and he arose from the altar as a new man, *Israel,* meaning "prince of God." He would be a man who would rule as God because he now realized his strength was from God and not from himself. In essence, he was rising to "walk in newness of life" (Rom. 6:4 KJV).

On the altar of altars, the Son of God was offered for us. As I look to this altar, I know, as Jacob knew, that God Almighty is also the God of me. As a believer, I have died with Christ, so I also live in Christ forever. To me, the altar of Calvary is a memorial of that truth. The personal revelation of the resurrection power is that when Jesus as God was raised from the dead so was a man!

Because Christ is risen, when we lay the old, false self on the altar, we are also raised to new life. And as we rise up off the altar, the real self that is at union with Christ is truly alive for the first time.

∞

*J*esus, I declare your lordship. You are not only the God Almighty of the universe. You are my God! I have said good-bye to my old self. "The life I live in the body, I live by faith in the Son of God, who loved me and gave himself for me" (Gal. 2:20).

255

identity

Complete in Him

From the fullness of his grace we have all received one blessing after another.—John 1:16

Our completeness as individuals comes from our being joined to Christ. He fills in our empty spaces, those holes and gaps in our makeup that result from sin, and makes us whole in spirit, soul, and body.

This principle of completeness is illustrated by the mystical union of Christ and the church as a parallel to that of man and wife. "And they will become one flesh," Genesis 2:24 tells us. To separate this fusion involves ripping and tearing, because the one has literally become a part of the other. Such a painful break explains why those who go through the grief of divorce often describe it by saying, "I feel like a part of me has died."

When we come to Christ, he pours his fullness into our emptiness— the holes and the gaps of our fragmented selves. That's really what it means to "receive from the fullness of his grace." He who is complete joins himself to those who are incomplete so that we might be altogether and entirely whole in him.

How do we receive his fullness? By accepting his love that surpasses knowledge, as the apostle Paul declared. As we discover and come to know the breadth, length, depth, and height of such a love, we experience "the fullness of him who fills everything in every way" (Eph. 1:23).

∞

Lord, thank you for the hope we have in you—the hope that there is no life so broken that you cannot mend and heal it. Thank you for your power to make us complete and whole and for your fullness, which is available for every wounded heart.

No Man Is an Island

For we are members of his body, of his flesh, and of his bones.
—Ephesians 5:30 KJV

"I don't need anybody. All I need is Jesus." Have you ever heard someone say this—or said it yourself? Usually it's expressed by those who have
experienced hurtful relationships. They have been burned one too many
times by someone they have trusted and loved.

God wants to be our source of strength. He wants us to rely on him
alone. But we have a need for earthly brothers and sisters too. There are
some aspects of the ministry of Christ that we cannot experience in a real
way except through a member of his body: someone we can touch, see,
and hear—his body, his flesh, and his bones. In this way, the love of
Christ is administered through our senses. We know him because we have
seen him in a brother or sister.

It was Barnabas, "the son of encouragement," who helped the apostle
Paul experience the blessing of the body. While many believers would not
receive Paul because of his former life of persecuting Christians, Barnabas
administered to him God's love and acceptance. Barnabas's kindness
advanced Paul's ministry in a definite way and fostered the mighty revival
at Antioch. Who knows what course the apostle Paul's life would have
taken had it not been for Barnabas?

God wants us to be interdependent, not independent. We cannot
touch the literal body of Jesus, but we can experience his love through a
believer's hug or touch; we can understand his grace and mercy through
another's forgiveness and understanding. You will find your true identity
through Jesus and his church.

∞

Lord, although you have revealed your heart to me through the members of
your body, sometimes I haven't recognized it—and have even rejected it. I
pray that I will not only freely receive but will freely give as I have been given.

identity

Weekend Reflections

No one is content to be a nobody, just a face or statistic. People go to great lengths to establish their worth. As someone said, "We take money we don't have to buy clothes we can't afford to impress people we don't like." Our real worth, however, should not be based on others' opinions or our own achievements but on the value God has placed on us.

1. Jesus said, "Are not five sparrows sold for two pennies? Yet not one of them is forgotten by God. Indeed, the very hairs of your head are all numbered. Don't be afraid; you are worth more than many sparrows" (Luke 12:6–7). What promises in Scripture prove to us that God places high value on human life?

   _____

   _____

   _____

2. We can't find out who we are by looking inward but only by looking up. What other false paths do we follow in trying to find ourselves?

   _____

   _____

   _____

3. Write down the lies you have believed concerning what God thinks about you, then write down the Scripture verses that refute those lies. For example: A lie: God is too busy to care. The truth: "He will not grow tired or weary" (Isa. 40:28).

   _____

   _____

   _____

   _____

Hope Remains

And now these three remain: faith, hope and love. But the greatest of these is love.—1 Corinthians 13:13

Listed right up there with faith and love, the two other essentials of the Christian journey, is another virtue that's often overlooked: hope. Most Christians know that we cannot please God without faith and that God's very essence is love. But how many sermons are preached on hope? Yet what an important virtue it is.

If there is one major reason that explains the increasing suicide rate, surely it is that more and more people are losing hope—and their purpose in life. Experts tell us that most depression can be best understood as anger turned inward. And what causes the anger? A situation or circumstance in which there is no hope for change. As Scripture teaches, "Hope deferred makes the heart sick, but a longing fulfilled is a tree of life" (Prov. 13:12).

How did Victor Frankl survive the horrors of a Nazi concentration camp? In a speech he explained, "I've never been here before; I've never seen any of you before; I've never given this speech before. But in my dreams, I have stood before you and said these words a thousand times." It was the hope of seeing those faces and telling that story of survival that kept him alive!

My friend, as long as you are breathing, there is still hope—hope that tomorrow will be brighter and that the sun will shine in your life again. To believe this is one of the essential virtues of the Christian life.

∞

Lord, my hope is in you. It isn't in my circumstances, in the government, my financial status, or any other worldly thing. Because I know you are alive, there is reason to be optimistic.

259

Endure for the Joy of It

Jesus…who for the joy that was set before him endured the cross.
—Hebrews 12:2 KJV

I'm sure you've heard the sarcastic statement after you've complained about bumping your head, "It'll feel better when it quits hurting." While this statement is said in jest, there is a principle here that rings true: Sometimes we have to hurt to feel better.

Consider a surgical operation. It is something most of us would never do for fun, but we endure the pain of surgery and recovery so that we can overcome a disease or have some other problem fixed. In the same way, we sometimes must suffer through spiritual surgery to experience the thrill of victory. For a divine purpose that we cannot see, God allows crises to come into our lives. No, it is not something we enjoy, but we know the hardship is building endurance in us and bringing us to maturity.

Jesus endured the cross for the joy that awaited him. Certainly he did not *enjoy* the cross, but he *endured* the cross. He gloriously triumphed over the agony of crucifixion by fixing his eyes, not on the pain and suffering, but on the joy to come. As it is written, "The joy of the Lord is your strength" (Neh. 8:10 KJV).

Father, *your* joy will be my strength, not *my* joy. I bless your name, for when my joy is empty, your joy fills me to overflowing. Give me a glimpse of the glory that awaits me on the other side of the crisis I must face.